D1371458

SAGA OF JESSE JAMES

OTHER BOOKS BY THE AUTHOR
The Day Jesse James Was Killed
Lawmen and Robbers
Younger Brothers
Gunslingers
Sam Hildebrand, Guerrilla
Great Lawmen of the West
Great Gunfighters of the West
Wild Women of the West
Badmen of the Frontier Days
Date with Destiny: Bill the Kid
Killer Legions of Quantrill
Forty Years on the Wild Frontier
Rube Burrow, Train Robber

SAGA OF JESSE JAMES

by

Carl W. Breihan

The CAXTON PRINTERS, Ltd.
Caldwell, Idaho
1991

Library of Congress Cataloging-in-Publication Data

Breihan, Carl W., 1915–
    Saga of Jesse James / by Carl W. Breihan.
            p.   cm.
        Includes index.
        ISBN 0-87004-327-7 : $14.95
        1. James, Jesse, 1847–1882. 2. James, Frank, 1844–1915. 3. Outlaws--
West (U.S.)--Biography. 4. West (U.S.)--History--1848–1950. 5. Frontier
and pioneer life--West (U.S.) I. Title
F594.J264   1991
364.1′552′092--dc20
[B]   91-12985
                                                                        CIP

Lithographed and bound in the United States of America by
The CAXTON PRINTERS, Ltd.
Caldwell, ID 83605
146945

Dedicated to our grandchildren
Danny F. Culbertson and Heather M. Culbertson

Ethel and Carl W. Breihan

Contents

Illustrations

Foreword Comments

by Homer Croy

Author of *Jesse James Was My Neighbor*

I never saw him but once. It was an occasion I will not soon forget, for he threatened to kill me. I did not want to be killed and I told him so, but that made no difference to him. I am happy to report that he did not kill me.

It was in the Highway Hotel, in Chicago, and it was a Sunday morning. The year was 1948 and I was getting material for my book on Jesse James and wanted to see Jesse in person. The man was then a hundred and one years old, he said. He was lying in bed, eating a breakfast consisting of whiskey and doughnuts. I can't imagine why anyone would want to eat doughnuts for breakfast, but this is what he was doing. I was not going to tell him what he should eat for breakfast, for, after all, it was his stomach and if he wanted to cram it with doughnuts, that was his business.

Now I will explain, for all this does not make sense. This particular and special Jesse James had lived most of his life under the name of J. "Happy Jack" Frank Dalton. And then suddenly, in the twinkling of an eye, he became Jesse James—no small feat.

He was discovered by a newspaper man living in a trailer in Lawton, Oklahoma. The newspaper was so excited that the day it released the story, it locked the doors to the building so that its rival would not know until the paper was on the street. The newspaper press associations flashed it from Lawton to Lhasa.

Well, it seemed crazy to a number of people who knew the true story of Jesse James, but the old gent was smarter than we had thought, for he got so much publicity that he drew a hundred dollars a day for saying he was Jesse James. State fairs, rodeos, and motion picture companies came running with money in their outstretched hands; he didn't have to pull a gun on them. I was at Northfield, Minnesota, when they were getting up a Jesse James Day. They wrote Dalton, asking if he would make a personal appearance. He would, but he would have to have a thousand dollars. This shook the good citizens to their foundations, for the original Jesse didn't get a cent.

The intriguing thing about this is that there have been six Jesse Jameses since the Kearney Jesse James was shot to death in St. Joseph, Missouri. Most of them lectured. Some people, who paid admission to hear them, came out muttering that the wrong Jesse had been shot. None of them ever made the success of it that J. Frank Dalton (alias Jesse James) did. He had a peculiar genius for being Jesse. He reduced Jesse James to Big Business.

I was astonished by the number of people

who were taken in by J. Frank Dalton of Goliad, Texas. One was a famous newspaperman, Robert C. Ruark, who did a daily column for goodness knows how many years. He interviewed the Lawton claimant and said he was the Real Article. I went on the air with Ruark, over Columbia Broadcasting System (Bill Leonard's Program) and we debated it back and forth. When it was over, Ruark still contended that this Jesse James was the One and Only. Ruark was a plenty smart hombre, so if the Gent from Goliad could pull the wool over Ruark's eyes, think what he could do to some clodhopper who didn't know any more about Jesse James than Billy Sunday did about sin.

Alias Jesse James lived until 1951. One of the things that plagued his life was the number of men who popped up and called him Pa. This didn't go well with alias Jesse James, so he asked his wife (alias Mrs. James) to go to Missouri and sue this latest pretender. This was done, with victory going to her.

Poor Jesse had been used to exploit all sorts of wares—even caves where he supposedly hid. There are in the United States eleven caves where he hid; that is, that's what the local Chambers of Commerce say. As a matter of fact, Jesse never hid in a cave in his life. He always said that to hide in a cave was like a ground squirrel hiding in the ground with only one way to get out and a man standing over it with a club. Instead, Jesse stayed with friends and kept hopping around from New York City to Paso Robles, thirty miles north of San Luis Obispo, California. But never a cave.

I think the most amazing thing about the Jesse James matter is that interest in Jesse is growing, not waning. One would think, in all the years since Jesse was shot down, that interest would be dying; instead, it is on its feet. How people chase him around. Jesse was never in Canada in his life, but Ontario says he lived there for a time under an assumed name. Kelwood, Manitoba, March,

1953, had a celebration for the man who knew Jesse when Jesse was hiding out in Canada. This one didn't even claim he was Jesse. It was revolutionary.

It is likewise amazing to find how people of Missouri have sympathy for Jesse. Reviewers of my book said I had sympathy, and I reckon I had. There was a lot to be said for the Clay County by; the banks were unregulated and could charge any old rate of interest they wanted; the railroads likewise were unregulated and could shake the contents of a farmer's pocketbook into their own grain sacks. So the people of Missouri didn't toss around in their sleep when Jesse and his boys robbed a bank. In fact some said that the people of Missouri turned over and slept like babies.

Jesse James had strange supporters, especially among Missourians. One of these was born in Lamar, Missouri. He went into politics where he got along nicely—in fact, became President. He said Jesse robbed the rich and gave it to the poor. Also said it was a good policy in so doing.

I'm not quite ready, myself, to say that stealing from the rich and giving to the poor is a fine policy, but I'll walk the rest of the way with him.

One of the myths about Jesse was that he became rich. This is hardly true for when he died his total cash assets amounted to $250. His widow was so poor that she could not bury him; for a time she accepted money to sit on a platform, with her two children, and let the audience look at her while a professional lecturer talked about Jesse. This proved that Crime Does Not Pay. I hope that all readers of this material will see the merit of this and try it out.

I shocked some friends by announcing that Jesse James was the best known Missourian who had ever lived, except President Truman. One of them said, in a roundabout way, that I ought to be horsewhipped. We disagreed on that, too. My friends said that Mark Twain was the best-known Missourian who ever lived. Then I pointed out that he was known only in the English-speaking world and that Jesse James, through the medium of motion pictures, was known the world around. Even in Arab countries, where most of the people couldn't read or write, they knew Jesse James and called him by name. It made me mighty proud of Missouri.

World name that he is, there is an immense amount of misinformation about him. Much of this is due to the "dime novels" that were written about him. In fact, there have been 450 copyrighted novelettes about him and Frank. Many of them were published while the boys were still kicking; a Johnstown flood came after. The title I like best is: *Frank Reade, the Inventor, Chases the James Boys with his Steam Man.* My sympathy was all with the James boys and I rejoiced when they escaped the foul monster.

I welcome all books on Jesse James. No one can read closely a book on him without getting a picture of the conditions in Missouri after the Civil War. They were truly dreadful. Brother shot brother. The very county where the boys lived was the bloodiest in the United States; the two sides were about evenly divided, for Missouri was a "Border State." The James boys were a product of this cauldron of hate.

Carl W. Breihan has fetched to light an immense amount of new material. It was unknown to me and I have been sleeping with Jesse James for years. Where he got all this information is beyond me.

One thing I do know and that is he did not get it from Robert F. James, Frank's son and Jesse's nephew. I courted him but he kept his mouth shut tighter than a Scotsman's pocketbook. All I got out of him was a charming smile. Once he talked beautifully about the weather. If I had to depend on him for information, I could have written all I knew on the back of a postage stamp.

There have been only three worthwhile books about Jesse James. One was by Robertus Love, entitled *The Rise and Fall of Jesse James.* It is now out of print and will cost you more than a television set repair bill. Another is James D. Horan's *Desperate Men.* If you don't know whose was the third, then I am too modest to tell you. Then along came Carl W. Breihan's, which is an exciting addition to the list.

Introduction

Let not Caesar's servile minions
Mock the lion thus laid low;
'Twas no foeman's hand that slew him,
'Twas his own that struck the blow.
John Newman Edwards

Out of the timber-studded hills of northwest Missouri rode Jesse and Frank James, casting shadows that were to endure and creating legends that grew to gigantic proportions.

Jesse was a legend in his own time, long before he toppled dead from a bullet fired by a traitor named Robert Ford. He spent some sixteen years of his life in armed robbery, but he never once saw the inside of a jail for all his crimes. He stole an aggregate of some half million dollars, yet he died a poor man.

There may have been two schools of thought regarding Jesse and Frank as citizens during their days as an outlaw team, but there is no question but that they came from solid stock. Their people were eminently respectable, with marked religious inclinations as evidenced by the number of ministers among them. Their ancestors, who settled in Goochland County, Virginia, were reputable persons, and they sprang from such ancestral names as Gardener, Hines, James, Mims, Poor, and Woodson.

Even today many of the backwoods people of several Missouri counties speak of Jesse and Frank in tones of almost reverence. In imagination they flash before their eyes. They see the Jameses and their guerrilla companions: "Bloody Bill" Anderson, George Todd, Bill Gregg, Quantrill, and others as they ride the outlaw trail. Outstanding in their minds is the vivid picture of Jesse riding his favorite horse Ebony . . . riding . . . riding into nothingness.

Jesse and Frank came upon the scene as the western border of Missouri was ablaze with burning homes and the grisly fruit of massacre hung heavy from the trees in the wake of the abolitionist fanatics: John Brown, James H. Lane, and James Jennison. Abolitionism, of course, was only a political force, plunder being the motivation.

Riding with William Clarke Quantrill in western Missouri during the Civil War, Frank and Jesse participated in many sanguineous and daring adventures. At that time they were just part of the vicious raiders, faceless and nameless men riding in the dead of night along the ravaged borders of Missouri and Kansas. These missions were to have a fateful influence on the lives of the brothers and their families.

They had been shaken with righteous indignation when the new Missouri State Constitution was adopted in April of 1865. It stipulated that no former Confederate or Confederate sympathizer would be permitted to practice any profession, thereby condemning them to menial labor or forcing them to leave the state.

Such was the background for a carnival of crime in which Jesse James and his brother Frank are supposed to have been involved.

Most writers tend to portray Jesse as having invented bank robberies and train holdups, but such is not the case. Of course, banks were looted during the Civil War by both sides but not by an organized group of bank robbers. Although the first crime was committed during the war it was not done by invading troops. This robbery occurred on the afternoon of Wednesday, October 19, 1864, when a large group of outlaws entered the town of St. Albans, Vermont, and looted every bank on Main Street. After the robbery the bandits made good their escape to their headquarters in Canada.

However, Jesse and his men did perform the first train holdup west of the Mississippi. This happened near Adair, Iowa, where today the citizens have erected a monument in commemoration of this historical event. The Reno brothers—John, Frank, Simeon, and William—of Seymour, Indiana, were the first train robbers in America. After a brief span of such robberies their careers were ended when all but John were lynched on December 12, 1868, in the jail at New Albany, Indiana. John spent nearly twenty years in the Missouri State Penitentiary for holding up and robbing the Daviess county (Mo.) treasurer's office in the spring of 1867.

No doubt robberies attributed to Jesse and his men were committed by other outlaws. It is now unlikely that any of the Missouri robbers participated in the train robbery at Ogallala, Nebraska. We know for sure that the Texas bandit, Sam Bass, killed at Round Rock, Texas, on July 21, 1878, engineered the job. The bank robbery at Riverton, Iowa, was committed by another Missouri outlaw named Polk Wells. Wells was captured and sentenced to ten

years in the Iowa State prison at Fort Madison. He escaped in 1882 and was returned in May of that year to serve a life sentence for murder. He was transferred on August 26, 1896, to the Men's Reformatory at Anamosa, Iowa, where he died insane on September 11, 1896.

They were a curious pair, this Jesse and Frank James. Jesse was happy-go-lucky, mischievous as Peck's bad boy, and active as the town joker. Frank was quiet, self-composed, intelligent, practical, and well-read. Only one instance is recorded that shows Jesse as being despondent. That was the time he tried to commit suicide in Kentucky because his sister Susan wanted to (and did) marry Allen Parmer, an ex-Quantrillian. I have never been able to learn the reason for the animosity between Jesse and Parmer.

Jesse was a flashy dresser for that period; Frank was more reserved and conservative in his style. Jesse' favorite suit was a coal black, tight-fitting outfit he took a fancy to when he robbed the stage near Lexington, Missouri. Its owner was an eastern schoolteacher who had come to Missouri to teach. Jesse forced him to disrobe and rode off with his prize. He wore this suit until it gave out. He always wore a pair of tight-fitting black gloves to hide his disfigured right hand with the missing fingertip.

When Jesse died in 1882, his legend did not. It has been exploited and nurtured and will probably endure until the end of time.

As in the lives of other famous or infamous characters, whose homes and graves became an important feature in the pages of history, the house where Jesse was killed in St. Joe was first used as a barber shop. The venture failed and the house was sold for taxes. In the thirties, a heated debate among citizens, businessmen and the clergy occurred as to whether the house should be destroyed or used as a museum. It was preserved for posterity. In 1949 it was moved to the Outer Belt near the Jesse James Service Station and Motel, and thousands of people visit it each year. Today it stands near the Pattee Museum in St. Joseph, Missouri. The old house is heavily insured and is sprayed twice a year with a wood preservative. At one time, it is said, a circus owner offered one hundred thousand dollars for the building.

The old James home in Clay County became a tourist attraction immediately upon Jesse's death. The original 275-acre farm had by now dwindled to 89 acres, and the house where Jesse was born, built partially in 1822, still stands. Visiting the house is like entering another era. Here is the home into which the Pinkerton detectives tossed several fire bombs. These were kerosene-filled railroad lamps with two brass wicks extending from the top of the rounded bottom part of the instrument. Dr. Samuel pushed one of these into the fireplace, causing the expanding gas in the container to explode. The explosion killed Archie Peyton Samuel, Jesse's half-brother, and shattered his mother's right arm so that it had to be amputated at the elbow. Here is also the farm where Jesse and Frank once plowed the earth, their mother doing likewise even with only one arm.

Jesse's descendants had little or no control over the property since Mrs. Samuel never legally divided it. Zerelda Samuel died in 1911 and left the farm to Frank James, who spent most of his later life there. When he died in 1915, the place was left to his only child and son, Robert Franklin James. He died in 1959 and left it to his second wife, May, who died in 1974. The property was boarded up for a while and left in a terrible state of disrepair before the Clay County Parks Department purchased it from Lawrence Barr, the remaining son of Jesse's daughter May James Barr, prior to his death in 1984.

Today the house has been returned to its natural state by the Clay County authorities, but even while it was boarded up the tourists came, exercising their own judgment about jumping the fence.

In March of 1949, Harry S. Truman had this to say about the Missouri outlaw:

> Jesse James was not actually a bad man at heart. I have studied his life carefully, and I come from that part of the country. Jesse James was a modern day Robin Hood. He stole from the rich and gave to the poor, which, in general, is not a bad policy. I am convinced that Jesse would have been an asset to his community, if he had not been diverted into a lawless life.

Frank James surrendered to Governor T.T. Crittenden following Jesse's death, and was acquitted by a jury at the famous trial at Gallatin, Missouri, in 1883. He had been tried for participation in the holdup of the Rock Island train at Winston and for the murder of Conductor William Westfall. Able counsel represented Frank, including Judge John F. Philips. His oration "brought down the rafters" of the old opera house where the trial was held, owing to the lack of room at the courthouse. Judge Philips also promised Frank to deliver the oration again at his grave. He did so when Frank died in 1915, and it was a classic piece of work.[1]

In February, 1884, Frank was arrested by federal Judge Krekel for alleged participation in the robbery of the United States Paymaster at Muscle Shoals, Alabama, in 1881. At Huntsville he was ably represented by General Leroy Walker, Richard Walker, and R.B. Sloan. Again, Frank was acquitted by the jury.

After his death Frank's body was taken to St. Louis, Missouri, for cremation, since there was no other crematory west of the Mississippi at the time. The ashes were placed in a copper urn, which, in turn, was put in a safe deposit box in the old New England Safe Deposit Company in Kansas City. In 1928 the urn was removed by Robert James to a vault in the Kearney Trust Company, Kearney, Missouri. There

---

[1]Cole Younger, a war-bandit buddy of Frank's, was lying ill at Lee's Summit, Missouri, at the time, and was unable to attend the funeral. Cole died a year later.

the ashes remained a closely guarded secret. Many have claimed that Frank's ashes were strewn over the old farm, but this is not true.

When Annie Ralston James, widow of Frank, died on July 6, 1944, her body was cremated and the ashes placed in an urn. Throughout her lifetime she remained true to her vow to Frank never to reveal anything to anyone concerning the activities of his outlaw life.

SAGA OF JESSE JAMES

Chapter One

The Real Jesse James

Who was this outlaw, Jesse James, whose name became synonymous with bold robbery over a hundred years ago and still symbolizes it today?

To what did Jesse owe the fame that a host of imposters found profit in claiming? Was it his personality? Or was it his innovative style and strategy in holding up trains and stagecoaches as they rolled across vast prairies and bank tellers as they glanced fearfully up through their windows?

No doubt both personality and innovation contributed to his reputation, but there were other ingredients also. Perhaps if there had been no Jesse James, Americans would have had to invent one, for he was a symbol that pioneer midwest America needed. To millions of Americans who read of his exploits, and to tens of thousands who knew someone who knew someone who was acquainted with someone in the James family, Jesse came to represent the courage, boldness, unrestraint, ingenuity, and manliness that are popularly associated with the settlement of the Mississippi Valley and the West.

It seems clear that Jesse really had these qualities. Moreover, the evidence is abundant that the yeast that made all these qualities rise together in fame was . . . a sense of humor.

Besides his sense of humor, Jesse also had a sense of justice. He was a man whose main occupational tool was a large caliber revolver that he didn't hesitate to use and he was generally accompanied by a troupe of highwaymen equally adept in wielding pistols, shotguns and rifles. Yet he was not indiscriminate in his choice of robbery victims.

"He robbed the rich and gave to the poor," was chanted like a catechism to several generations of midwest American children. The best authorities on the life of this handsome outlaw agree that there was considerable truth in the legend.

Jesse James spent about sixteen years of his young manhood in armed robbery, with great success escaping the law, but with no particular accumulation of wealth. He died poor. But even at his death, he had come to stand for a crude form of social justice in the minds of many people, just as Robin Hood symbolized a movement for social justice in medieval England.

Many nations have counterparts of Jesse James in their mythology: they are brave; they are protesters against circumstances that trap the poverty-stricken; they are clever; and they stoutly hold that laws are made for men, not men for laws. They are not products of slums, either medieval or modern, but come from families of substance if not of means. They all have that leavening sense of amusement at the predicament of wealthy victims of their holdups.

Historians cannot always speak with certainty on banditry in other centuries and other countries; historical records are too unreliable. Ample documentation exists on Jesse James, however, to provide an accurate portrayal of his career in outlawry. There were also plenty of people—neighbors, acquaintances and relatives—who knew Jesse, Frank, or his family from 1860 onward, and could supply the classic ingredients for a romance on his life. It might even be said that the portrait many skeptics doubted was actually a good likeness.

Like many Missourians, Jesse had Kentuckians for parents, just as a generation earlier the aristocracy of Kentucky had Virginians for parents. The Reverend Robert Sallee James, Jesse's father, was a Baptist preacher who received his training at Georgetown College in Kentucky, one of many small colleges established on slender financial bases in the early 1800s. Robert James's ancestry goes back to 1777 when the James, Poor, Mims, and Woodson families were residents of Goochland County, Virginia. His other ancestors were of the Ferris, Hines, Gardener, Martin, Porter, Pryor, and Weldy families.

Robert Sallee James's parents were John James and Mary Polly Poor, who were married in Goochland County on March 26, 1807. The Reverend Lewis Chaudoin officiated. In 1811 the couple moved to Logan County, Kentucky. Eight children were born of this union. Mary was born September 28, 1809, in Goochland County. The rest of the children were born in Logan County. William was born September 11, 1811; John R. on February 5, 1815; Elizabeth on November 25, 1816; Robert Sallee on July 7, 1818; Nancy G. on September 13, 1821; Thomas Martin on April 8, 1823, and Drury Woodson, born November 14, 1826. The girls later married into the John W. Mims, Tilman Howard West, and George B. Hite families.

When Robert James was nine years old his parents died; consequently, he was

Zerelda James Samuel (rare copy from original tintype).

raised by his sister, Mary Mims. Little is known of his early life, but in 1838, he entered Georgetown College and received his Bachelor of Science degree in 1842.

At Georgetown, Robert James met Zerelda E. Cole. She was born on January 29, 1825, in Woodford County, Kentucky, the daughter of James and Sallie (Lindsay) Cole. Zerelda attended the Catholic convent

Reverend James and Zee Cole were married in the home of Judge J.M. Lindsay, guardian of Zerelda Cole.

Reverend James and Zerelda Cole were married in front of this fireplace.

at Georgetown, although not a Catholic herself. Zerelda was only two years old when her father was killed falling from a horse. She had one brother, Jesse Richard Cole. At the time she met Robert James, she and her brother were staying near Georgetown with their uncle, James Madison Lindsay, at Stamping Ground, Scott County, Kentucky.

Zerelda's mother eventually married a widower named Robert Thomason who had six children. Zerelda hated the children and refused to accompany the new family to Clay County, Missouri. Thus it was that she remained under the guardianship of James Lindsay.

On December 20, 1841, Robert James executed a marriage bond in Scott County for his marriage to Zerelda, with the penal sum of fifty pounds in British currency— not tobacco—as some romantic writers would have us believe. Since Zerelda was only seventeen, she had to have her guardian's consent before she could be married. James Lindsay gave his consent and on December 28, 1841, Robert and Zerelda were married by the Reverend Y.R. Pitts, in front of the fireplace at the home of her uncle. This house still stand near Stamping Grounds. The record of the marriage is still legible in Marriage License Book A, File

This was the home and spring house where Reverend and Mrs. James lived for about one year prior to going to Missouri. The home was situated between Lexington and Frankfort, Kentucky on the old Frankfort Pike, Franklin County, Kentucky.

Jesse was born in the James home at Kearney, Missouri.

Number 358, in the office of the Clerk of Scott County, Commonwealth of Kentucky.

The newlyweds lived for about a year in a small house between Lexington and Frankfort, Kentucky, on the old Frankfort Pike. Then in the summer of 1842, Robert and Zerelda visited her mother and stepfather, Robert Thomason, in Missouri and decided to settle there. Following Robert's graduation, they did just this on a farm near Kearney, in Clay County, Missouri. Soon after, the Reverend James decided to further his education so he returned to Georgetown until 1843 when he received his Masters degree. Many people have questioned why the Reverend made no trips home during that time but it must be remembered that the winter of 1842-43 was very severe. Bitter cold temperatures and swollen rivers made travel difficult.

Robert went back to his Missouri farm and divided his time between tilling the soil and saving souls. His work prospered both in the ministry and on the land. He was apparently a vigorous worker for the Lord and established the New Hope Baptist Church. In 1845, he bought a 275 acre farm from Jacob Gromer who had started

In 1873, a photo was taken of the James home at Kearney, Missouri.

Reverend Robert Sallee James, father of Jesse and Frank.

Courtesy of Stella James

Frank James, age 54.

Frank James, 1870.

the buildings in 1822. The farm was well-stocked at a later date and run by seven slaves. (This is the oldest house in Clay County today.)

The young minister took New Hope Church into the North Liberty Baptist Association in 1844, and then established other churches. He helped organize the William Jewell College at nearby Liberty, was a member of its first board of trustees and during this time, accumulated one of the best libraries in the frontier state.

Some of his churches are still in existence, monuments to a Bible-carrying man riding horseback on a circuit along dim-wooded frontier trails. His monuments are as real as, although lesser known than, the

Mrs. Samuel (seated) and Mary James at the James homestead.

legends perpetuating his horseback-riding, pistol-carrying sons.

Frank was the first child born to this marriage. He was born in Clay County, Missouri on January 10, 1843.

There is an unpardonable conflict of opinions on Frank's and Jesse's birthplaces and birth dates. The errors can be traced back to slipshod research by the earliest students of James history. The records of the original Jameses who settled in Missouri give the authentic dates. Also, the United States census of 1860 lists Frank James by his full name, Alexander Franklin James,[1] and gives his age as sixteen when the census

[1]Frank's mother was a great admirer of Alexander Hamilton and Benjamin Franklin; this explains her naming her first son Alexander Franklin.

Room where Jesse James was born.

was taken on June 26. The 1850 census corroborates these facts.

The second child, Robert James, was born on July 19, 1845, and died in infancy. His mother's grief over his death caused her to bear a certain resentment toward her third child, Jesse Woodson James, who was born September 5, 1847. It was some time before Zerelda could reconcile herself to this replacement of her lost baby. Though nearly five years younger than Frank, Jesse was destined to be the leader of the pair throughout their career.

The fourth child was a girl, named Mary, who was born October 3, 1848. She died August 17, 1866.[2]

One more child was born to this minister and his wife. Susan Lavenia James was brought into the world on November 25, 1849, when news of the discovery of gold in California gave rise to a national stampede. Whether they were simply adventurous, unattached, or seeking their fortunes, Americans by the scores took off for the western mountains and the Pacific Coast.

Living in Missouri, Robert James was not far from Independence and St. Joseph, two jumping-off points on the frontier for overland journeys to the goldfields. All around him were men who had come from Kentucky, Virginia, and Pennsylvania to settle in Missouri. Now they were pulling up stakes and heading for Sutters Mill and other California hamlets whose names signaled magic to those who sought quick wealth.

The preacher resisted the lure of the gold rush for some time, but on April 12, 1850, he could withstand the tide no longer. On that day he set out for California with his friend, William Stigers of St. Joseph, leaving his family until he made his fortune.

The trip took nearly three months, about average time for a fast caravan. Robert James arrived on the Pacific Coast on July 14, 1850. Several letters were sent to Zerelda James from Reverend James, the last being dated July 19, 1850, stating they had reached their destination five days earlier. By August 19, he was dead at age thirty-two of a malady characterized by intense fever. His death occurred at a mining camp in California called Hangtown,

---

[2]The author acquired this information while perusing some papers left to him by William Stigers, of St. Joseph, Missouri. Since no one ever alluded to the existence of another girl, it's possible she bore some abnormality that the family wished to hide.

Reverend James died in Hangtown, California.
Courtesy of the California Historical Society

now more euphoniously known as Placerville.

It is said that Jesse and Frank James searched for their father's grave in later years. It is certain that other descendants of Robert James made efforts to locate his burial place as did this author, but in the anarchy of western mining camps, it was fruitless to expect the grave of one lone seeker of the golden fleece to have been marked.

Why the gentle Reverend Robert James would ever take the dangerous journey to the goldfields remains a matter of speculation. Some people thought he wanted to do missionary work in the camps. Others thought he was beguiled by the prospect of wealth and wanted a respite from Zerelda's constant scolding. The Reverend James's brother William offered what is probably the most precise reason when he said in 1882:

> Robert's wife was a peculiar woman. She made objections to her husband's riding over the country doing his minister work, he being absent from home a large portion of the time. Robert determined to go to California, intending to return home in twelve months, when he hoped to find things a little pleasanter at home.

William Stigers returned to Kearney and remained a close friend of the James family. He eventually moved to his other home in St. Joseph, from which his family counseled and comforted the Jameses at every opportunity. Unfortunately, there is no record of what he reported on his return from California.[3]

The preacher's widow, Zerelda, found life on the backwoods Missouri farm rough going, especially with four small children. On September 30, 1852, she married Benjamin Simms, a neighbor-farmer. The marriage was probably never meant to last. For one thing, the children didn't like their

---

[3]Bill Stigers, grandson of William Stigers, was a good friend of mine and a big help in the preparation of this work.

Dr. Reuben Samuel (rare copy from original tintype).

new stepfather, and then Simms foolishly demanded that Zerelda put all her property in his name. To approach a person like Zerelda with such a proposal was a bad move on Simm's part. Divorce proceedings were about to begin when Simms was killed falling from a horse. Zerelda then went back to using the name James.

In 1855, Zerelda married Dr. Reuben Samuel, also a native of Kentucky, and four years her junior. He was born in 1828. This marriage was a success since Zerelda found it easy to dominate the mild-mannered Dr. Samuel and all the children liked him. Zerelda and Dr. Samuel had four children:

Sarah L. was born on December 26, 1858, married William A. Nicholson, and had three sons. She died on July 14, 1921.

John T. was born on December 25, 1861,

Dr. Reuben Samuel.

Courtesy of Stella James

Zerelda Samuel, mother of the James boys. Note her missing arm, the result of the Pinkerton detectives' raid on her home.

married Norma Lena Maret, and died in 1934, leaving no children.

Fannie Quantrill was born October 18, 1863, married Joe C. Hall, and had three children. She died on May 3, 1922.

Archie Peyton Samuel was born on July 26, 1866, and was killed on January 26, 1875, when Pinkerton detectives assaulted the Samuel home.

In her later years Zerelda was a woman of stern visage, with a chin firmed against the onslaughts of a life having many bitter moments, and eyes showing the courage of a hawk. She brought her children up strictly, as was the custom in backwoods Missouri where church was the center of a family's social life and pistol-toting was the norm.

Mrs. James-Samuel had an almost idolatrous worship for her children, especially Frank, whom she called Mister Frank on all occasions. Jesse either called him Frank or Buck, his nickname. Anyone who uttered

anything against Zerelda's boys was in for trouble. Undoubtedly there were folks who felt that her protectiveness exceeded the bounds of healthy discipline. Zerelda claimed that her second marriage went awry partially because of Simm's dislike for the children. However, her marriage to the meek Dr. Samuel worked out very well—he stood by the boys at all times and gave them guidance, too. When Frank and Jesse later assumed the pistol and mask, folks knew it was not for lack of upbringing.

According to their contemporaries, even as children the James boys were strong-willed; only their mother's stern management kept them under control. The neighbors' opinions were divided; since most of these opinions were expressed after Jesse and Frank were hardened highwaymen, they were doubtless colored by events. Some felt that Jesse and Frank's behavior was average; others felt it was above average and still others shook their heads with an "I told you so" air and claimed they had been wild bad young 'uns from the start.

Both Frank and Jesse displayed a notable aptitude for forming friendships even in their childhood. They were considered leaders in the youthful pranks around the neighborhood.

Since wild game formed a large part of the diet of farm families in the Missouri Valley, guns were standard household equipment. Naturally Jesse and Frank learned how to use firearms early, first mastering the shotgun and then becoming expert pistol handlers. In an age of deadly marksmanship with revolvers, they ranked with the best.

A typical example of Jesse's respect for the opposite sex is shown in the following note from Miss Goula Wright, of San Diego, California:

> My grandmother, Martha Ann Jeffries, went to school with Jesse at Kearney. One day her lunch was gone and she went around looking at what the other children were eating. Jesse asked her about it and she told him her lunch was missing. He found the boy who stole it and Jesse made him apologize to my grandmother, after giving him a thrashing.[4]

---

[4]Miss Wright sent this note to the author in 1970.

The 1850s were turbulent years in Missouri and the Kansas country. Tempers flared constantly as the dispute raged over slavery and states rights.

The James boys listened to fiery talk from abolitionists and would-be secessionists. The tension swelled so that men—not wild turkey in the woods nor deer along the streams—gradually became targets of the frontier pistol and rifle. The usual discussions around the supper table focused on John Brown and his sons' exploits, their killings and raids, and the ultimate capture of Brown at Harpers Ferry by Colonel Robert E. Lee. News of Brown's hanging stirred the imagination of young men in Missouri, and when the conversation shifted to talk of war, their blood began to boil. Many were eager and ready to take sides, should the conflict begin.

Anyone hoping to understand the circumstances surrounding the lives of the Jameses must undertake a careful study of pre-Civil War days and the period of Reconstruction.

Chapter Two

War Sets Jesse on the Road

No other war in which our nation has engaged has aroused such bitterness as the Civil War. In no place did the passion arise earlier and last longer than in the Missouri-Kansas border territory.

Georgia and South Carolina remember General William Tecumseh Sherman. New Orleans remembers General Benjamin Butler. Proportionately, the Missouri counties south and east of Kansas City still have more unreconstructed rebels per square mile than the Deep South. Jackson and Clay Counties in Missouri were settled by people largely of southern sympathies—people like Dr. Reuben Samuel and his adopted James family. Eastern Kansas, on the other hand, was the scene of early demonstrations by John Brown and numbered many other abolitionists among its population.

By the time the Civil War officially began, many slavery haters had become wandering bands of armed guerrillas called jayhawkers[1] or redlegs. Out of a misguided sense of duty, or sometimes out of sheer sadism, these bands harried southern sympathizers. Their purpose was not so much to subjugate the South as to annihilate William Clarke Quantrill and his rebel band.

The principal leaders of the jayhawkers were General Jim Lane, Colonel Charles R. Jennison, James Montgomery, and a man

[1]The word "jayhawk" was coined around 1858 and referred to a fictitious Kansas bird. The word is also a nickname for Kansas.

William Clarke Quantrill (rare copy from original tintype).

named Anthony. Jennison, a former doctor from Leavenworth, Kansas, was commander of the 15th Kansas Volunteer Cavalry.

General Lane marched his men out of Kansas and into Missouri to outfit them all with the blue uniforms of the Union Army. They returned to Kansas City with the United States banner waving at the head of

William Gregg, aide to Quantrill. He later wrote a manuscript of his activities.

their column. En route they burned the town of Osceola, Missouri, on September 23, 1861, and drove hundreds of wagon-loads of spoils along with them.

Such attacks brought about the formation of pro-Confederate bands, the most notorious led by William Clarke Quantrill. Quantrill's original band was formed during the winter of 1860, and included William Haller, James and John Little, Edward Koger, Andrew Walker, John Hampton, James Kelly, Solomon Basham, George Todd, and the two brothers, Oliver and George Shepherd. By the spring of 1861, Quantrill had succeeded in swelling his ranks by the enlistment of David Pool, John Koger, William Gregg, Cole Younger, and John Jarrette, who was Younger's brother-in-law. Younger had been forced to leave home because of trumped-up charges issued against him by Captain Walley of the Missouri Enrolled Militia.

Quantrill was a mixture of patriot and brigand. He had been born in Canal Dover (now simply Dover), Ohio, and went to Kansas as a young man. In Kansas he got into trouble and was thrown out almost immediately. He was humiliated and resent-

Captain John Jarrette, Lee McMurtry, and William Hulse.

ful, and felt that the people of Kansas had treated him shabbily. Quantrill's bitterness for the state grew until it was all-consuming.

In this light, the Civil War was made to order for Quantrill—he eventually purged his entire distorted hatred by taking out his homicidal viciousness against Kansas. His excuse—which was a lie—was that his oldest brother (his family's first born) had been murdered by Kansans. The lie gradually became real in Quantrill's mind and gave him his excuse for guerrilla attacks.

Since he was completely incapable of taking orders, it was natural for Quantrill to organize his own band. He led his men to fight in the Battle of Carthage, Missouri (sometimes referred to as the Battle of Dry Forks), on July 5, 1861. It was the first significant confrontation in Missouri by Union and Confederate sympathizers.

At Carthage, Quantrill was under the immediate command of Stewart's cavalry. Cole Younger was serving in the state guard, having temporarily gone there from Quantrill's band.

At the outbreak of the war, Missouri's Governor Claiborne F. Jackson went to the field dressed in the uniform of a Confederate general. At Carthage, General Franz Sigel assured his Federal batteries that there would be no serious combat; a few rounds of grape and canister would quickly disperse the Missourians. He was in for a surprise.

General Jackson figured it was nearly impossible to get his Confederate cavalry and guerrilla aids in position under General Sigel's fire. He ordered the infantry to charge the enemy, and the cavalry to come up at the same time in support. As a result, the Federals retreated across Bear Creek—a wide and deep stream—destroying a bridge in their crossing. About a mile beyond the creek they took a stand behind a skirt of timber.

Before Jackson's men could attack, they had to cross an open field while being exposed to raking gunfire. The cavalry, including Quantrill and his men, dismounted and advanced with the infantry. They threw a pile of timber into the stream and crossed over. After an hour's heavy fighting, the Federals abandoned their position and retreated to Carthage, fighting as they ran. At Carthage they made another stand, forming ambuscades behind every cover. Then darkness fell and General Sigel and his men fell back to Rolla, Missouri, about forty miles from the scene of the first fighting that day.

Over a month later, on August 10, 1861, Confederate troops under Generals Sterling Price and Benjamin McCulloch defeated General Nathaniel Lyon and his troops in a desperate battle at Wilson's Creek (or Oak Hill), Missouri. General Lyon was killed and his troops fell back to Springfield. Frank James fought here under General Price in the Confederate State Militia. Quantrill was also there—he fought spectacularly, always getting out in front with his blazing red shirt a target for the enemy.

Although the Wilson Creek victory offered the Missourians an opportunity to assemble a grand campaign, Price and McCulloch couldn't agree, so McCulloch returned with his men to Arkansas. Even during the battle the two men argued about which of them should be in command. McCulloch insisted he ought to command both Price's and his troops since he was a regular commissioned Confederate general and Price was only a general in the state militia at the time. He later became a Major-General in the regular Confederate army.

After the Battle of Wilson's Creek, Frank James was found in a hotel in town, where he was laid up with the measles. He was immediately arrested for taking part in the fighting, regardless of the measles. He was given a field parole, meaning he swore never to take up arms again on either side. This promise rankled with Frank and on his return home, he spent his time bragging about how the Confederates had whipped the blue-bellies at Wilson's Creek. To emphasize his speech, he waved a pistol menacingly in the air. Frank was subsequently arrested and thrown into the Liberty jail. His mother used her influence with local authorities, and Frank was released. Soon after the Battle of Lexington on September 19, 1861, Frank James joined Quantrill's raiders, in direct violation of his parole.

The jayhawkers and redlegs in time acquired an official status of a sort and came to be called variously the Federal Militia, Home Militia, or Home Guards. There is no evidence that these somewhat informal military groups molested the James family, despite its known southern sympathies, until Frank James joined Quantrill's guerrillas. Frank's enlistment in that daring group, however, drew his whole family into the orbit of political passions.

Early in 1863, a militia band appeared at Dr. Samuel's home and demanded the whereabouts of Frank and Quantrill whom they presumed were hiding somewhere on the farm. Jesse and Dr. Samuel, who were plowing, said they had no knowledge of their hiding place, but they were not on the farm. The militia resorted to a violent form of torture to extract information; they fastened a rope about Dr. Samuel's neck and strung him up to a tree. Apparently they intended the hanging to be fatal, but after they left he was taken down and revived by his family. Even so, he bore rope burns on his neck for many years.

That same day, Jesse, then a boy nearly sixteen, was jabbed with bayonets and beaten with ropes by militiamen, but he released no information. The militiamen gave up hard, however, and a short time later they put Jesse in jail at Liberty, Missouri, because of his sympathies for Quantrill's men. That was the only time Jesse is known to have seen the inside of a cell. Ironically, it was for no offense against the law—it was simply one incident in the

border warfare. He was soon released, but the family's freedom was short-lived. The next time the militiamen rode up they hauled Jesse's mother and sister, Susan, off to the St. Joseph jail. Susan was just a girl in her teens. It was nearly a month before they were released, and only then because Susan had contracted pneumonia.

Fierce family loyalty raged within Jesse; he became a demon. His motive was the epitome of simplicity . . . to kill as many Union soldiers as was humanly possible. He rode away to join Frank in Quantrill's band. At first Quantrill refused to accept Jesse, saying he was too young, but the boy flatly refused to return home. The deadlock was broken when Bloody Bill Anderson agreed to take Jesse into his unit of the Quantrillians. Frank was also a member of Anderson's group, and Jesse kept to his side for guidance. Anderson later remarked, "That boy is the best fighter in the group. He's not afraid of the devil himself."

Thus Jesse's days of shooting rabbits and wildfowl on the family farm were ended. One of his earliest missions, in May of 1863, was to participate in an attack by a band of twelve guerrillas on the Yankee-sympathizing town of Richfield, Missouri, on the north side of the Missouri River. The small Federal garrison was defeated by the guerrillas; several of them killed Captain Sessions, commander of the garrison. It was a bitter, bloody education for a young man, his baptism of fire.

This ignominious defeat aroused the area commander of the Federal forces. He sent a new garrison from Plattsburg, Missouri, to track down the guerrillas. The Confederate grapevine was functioning perfectly though, and Jesse learned about the dispatch from his mother. Such a shift of forces left Plattsburg poorly defended so Anderson's band—Jesse included—descended on the town and captured a large supply of guns, ammunition, and money.

Sometimes northern sympathizers would set off a reign of terror and sometimes

"Bloody Bill" Anderson, as guerrilla.

southerners would instigate one. When jay-hawkers wantonly sacked and burned the town of Osceola, Missouri, Quantrill's band retaliated by laying waste to the town of Lawrence, Kansas. Quantrill also chose Lawrence since he wanted to get back at the Kansans for their alleged mistreatment of him. An ostensible purpose of the Lawrence raid was to capture and put to death General James Lane, a man bitterly hated by the guerrillas for his indiscriminate raids into Missouri. A close accounting of the raid showed 154 of the best buildings in the business section and residential districts destroyed, and a property loss of a million and a half dollars, an appalling sum for those days. August 21, 1863, was indeed a black day for Kansas, for 185 men and boys died violently.

The Lawrence raid was one of the blackest episodes of the border warfare, and researchers have tried hard to establish whether or not Jesse James participated. It seems that he did not, although Frank

James was there that day. The evidence that Jesse was not in Lawrence at the time of the pillaging hinges largely on the testimony of Captain Harrison Trow, a well-known member of Quantrill's group, and the memoirs of Cole Younger, who was later one of Jesse's partners in outlawry.[2]

As members of Quantrill's guerrillas, Jesse and Frank became accustomed to the sound of shots in the dark, ambushes along the forest-bordered roads in the Missouri country, and the sight of violent death.

This guerrilla warfare grew even more rugged, and at Flat Rock Ford, near the

---

[2]Cole Younger, whose reputation for ruthlessness was widespread in later years, was oddly enough something of a man of mercy that day in Lawrence. He is credited with successfully pleading for the lives of several citizens taken prisoner. This act of charity repaid him handsomely many years later, for some of these men became prominent in the attempt to obtain a pardon for him after he was sentenced to prison in Missouri for his part in the ill-fated raid on the Northfield bank.

Grand River, on August 13, 1864, Jesse James nearly met his death. About 65 encamped guerrillas were surprised by 300 Federal soldiers and about 150 redleg partisans. In the attack Jesse was struck in the lung by a musket ball. The guerrillas retreated hurriedly, leaving Jesse where he had fallen. They figured he'd never survive, but he crawled into a nearby field and hid. His friends, Gooly Robertson, Nat Tigue, Ol Shepherd, and Peyton Long were determined to save him. Jesse, however, expected to die so he handed Peyton a plain gold ring, with instructions to give it to his beloved sister Susan. Then he told the men to leave as there was no use in their getting killed too.

But Jesse didn't die. He was later rescued and nursed back to health by Mrs. John Rudd and Mr. and Mrs. S. Neale, in Carroll County.

Chapter Three

Centralia and Beyond

On the morning of September 23, 1864, fifty guerrillas were camped near the Howard-Boone county line. Another band joined them. This detachment was under the command of Captain Tom Todd (no relation to Captain George Todd).

Captains George Todd and Bill Anderson called on Captain Tom Todd to formulate a plan of action. After a few minutes reflection, he proposed a raid by the three companies through the northern parts of Howard and Boone Counties. They would tear up the North Missouri railroad, cut the telegraph wires, fight at every favorable opportunity and in George Todd's language, "raise Hell generally." This would draw the Federals from the river and afford the guerrillas an opportunity to cross at Rocheport in safety.

Fayette was directly in the path of the guerrillas. The Todds wanted to march around it, but Anderson urged an attack on the town and, if possible, capturing and avenging the deaths of six of his men killed by the Federals while they were sleeping in a barn a few days earlier. Anderson's counsel prevailed and a charge was ordered, the Todds going to the left and Anderson to the right of the courthouse.

The guerrillas were in town before the Federals were aware of them, howling and yelling like wild Indians and shooting in every direction. On through the town they tore like a hurricane, receiving a volley as they passed the courthouse. Converging in the northwest, the guerrillas re-formed scarcely out of reach of the enemy's long-range guns. They charged the Federals' camp furiously, but anticipating just this, the soldiers took refuge in an old double log house, some brick dwellings, and a deep gully. They poured such a withering fire into the ranks of the guerrillas that they were forced to beat a hasty retreat.

The soldiers were armed with short-barreled, long-range guns. Had it not been for their poor marksmanship, the guerrillas probably would have lost quite a few men. As it was, six of them were left dead on the field.

From Fayette, the guerrillas marched about twelve miles and camped outside Huntsville. They held an election to choose an officer to command the three companies. Captain George Todd was chosen. The next day, two of them were sent into town to demand a surrender. The response was that the guerrillas had ample opportunity to attack if they wished. Recalling their experience of the day before at Fayette, however, the guerrillas decided against taking on soldiers who were defending brick houses.

The march toward Jefferson City was resumed, and on September 27, 1864, the guerrillas were southeast of Centralia. At ten o'clock that morning, in a haze of dust and the sound of galloping horses' hooves, Bloody Bill Anderson and a part of his company rode boisterously into Centralia. Some of the men wore long linen dusters; others wore uniforms of various types. At first the citizens weren't sure just who they were or why they had come. They did notice, though, that the roughnecks were a motley group, most of whom wore their unkempt hair long—almost to their shoulders—and were heavily armed with a sinister array of big Navy Colts in their belts and waistbands.

Then it was whispered around that the hard-visaged man commanding the company was none other than the notorious Bloody Bill Anderson. Men and women hurried into their homes for safety. When the invaders began entering and looting the stores, the storekeepers and other businessmen fled out the back way, thinking not of their goods but of their lives.

Anderson walked erect and brazenly into a saloon. In minutes, he and his men had taken over the place. They broke open a barrel of whiskey and started drinking, using shoes and women's slippers in lieu of glasses. (They'd taken the shoes from one of the nearby stores.)

When the drinking orgy was at its height, the Columbia stagecoach arrived in Centralia, bound for Mexico, Missouri, where the passengers were to attend a political meeting. Riding the stage were some prominent people: Major James Rollins (a Congressman), James H. Waugh (sheriff of Boone County and afterwards a well-known banker), John M. Samuel (a former sheriff), Henry Keane, Boyle Gordon, Lewis Shaw, and Lafayette Hume. The stage was brought to a halt by the outlaws and all the passengers robbed of their money, jewels, and other valuables. Anderson made no distinction between northerners and southerners when he robbed. The occupants of the stage, though, saved their own lives by giving false names to the raiders.

The stagecoach was then permitted to continue its journey. Later on, near eleven o'clock, the Wabash Railroad's regular passenger train was seen approaching the town. The guerrillas dragged up crossties, threw them on the rails, and hurriedly concealed themselves. The engineer, seeing the obstructions and also noting that sections of the town were on fire, brought his train to a stop. The raiders fell in on either side of the train, firing their heavy revolvers and threatening the engineer and other trainmen with instant death. Anderson and his men then went through all the coaches and abducted twenty-six Union soldiers, some of them ill and others being mustered out of service.

Lieutenant Peters saw what was happening; he quickly discarded his uniform and cap, wrapped himself in a blanket and darted out under the burning depot. He was captured by two of the guerrillas and led to the spot where the execution of the soldiers was to take place. Of the twenty-seven soldiers of the Union Army who had been on the train, only one escaped death. He was Sergeant Thomas M. Goodman, who was kept alive as a hostage to be offered in exchange for Cave Wyatt, one of Anderson's men who had been captured a short time before on a train en route to St. Louis. Sergeant Goodman later managed to escape from the guerrillas and Cave Wyatt was hanged in Kansas City.

The other poor wretches were marched to the edge of town and lined up. Eyewitnesses claimed that Anderson himself shot all of them, a freshly loaded pistol being handed to him as fast as he emptied the one in hand.[1] No amount of pleading saved one life, and not one word of pity or protest was uttered by any of the guerrillas. On the contrary, they all seemed to gloat over the ruthless massacre of the Union soldiers by their monster chieftain.

[1]Whether or not Anderson personally killed twenty-six soldiers at Centralia has always preyed upon my mind. Checking further I find that a different story unfolds. In the *History of Boone County* twenty-six pages are devoted to this subject, possibly biased by the sentiments of the author, W.C. Todd, a cousin of Captain Tom Todd.

After plundering from the train everything of value, Anderson's men set it on fire. They ordered the engineer to start the engine, pull the throttle wide open and jump off. Farther up the road, he gathered the injured and terrified passengers into the cab and tender of the locomotive, uncoupled the engine from the burning cars, and rushed to the town of Sturgeon.

The soldiers in Sturgeon, after hearing the story, hastily prepared for an attack. Instead of immediately charging after the guerrillas, they tried to strengthen their position in the town. They had heard that Major A.E.V. Johnson and three hundred soldiers were en route to Centralia, and they thought it better judgment to let the regular army battle with the murderers.

Great apprehension prevailed in the little town of Sturgeon, where it was feared Anderson's men would attack next. Late that afternoon a lone rider came galloping into town. He was unarmed and his uniform was in tatters—literally torn from his body. Only the remaining shreds of his pants identified him as having been in Johnson's command. The soldier was verging on collapse from shock and exhaustion. He told haltingly of the guerrillas' assault on Centralia: citizens were killed outright, stores and homes looted, and the town burned. The citizens of Sturgeon accordingly went and recovered the bodies. They brought them back to Sturgeon and

The report reads in part, "Anderson and his men immediately went through the cars, taking off twenty-seven federal soldiers, twenty-six of whom were killed . . . "

The descendants of Sergeant Thomas M. Goodman, living in Iowa and in California, essentially offer the same account as W.C. Todd. Also, in his small booklet, *A Thrilling Record*, Sgt. Goodman reported, "After I had stepped out of line at the request of Anderson, who had asked for a volunteer sergeant, he assigned me a post to the rear. Just then a volley from the revolvers of the guerrillas in front, a demoniac yell from the surrounding men, mingled with cries and moans of pain and distress from my comrades smote upon my ear."

I suspect that these two reports would negate the idea that Anderson did all of the killing personally.

put them in the church which was converted quickly into a makeshift morgue.

Major Johnson, who was stationed at Paris, in Monroe County, received news of Anderson's attack on Centralia when it first happened. He believed that Todd's men were also involved with Bloody Bill and he made plans to attack them all.

He found their trail south of Middle Grove and followed it into Centralia where he saw the bodies of the soldiers who had been massacred. The town itself was in ruins. Furiously, Johnson ordered an attack on the guerrillas who were then only a few miles away. He had received strict orders from General Clinton B. Fisk to weed out all the guerrillas in his territory.

Had the Major known of the deadly accuracy of his opponents—their swift and ruthless way of charging a foe and their death-dealing revolvers—he might have wisely chosen to ride to Sturgeon and safety, deciding it was in his better interest to leave the raiders unmolested.

He had never witnessed or experienced this kind of combat. The guerrillas went into battle at full gallop. When they were within gun range of the enemy, they let loose with a terrifying rebel yell. It was enough to curdle one's blood. Then, with increasing speed, they fired a deadly barrage of heavy caliber bullets, often firing with both hands. They always carried several loaded cylinders in their pockets or tied to their saddle horns; when the revolver was empty, they cunningly used some sort of trick practiced and perfected whereby the empty cylinder was knocked out and the loaded one swiftly injected. Their aim was near perfect—most of their victims died shot through the head. These weapons were not the cartridge type, but the cap-and-ball percussion type, hence the use of interchangeable cylinders.

Major Johnson rode down Centralia's main business street on his fine horse, the impressive Knox County militia regiment close behind. Suddenly, a young woman dashed out and threw her arms about the neck of his horse, begging him not to fight Anderson's guerrillas. ''Those devils will kill all of you, sir! I beg of you, turn around and run for your lives! I saw Anderson and his gang and what they did here today, and it was ghastly beyond description. Please retreat before it is too late, Major!''

Johnson was impressed by her pleas, but he replied calmly, ''My good woman, much as I appreciate your concern, I have orders to attack those cutthroat guerrillas. Surely you would not have our soldiers run from those murderous swine. Look what they did to your beautiful town. They must be annihilated, so that their outrages cannot continue. Do not worry, miss. We will bring Anderson's head back on a rail within a few hours.''

With that Major Johnson and his forces rode out of Centralia on the trail of the guerrillas.

W.C. Todd, a cousin of Captain Tom Todd who was there that day, reported that when Major Johnson left Centralia, Captain George Todd sent a scout, John Thrailkill, to ascertain the strength of Johnson's troops and armament. Thrailkill rode close to town and through his field glasses saw 103 men in line, two abreast, making a total of 206 men armed with what looked like Enfield muskets. He conveyed this information to Captain Todd, along with word that about 25 soldiers had been left in town. Thrailkill was then ordered to decoy the enemy to their position.

Todd ordered his main detachment to fall back into the timber and then charge when he gave the signal. He went up on a rise where he could get a clear view of the Federals and still be seen by his own men. There he waited, ready with fifty men. Anderson stayed to the right with sixty-five picked men, and Captain George Todd's company of eighty men formed the center. George Todd always chose the center of an attack—this time was no exception.

Thrailkill and his ten men rode close to Centralia and exchanged a few shots with the Federals. Johnson sent some of his men to attack them, but the wily Thrailkill fell back for a mile, and then wheeled and charged the soldiers, sending them scampering. At that Johnson left about twenty men to guard the wagons, mounted the balance of his soldiers, and took off in hot pursuit. Thrailkill paused now and then to exchange a few shots while he led the Federals into the Todd ambush. How Johnson could have been maneuvered into such a trap remains a mystery. He must have figured that Todd's main troops were nearby, or at least suspected that the purpose of Thrailkill's small group was to lead him somewhere.

About three miles from town, Major Johnson ordered three-fourths of his men to dismount, leaving every fourth man to hold four horses, as was the custom with mounted infantry. At the same time Thrailkill had ridden up to Captain Todd, who was watching from the rise. Now Thrailkill and his ten men dismounted and tightened their saddle girths for the main charge. This could have given Johnson the idea that Todd and Anderson planned to fight on foot. He should have known better. The guerrillas, with years of mounted warfare to their names, certainly would not resort to infantry tactics now.

Major Johnson, riding in front of his foot soldiers, advanced about a half mile. He raised his Dragoon pistol and shouted, ''You damned cowards, wait for us. Why don't you come back and fight instead of running like scared rabbits, you women-killing bastards?''

Todd calmly waited to allow Johnson ample distance from his horses before ordering an attack. He then raised his hat three times before putting it on his head. This was the prearranged signal. One can imagine the Union troops' surprise and consternation when they saw three companies come galloping over the rise, many of the riders with their horses' reins in their teeth and a heavy Dragoon revolver in each hand. Once they were within gun range of the enemy, the familiar, blood-chilling rebel yell was raised. The soldiers fired a volley at eighty yards, but most of the bullets passed harmlessly over the heads of the advancing guerrillas, leaving only three dead and three wounded.

At about forty yards from the huddled Union troops the entire front of the racing horde of guerrillas was one solid mass of flames from their guns. The smoke rose and disclosed by later count fifty-seven soldiers dead on the ground, and the rest in wild flight. In short order they, too, were motionless on the ground. Major Johnson was also slain, having been singled out by the gaunt young man who later became the famous bandit, Jesse James.[2] For just one shocked moment those soldiers who'd been left holding the horses stood petrified, as if they'd seen a legion of ghosts appear from nowhere. They turned and galloped madly toward town with the guerrillas in hot pursuit. Anderson and Arch Clements, led the charge against those Federals who were left and shot them too.

A few of the guerrillas in the field reached Centralia and prepared to fight those Union soldiers who had been left there. Approaching the town, the guerrillas faced a short line of Federals waiting for them. Anderson, standing at the head of his men, surveyed the situation with his fiery black eyes. Quickly he ordered a charge. Most of the soldiers were slain in the first assault. One of Johnson's men who miraculously escaped the carnage reported on the men who'd been left in Centralia:

> Lieutenant Jaynes was the first to arrive from the fight; he told us they were whipped, and that we had better move to Sturgeon, which we did at a dead run. All the men (who) escaped, as far as I know, went to Sturgeon except two who made their

"Bloody Bill" Anderson in death.

way to Paris. Fifteen of those left in town to guard the wagons were killed. I think about fifteen to eighteen in all escaped.

The battle produced one significant result: the Federal commanding officer in St. Louis, General Douglass, clearly realized he was dealing with organized bodies of Confederate troops, rather than roving bands of outlaws. He ordered his field commanders to treat all captured guerrillas as prisoners of war.

Many historians refer to this battle as a massacre; such is not the case. True, the

---

[2]The belt and revolver that Jesse took from Johnson's body can still be seen in the old homestead at Kearney, Missouri.

murder of the soldiers taken off the train at Centralia was a massacre, but the defeat of Major Johnson and his troops was the result of a well-planned and executed ambush, not the indiscriminate slaughtering of unarmed men.

Some apologists for Bloody Bill Anderson claim his slaughtering the soldiers in Centralia was in retaliation for the murder of his sister by Federal soldiers and the sacking of the town of Osceola, Missouri. It was said, "That Quantrill sometimes spares; Anderson, never." For each soldier he killed, Anderson tied a knot in a silk cord he wore about his neck. When he was killed on October 27, 1864, near Orrick in southwest Ray County, Missouri, the cord was knotted fifty-four times. Four days before that, the gallant Captain George Todd had met his death during a skirmish near Independence, Missouri, when a Spencer rifle ball pierced his neck.

The cold-blooded murder of the soldiers taken from the train in Centralia has gone down in history as one of the most atrocious crimes of the era, followed by the execution of ten reputable citizens of Palmyra, Missouri, on October 18, 1862, by Union General John McNeil.

Shortly after the Centralia affair, the guerrilla force itself fell into an ambush. During this fray, Jesse's horse was shot from under him and he was wounded in the left side and arm. Despite his wounds, he was credited by fellow guerrillas with shooting several Union soldiers.

Not long afterward, a group of men with whom Jesse rode and fought camped about four miles from Independence, Missouri. Among other attractions, the town had a house full of gay girls who entertained Federal officers for a price. Jesse, a handsome, clear-skinned, slender youth, assumed one of his earliest disguises—the dress of a girl—and went calling on the madam of the house in search of information. That night an even dozen Federal officers decided to call on the hospitable

General John McNeil, called the "Butcher of Palmyra."

girls, but were ambushed and killed as they approached the brothel.

Quarter was seldom granted in this vicious semi-freelance backwoods fighting. The brothel episode was soon followed by the Confederate guerrillas penning up eight Federal soldiers in a barn, setting the barn on fire and shooting the men as they fled the smoke and flames.

On still another occasion, the guerrillas found eleven Federals in a house. Ten were killed outright, but in the confusion, one escaped. When he was found later, he was sent to some nearby woods to be shot. Some people claim that Frank James was assigned the executioner's role, but it is more probable that Arch Clements was given the task. Even though he was a guerrilla hardened to killing, Arch could not stomach this particular chore so he fired a shot into the air and let the man escape.

General Jo Shelby.
*Courtesy of Missouri State
Historical Society*

It was about this time that guerrilla bands began falling on hard days. Confederate organized forces under General Sterling Price and Jo Shelby had retreated from Missouri, leaving the Federal troops free to search out and exterminate the remaining guerrillas. With no protection from the Confederate Army, the bands drifted apart.

Jesse James went south to Texas with Lieutenant George Shepherd, and Frank went into Kentucky with Quantrill.

During a ragged march through the Cherokee nation (now Oklahoma), the company of which Jesse was a member encountered a troop of Federal militiamen commanded by Captain Emmett Goss. Jesse

General Thomas Ewing, Jr., Union forces, issued Order No. 11 after Quantrill's raid on Lawrence, Kansas.

fostered a particular enmity for Goss, though the reason is obscure. It was symptomatic of the border warfare bitterness and perhaps of Jesse's deep-seated disregard for an enemy's life. At any rate, Jesse singled out Goss and sent bullets through his head and heart.

Jesse remained in Texas for the winter of 1864–65. In the spring he headed back to Missouri with a small party of guerrillas. He killed two foes on his circuitous route: a Federal soldier named Harkness who was said to have harried Confederate sympathizers, and a former Union soldier named Duncan.

On Palm Sunday, April 9, 1865, General Robert E. Lee surrendered to Lieutenant General Ulysses S. Grant at Appomattox Court House, in Virginia. Later that month, Confederate guerrillas were surrendering to Federal Major Rodgers in Lexington, Missouri, and on April 23, Jesse rode at the head of one of the surrendering troops, carrying a flag of truce. He was leading the group for a conference with Major Rodgers to negotiate a surrender. As the group rode past the old brick school, they saw a detachment of Union cavalry coming up the Salt Pond Road, seven miles from Lexington. The approaching soldiers were apparently drunk and, without warning, they fired.

Startled by the sudden attack, the guerrillas returned the fire, and then scattered and ran. Jesse was hit in the lung by a minie ball—the same lung he'd been shot in before. He stayed in his saddle, though, and fled south along Prairie Church Road. Past the A.A. Young farm, he managed to find an old drift coal mine on Garrison Creek. Later, he made his way to Dr. Barnett Lankford's home where he was given food and treatment, and within two days, was on the road again through Johnson County to a place eight miles southeast of Clinton, in Henry County, Missouri.[3]

Here he learned that his mother had gone to Rulo, Nebraska, and was teaching school there. She had removed herself from Missouri after the Lawrence raid, when General Ewing's General Order No. 11 commanded all Confederate sympathizers to move within a certain distance of a Federal post or leave the state. Zerelda had chosen to leave. Jesse joined her in Nebraska traveling on a flatboat provided by Major Rodgers, of all people.

A week after the shooting, Dave Pool and forty other guerrillas surrendered and told how Jesse James had been wounded. Provost Marshal Rodgers did not bother to list Jesse's name among those who sur-

---

[3]John L. Jones, later of Cottonwood Falls, Kansas, a private in the Third Wisconsin Cavalry, claimed the distinction of having fired the last shot of the Civil War in Missouri by wounding Jesse James.

rendered. He stated he had seen the boy and was certain he would die. This omission made Jesse James a hunted man right off the bat.

In Nebraska, Jesse thought he was dying and asked to be taken back to the Missouri homestead. He said he wanted to die on his native soil. Though somewhat apprehensive of the wrath of the Federal troops who had ordered her from her home, Mrs. Samuel started back to Missouri with Jesse. They got as far as Harlem, Missouri, a place across the river from Kansas City, where Jesse again saw his cousin, Zerelda Mims. It was "Zee" who assumed the task of nursing him during his long recovery.

Zee was twenty years old at the time, an attractive young woman, and Jesse's double-first cousin. He fell in love with her, and

eventually married her at the Clay County home of W.B. Brander. His uncle, the Reverend William James, reluctantly officiated. Jesse's marriage to Zee took place in Kearney, Missouri, on April 24, 1874, and lasted until his death.

Meanwhile, during the winter of 1864-65, Frank James was in Kentucky with Quantrill, who ambushed a company of the enemy near Hartford and, in turn, was ambushed near Smiley. Frank was off on another mission on May 10, 1865, when Quantrill and his men were trapped in a barn during a heavy rainstorm. Frank did return to the Wakefield House, where Quantrill and his men had been taken temporarily. The guerrilla chief begged his men to surrender. Quantrill was later transferred to a military hospital in Louisville,

Wakefield Farm. Quantrill was wounded and taken to this house.

Courtesy of W.A. Zink Collection

since Captain Edward Terrell, whose men had wounded the guerrilla leader, feared his men would try to rescue him. Quantrill was later admitted to the Catholic hospital in Louisville, where he died on June 6, 1865.

On July 26, 1865, Captain Henry Porter of Quantrill's band did surrender to Captain Young of the United States Army, at Samuel's Depot, Nelson County, Kentucky. With Captain Porter were Bill Hulse, John Harris, John Ross, Randall Venable, Dave Hilton, Bud Pence, Allen Parmer, Lee McMurtry, Ike Hall, Bob Hall, Payne Jones, Andy McGuire, Jim Lilly, Jim Younger, and Frank James. This was Frank's second surrender. The first had been at Wilson's Creek in Missouri, when he had been paroled after taking a solemn oath never to take up arms against the government. This made Frank James a parole violator. Had Captain Young known this, Frank's career would have been terminated at once, without ceremony or trial. Jim Younger, brother of Cole, was confined to the military prison at Alton, Illinois, for some unknown reason and was released near the end of 1865. Others who accompanied Quantrill into Kentucky surrendered a short time later.

1903 Convention of "Quantrill's Band" at the Old Blue Church in Blue Springs, Jackson County, Missouri. Last man to the left in the last row is Frank James. George Shepherd is to the right of the young boy. The young boy is B.J. George, Sr., son of Hi George, Quantrillian (enlargement of original group photo).

Chapter Four

The Birth of Outlawry

The Civil War had ended but old animosities festered along the border country of Missouri and Kansas. Jesse had surrendered honorably at the end of the war, but his wound at the hands of a Federal trooper resulted in his being unofficially consigned to the dead. Moreover, since his name did not appear on the roster of surrendered Confederate guerrillas, he was fair game for the semi-official state enrolled militia as they endeavored to enforced the Reconstruction Act one way or another.

In Missouri, the terrible warfare left scars wide and deep and bloody. They were still tender when the banners of the contending armies were furled. At least it seemed so to Frank James who postponed his return to Missouri. He had played a conspicuous part in the war, and on account of Centralia, he was on the list of the proscribed. As far as Jesse and Frank James were concerned, the war had not really ended where actual hostilities were involved. Although Frank longed to return to Kearney and the farm, he was reluctant to do so and remained in Kentucky for a time.

To make matter worse, on April 8, 1865, the state of Missouri adopted the Drake Constitution. Why such an amendment to the newly-formed Constitution was adopted has never been explained. It stipulated that all Confederate soldiers or Confederate sympathizers were forbidden to practice any professions or act as deacons in any church under heavy penalty. The amendment held Confederates fully responsible for acts committed while they were either soldiers or civilians, yet granted full amnesty to all Union soldiers for their acts after January 1, 1861.

In August, Frank decided to return to Missouri. He and three other Missouri-bound friends were passing through Nelson County when they decided to stop over in Brandenburg, Meade County, Kentucky.

On the night of August 27, 1865, at about nine o'clock, the four men, mounted on exceptionally fine looking horses, rode up to the hitching rack in front of the Ashcraft Hotel in Brandenburg. They were: Frank James, Cole Younger, Clell Miller, and Andy McGuire. They dismounted, tied their horses, and stomped into the hotel lobby, almost colliding with the handyman, a young black lad named Charles Jackson.[1]

Now, a number of nearby Larue County residents had been losing valuable horses and everybody was on the alert for possible thieves. The sight of four strangers on such splendid mounts led the townsfolk to believe that they must be the horse thieves. Some of the citizens gathered on the porch of the hotel and when the four ex-guerrillas stepped out, they were accused of being horse thieves. There was not a shred of evidence, but no one stopped to reason. A

---

[1]Jackson later reported the incident, along with a Mr. Boling who was seated in the lobby at the time.

blacksmith, George Smith, attempted to arrest Frank James and the shooting began. Smith succeeded in shooting Frank in the hip.

While Clell Miller and Andy McGuire held the crowd under their guns, Cole Younger assisted Frank in mounting and then they too drew their guns and covered the mob. The four galloped out of Brandenburg. Some twenty miles from Brandenburg, Frank's hip was treated in the cabin of a friend on Otter Creek. Dr. Henry K. Pusey, of Garnettsville, was the attending physician.

The Radicals controlled the Missouri state government. The men who had gone away to fight for the Confederacy, the guerrillas, and the southern sympathizers found themselves officially stamped third-class citizens. Such were the conditions in Missouri when the Jameses and Youngers returned to their homes and tried to live in peace.

Jesse James, according to his family and friends, wanted to live a peaceful life. He would not be, he said, driven from Clay County, his home. His mother supported his determination and warned him never to surrender to anyone accosting him on the pretext of being a law enforcement officer. Some of the men who had ridden with Quantrill, she said, had been forced to surrender on trumped-up charges. Even though the war was over, they'd been taken from the jails and hanged by Federal partisans.

Jesse knew from experience that former members of the Confederate army—especially former guerrillas—could not be too cautious in postwar Missouri. His friend, Henry C. Campbell, for instance, had fought in General Price's Missouri division and had returned to live in Cooper County after surrendering to the victorious Union army. Near Campbell's home lived an ex-Federal soldier who owed him money. Campbell went to collect and was attacked by fifteen Federals. Fortunately, when he fled, Jesse and several neighbors spotted him; they ambushed the soldiers and rescued Campbell.

Another of Jesse's friends, Arch Clements, was in a rescue party that found four of General Price's former soldiers hanging from a tree, victims of another atrocity committed by Federal militiamen. The hanging had just occurred, luckily, and because the men had been pulled up from the ground slowly, not yanked from the backs of horses, their necks weren't broken and they could be revived.

Jesse retained a strong sense of justice for the downtrodden. At one point he protected a black boy who was in the care of General Jo Shelby's family in Lafayette County, Missouri. One day some white boys beat the black boy up. On his return trip, the black boy carried the general's old revolver and when the contention started up again, he nipped the white bully in the leg.

A mob formed and prepared to lynch him. Jesse, a mere stranger to the mob, pleaded with them to spare the boy's life, but his words had no effect until someone in the group recognized and identified him to the bunch. His reputation already commanded respect. Consequently, the black boy was taken to Lexington, tried, and acquitted.

The former guerrillas shared a deep sense of loyalty among themselves and their families. The frequently-told story of his ingenious aid to the widow of James DeHart illustrates this strong feeling. The widow, alone and penniless on a small farm in Tennessee, was expecting the sheriff and a loan shark banker to foreclose the mortgage on her farm. Just by coincidence, on the day this distressing event was to take place, Jesse and a companion rode by the farm, had lunch with the widow, and inquired concerning her obvious despondency.

She explained that DeHart had died and the sheriff was going to take away her farm. Since DeHart had been Jesse's friend, it was easier for him to listen to the tale of woe. Jesse handed the widow the $500 she needed to pay off the mortgage, cautioning her to get a full receipt for the money and a release of the mortgage. Then he and his companion were on their way. Several hours later Jesse held up the banker and sheriff as they returned from their visit to the widow, and the money used to pay the mortgage found its way back into Jesse's pocket.

February 18, 1867, was a bitter night. Jesse was at the Samuel homestead in Kearney when a party of six militiamen rode up to the house. Although still suffering from the wound in his lung, Jesse fought them off with a revolver in each hand. Some accounts contend that Jesse killed several of the soldiers that night but there is no evidence of this.

Jesse believed that the militia would continue to molest him, so he went into hiding until the spring and then embarked on a series of travels taking him, among other places, to New York, to the Isthmus of Panama, and then on to California. In California, he stayed with an uncle, Drury Woodson James, who owned the La Panza Ranch in San Luis Obispo County.[2]

[2]Drury Woodson James was one of the organizers of the town of Paso Robles, California, which was incorporated on February 25, 1889. He had a half interest in the Paso Robles Hot Springs and Rancho with Daniel D. Blackburn. Drury James and Daniel Blackburn donated land for the city's park, and Drury donated land for a public school—the present site of the Paso Robles High School. He was county supervisor of San Luis Obispo for many years, a school trustee, and a member of the state legislature. He was the overwhelming choice for the gubernatorial nomination for the Democratic Convention of 1877, but on the strong objections of his wife, he refused the nomination.

Frank James had preceded Jesse to their Uncle Drury's ranch. Both young men were still recovering from bullet wounds and led quiet lives. After a year, Jesse returned to Missouri, but within a short time he was again the victim of former Union soldiers who couldn't let the violence of the Civil War die.

Even though General Lee had surrendered, the North hadn't finished beating on southerners and the atmosphere generated by such incidents invited further violence. Those returned Confederate soldiers and ex-guerrillas who had slow, even temperaments patiently bore the rebuffs and harassments of the triumphant redlegs, Home Guards, and state enrolled militiamen. Men of hot and headstrong dispositions like Jesse, however, felt that society had turned against them and that a life of outlawry was justifiable under the circumstances. Such was the background for the series of bank robberies in which Jesse James and his brother Frank were involved.

Chapter Five

Postbellum Crime

LIBERTY, MISSOURI

On February 13, 1866, a band of armed men rode into Liberty from several directions. They met in the square, where their leader deployed them at strategic points. It was quite early in the morning so no one paid any attention to the two men who entered the Clay County Savings Association building. They confronted the cashier, Greenup Bird, who was alone in the bank except for his small son. Under threat of instant death to himself and his son, Bird was ordered to open the vault and the robbers stuffed their two saddlebags with $58,000.[1]

Outside was a young lad named George Wymore who was on his way to William Jewell College with Henry W. Haynes. Bird thrust his head out the window as the robbers hastily left, and called out to Wymore, telling him of the robbery and asking him to raise an alarm. Wymore began yelling, "Robbers! Robbers!" As he did so the bandits began firing and yelling with savage fury. Haynes quickly took shelter behind a tree, but Wymore was not so fortunate—he was hit by four bullets and killed.

---

[1]Even today tourists can walk into the bank vault from which the money was taken.

LEXINGTON, MISSOURI

Soon another robbery occurred and the people of Missouri began to wonder about the security of the country banks. On October 30, 1866, between noon and one o'clock, the banking house of Alexander Mitchell & Company, in Lexington, Missouri, was robbed of $2,011. There were four robbers and to carry out their bold plan, they had chosen the lunch hour when no one was in the bank except J.L. Thomas, the clerk.

A few minutes before they came in, Thomas was standing in the doorway of the bank, when he noticed a couple of strange men approaching. Thinking they were coming into the bank, he stepped back and was writing a letter at a desk when they entered. One of the men placed a fifty dollar 7–30[2] bond on the counter and requested the discount on it. Mt. Thomas did not like the laughing manner in which the request was made and replied that the bank was not buying that kind of funds.

Just then the two other robbers appeared. In an instant, Mr. Thomas was surrounded by four revolvers. The thieves warned him that he'd die if he didn't obey orders to the letter. In the cash drawer, they found $2,000 as well as $11.50 in silver. They

---

[2]7–30 was a government bond (they had probably stolen it) with interest coupons attached. The outlaws probably were willing to sell it at less than face value.

Left to right: Fletcher Taylor, Frank James, Jesse James, 1866.

claimed there was an additional $100,000 in the bank, and that if Thomas valued his life he would tell them where it was. Thomas denied there was that much money in the bank. The bandits searched him for the vault key, but he didn't have it so they left. As they did, they warned Thomas not to call out any alarm under pain of death. Quickly, they reached their horses which they'd tied in a nearby alley, and were gone.

Soon twelve armed citizens, including Jesse Hamlet, David and John Pool, James Cather and Hedge Reynolds, started after the bandits. They spent two days on a fruitless search. The trail led down the road to Wellington. After a brisk ride of several miles, Dave and John Pool found the robbers and fired. The Pool boys reported five thieves in the party when they saw them, but they were unable to get close enough—the outlaws' horses were too fast.

It was a bold robbery and one that stirred the countryside. Thomas described all the men as well under thirty years old. The

Liberty, Missouri bank as it appears today. It was robbed by outlaws on February 13, 1866.

Courtesy of J. Wymore

Thomas Little was with the James brothers at Liberty. Little was a guerrilla under Quantrill. Later, he was hanged at Warrensburg, Missouri after the Richmond, Missouri bank robbery (from original tintype).

descriptions easily fit both Frank and Jesse James but there was also talk that the band might have been made up of Kansas "redlegs," leftovers from the war.

The Younger brothers loudly asserted they had nothing to do with these robberies. They were friends of the Jameses, nevertheless (or were supposed to be), and their names went down as accomplices in this as well as in many robberies to follow. Suffice it to say, large sums were offered as reward for the capture of any of the Youngers, dead or alive.

RUSSELLVILLE, KENTUCKY

The Missouri outlaws decided to extend their operations outside the state. Their first target was the Southern Deposit Bank

Southern Bank of Kentucky, Russellville, March 20, 1868.
Courtesy of R.F. James

in Russellville, Kentucky. At the time, Russellville was a little, quiet, and beautiful village in Logan County. Its people were peaceful and decent, and it was a center of wealth.

Nothing exciting ever happened in Russellville; things moved in a routine fashion. Thus, citizens barely noticed a well-dressed man riding a superb mount, stopping before the private banking concern of Nimrod Long and George Norton. It was Long and Norton, years earlier, who had paid tuition for one struggling minister in the Baptist church in Georgetown, Kentucky. Yes, the minister was Robert James, father of Jesse and Frank.

This stranger, who said his name was Henderson Colburn, stepped into the bank and asked Long to redeem a 7-30 note in the amount of $500. Long, president of the bank, grew suspicious when the stranger offered to sell the note at par when the interest coupons were still attached. Colburn claimed to be from Louisville and Long, knowing full well that such a note

was at a premium in that city, refused to buy it.

There are many versions of what occurred in Russellville at noon on March 20, 1868. A great grandson of Nimrod Long reported that eight men were involved: Frank and Jesse James, Cole Younger, Jim White, George and Oliver Shepherd, John Jarrette, and Jim Younger. These men had spent the entire previous week in Russellville, buying every fast horse and gun in town, and looking the situation over.

At noon, Mr. Long was at home eating lunch when he heard the shots. He jumped up from the table exclaiming, "They are robbing the bank!" He ran down the street and entered the bank through the side door where his office was located. Jesse James confronted him and they scuffled. Jesse shot at him twice, but the bullets just grazed his head.

Jesse just returned to the front of the building and told the other bandits he'd just killed the bank president. The gang succeeded in tying up the bank cashier,

Morton Barkley, and scooping up $14,000. They failed to seize the $50,000 in the vault, though, and during their getaway, dropped a one-hundred-dollar bill.[3]

Several of the bandits sat astride horses in front of the bank. When Mr. Long ran out shouting that robbers were in the bank, they took a few shots at him but missed. All the robbers galloped out of Russellville along the Franklin Road, riding through an old covered bridge and disappearing into the wilderness.

A second account states that Long was in the bank when Colburn and another robber entered. They held a revolver to Long's temple and demanded the money. In a surprise move, Long wheeled around and leaped for a door leading into a rear room. Colburn did not fire. He seemed astonished and irked at the banker's efforts to escape the menace of the gun. Long reached the back door and a bandit fired two shots but the bullets just grazed his head. The banker tore through the rear exit yelling for help. Two of the mounted robbers fired, but missed him again. This time, though, Long was able to round the corner and escape.

Inside the bank, Colburn and his companion were busy keeping guard over the two clerks and stuffing money into the infamous grain sack. A citizen named Owners got an old six-shooter and blazed away at the robbers, but a volley from the bandits quickly sent him scurrying. Not a single shot had struck a target.

About twenty minutes after the gang of robbers had dashed from town in the direction of Gallatin, a hell-bent posse of some fifty Kentuckians took off in pursuit, but the effort was fruitless. The desperadoes were riding splendid mounts; the towns-people were trying to overtake them with old farm plugs and buggy horses—there wasn't a capable animal in the lot. Also, while the peaceable townspeople were most reluctant to venture into brush and thicket,

the fearless ex-Quantrillians could ride pell-mell through anything.

The posse returned wearily to Russellville after trailing the bandits as far as the Mississippi River. The robbers crossed there and hid out in the rugged hills of southeast Missouri.

The first account of the robbery sounds more reasonable for it seems impossible that expert marksmen should fire at Long so many times and at such short range without killing him. Yet both reports more or less agree. There are also disputes over how many bandits participated; some say twelve and some say six men were involved.

Around Russellville, the news of this daring raid on the bank spread far and wide. Names of all Missouri bandits were constantly on the citizens' tongues. Many of them had heard of Jim Younger and Frank James because they rode with Quantrill in Kentucky in 1865 and left a gory record. Jesse James and Cole Younger, though, were just vague newspaper names to them.

There was much speculation on the identity of the raiders. Friends of the James boys declared it was impossible for Jesse to have participated. They maintained that he was in Chaplin, Nelson County, more than fifty miles from Russellville, when the robbery happened. Jesse himself, that nervy bandit, wrote to the *Nashville American* in which he claimed to be at the Marshall House in Chaplin at the time of the robbery. However, the date Mr. Marshall stated Jesse was in his hotel did not agree with the date of the holdup. For Jesse to ride over fifty miles on horseback in six hours was far from impossible; many times his alibis hinged on this fact. It was also noted that Jesse was seen in Chaplin the day after the robbery.

As for Frank, friends said he was still suffering from a hip wound he received in Brandenburg, but it was no secret he could ride a horse with his injury. He'd made several recent trips on horseback between the Sayers' home in Nelson County to his

[3]The hundred-dollar bill was later retrieved by a Mrs. Grubbs and returned to Nimrod Long.

relatives' home in Logan County. Citizens who claimed he was a horse thief shot at him.

Some people were sure that Jesse and Frank were staying with a Mr. J.D. Thompson (La Panza Ranch) in San Luis Obispo County, California, at the time of the Russellville robbery, but they were mistaken, for the brothers had been seen with relatives in Logan County, just a dozen miles from Russellville.

Nimrod Long hired the famous Louisville detective Delos Thurman "Yankee" Bligh to track down the robbers. Bligh had often remarked that his life's ambition was to meet Jesse James, and that if he did, he would be ready to die. One day Bligh met a man at the Jeffersonville, Madison, and Indianapolis railroad depot at 14th and Main Streets, in Louisville, and had an interesting talk. Afterward, he told friends about the fine gentleman he had met. A postcard arrived from Baltimore several days later:

> Dear Mr. Bligh:
> You have been quoted as saying on more than one occasion that if you could only meet Jesse James, you'd be content to lie down and die. Well, Mr. Bligh, you can now stretch out, lie down and die. The gentleman you met the other day in the R.R. depot at Louisville was yours,
> Sincerely,
> Jesse Woodson James

Highly indignant at this affront, Bligh began following clues that put him on the trail of Oliver Shepherd. Shepherd had quietly left Kentucky for his home in Jackson County, Missouri. Learning of this, Bligh and William Gallagher, another detective, notified authorities in Jackson County to be on the alert for the robbers.

The usual story of Oliver Shepherd's death is that when the officers approached his home he chose to fight it out with them and was killed in the fray. According to Margaret Shepherd, however, the lawmen came to her grandfather's home on April 4, 1868, and called to Oliver to throw down his weapons and surrender.[4] Oliver showed no resistance on account of his family and respect for his brother's home. He threw his guns and gun belt into the yard and went out with his hands over his head. He was shot as he approached the woods. Later on, twenty bullets were found in his body instead of the usually reported seven.

Although warrants and requisitions were out for the arrests of Cole Younger, Jesse James, John Jarrette, and Jim White—all thought to be participants in the Russellville robbery—none of the men were ever arrested. George Shepherd, who spent some time in the Kentucky State Prison, was an exception. Law officers raided the Younger residence, but found only the youngsters, John and Bob, there.

Jesse returned to Missouri right after the Russellville affair. He rode from Chaplin in Nelson County, Kentucky, to Clay County, Missouri, where he was seen around the beginning of April. It is no wonder that he and the other bandits were able to escape the Kentucky posse. Jesse knew every path in the rugged hills of southern Missouri. Moreover, friends of the Jameses were numerous in early post-Civil War Missouri. It was on the advice of one of these friends, Dr. Joseph Woods of Kansas City, that Jesse decided to visit his uncle in California.

In May, 1869, Jesse left his mother's home near Kearney on his way to New York. On June 8, he booked passage on the steamer *Santiago de Cuba*, bound for Aspinwall.[5] From there he took a steamer to San Francisco. At this time, Frank was hiding out in the Sayers' home in Nelson County. It was considered unsafe for him to

---

[4]Margaret Shepherd, a niece of George Shepherd, related this to the author. Her father was an eyewitness to the affair and was present when the doctor counted the bullet wounds. Her grandfather kept Oliver's guns and cartridge belt.

[5]Aspinwall is now called Colon. It is in north central Panama on Limon Bay, the north entrance to the Panama Canal.

remain in the area, however, so Frank too went off to visit his uncle in southern California (San Luis Obispo County).

Jesse and Frank met in Paso Robles at their uncle Drury Woodson James's Sulphur Springs spa and visited some of the Nevada mining camps in the autumn. Their stay at the spa had done wonders for their health and they were again anxious to be on the move.

After bidding farewell to their relatives and friends in California, Jesse and Frank boarded an eastbound train and in due time were back in their old haunts in Missouri.

Frank, grave, self-possessed, lithe of figure and gracious in manner, had a warm hand and a winning glance for those whose friendship he desired. He was scholarly, this rough fighter of the border, and could speak German and Spanish fluently, as well as quote Shakespeare.

Jesse, smiling and warmhearted, made friends easily and loved practical jokes. He was cautious, and his keen judgment prevented his social abilities from leading him into conversational pitfalls. His education was meager, about the fifth grade. At times he could be moody and anxious to exact revenge on anyone he thought had betrayed him.

GALLATIN, MISSOURI

It was noon December 7, 1869, when two young men on spirited horses rode up to the door of the Daviess County Savings Bank in Gallatin, Missouri. One dismounted and handed the bridle rein to the other, asking him to hold his horse for a minute. He then quickly entered the bank. A young man named James McDowell was in the bank on business. The cashier, John W. Sheets, formerly a captain in the Missouri Federal militia, was behind the counter.

The stranger, who looked like a well-to-do stockman, took a one-hundred-dollar bill from his pocket and asked the cashier to change it. Sheets took the bill, walked back to the safe and took out a handful of bills. He was counting the change when the stranger pulled out a navy revolver and shot

Daviess County Bank, Gallatin, Missouri was robbed by the James gang on December 7, 1869.
Courtesy of R.F. James

the cashier through the heart, at the same time grabbing the money and stuffing it in his pocket. He fired a second shot immediately, which went through the cashier's brain. Before the startled McDowell could recover his senses the deadly revolver was on him, holding him at bay.

The robber went behind the counter, plundered the safe and till, and secured about seven hundred dollars in currency. Thomas Lewis, the eighteen-year-old brother-in-law of Captain Sheets, ran into the bank and saw the outlaw pulling Sheets' body from under the counter. Startled, the outlaw fled into the alley and attempted to mount his horse, but the animal jerked away. Lewis darted from the bank, but the outlaw threatened him with his revolver.

The horse moved abruptly and threw the robber. He fell to the ground and was dragged about thirty feet, head downward, and with one heel caught in the stirrup. He succeeded in disengaging himself, however, and for a moment he lay prone while the animal went racing off in the distance.

The whole incident occupied just a few minutes, but by that time a dozen townsmen had snatched up weapons and were racing toward the bank. They opened a lively fusilade, but the mounted bandit instantly rode back to his fallen comrade, who leaped up behind him, and together they galloped away.

About a mile southwest of town the fugitives met Daniel Smoot, riding an excellent saddle horse. Without hesitation they approached him and, with the muzzle of a revolver an inch from his nose, told him to dismount. Smoot took to the brush with great alacrity, and the two robbers were once more equipped. They seemed to have little fear of capture after obtaining Smoot's horse.

Between Gallatin and Kidder they conversed with several people, boasting of what they'd done. At one point they met the Reverend Helm, a Methodist minister, and pressed him into service at gunpoint, forcing him to guide them around so as to avoid Kidder. Upon leaving the minister, one bandit informed him that he was Bill Anderson's brother and had killed a man named S. Cox, if he hadn't mistaken the man. He claimed it was an act of vengeance for his brother Bill's death.

Undoubtedly the robber was framing a tale based on some fact of old guerrilla warfare to demonstrate that the raid on the bank was not for plunder alone. Bloody Bill had been killed by a volley in an ambush by Federal soldiers during the war. Furthermore, the cashier (Captain Sheets), had been an officer in the Missouri Federal militia and fought several battles with the guerrillas.

The sheriff at Daviess County found the outlaws' skittish horse and identified it as the property of a young man named James, whose mother and stepfather lived about four miles from Centreville, Clay County (now Kearney), near the Cameron branch of the Hannibal and St. Joe Railroad. The escaped robbers were also traced across the Missouri River into Clay County.

Reports stated that the James boys were dangerous killers, having had a lot of experience with Quantrill's raiders during the Civil War. A thorough inquiry was conducted to verify the identity of the robbers; most people did not doubt that Jesse and Frank James had been the pair. Later on, of course, Jesse claimed he sold the recovered horse to Jim Anderson some time before the robbery.

Hearing that they were accused of the Gallatin crime, Jesse and Frank boldly rode into Kearney and denied the charge. They avoided Gallatin, though, because a warrant had been sworn out for Jesse's arrest there. The boys' display of wrath and injured innocence convinced most residents. Even the governor stated publicly that he didn't believe the James boys had anything to do with the Gallatin robbery.

Once it was definitely ascertained who the robbers were and where they were from, two Gallatin citizens, thoroughly armed, rode to Liberty, Clay County. They called on Captain John S. Thomason, former sheriff of the county and an ex-officer of the regular Confederate army. Captain Thomason felt that for the honor of Clay County he should lead an expedition to find the robbers and return them to Gallatin for punishment. Accompanied by his son Oscar and the two men from Gallatin, he started for the Samuel residence, some twenty miles from Liberty.

Approaching Dr. Samuel's residence called for some strategy. The men from Gallatin watched the house from the woods, while the captain and his son dismounted at the front gate and walked very deliberately to the door. Before reaching it, however, a little back boy named Perry ran by. Just as he reached the stable, the door opened suddenly and out galloped the two robbers on splendid horses, with pistols drawn. The Gallatin party in the woods opened fire on sight. The ex-sheriff and his son followed suit, as did the James brothers, but no one was hit. Then the chase began.

Thomason's horse, a fine animal, was the only mount to clear the fence, so while the other pursuers used the gate, the captain found himself some distance from his men. Thomason was riding like the wind, and he gained on the robbers, well-mounted as they were. Several shots were exchanged, but the speed was too great for accuracy. Carried on by the heat of the chase, Mr. Thomason was soon far in advance of his supporting column, and, in fact, hotly pursuing two desperadoes with nothing but an empty revolver.

Just what really happened will probably never be known, as there were no witnesses but the principals, who chose to remain silent about it. A short time afterward, Mr. Thomason returned to Dr. Samuel's house on foot, evidently having made a forced march through the woods. The horse he had been riding was later found, shot dead. He took a horse from the Samuel barn and

started for Kearney. He had hardly been gone ten minutes when Frank and Jesse returned to the house. When they learned from their mother than the captain had the nerve to come back there, they went after him, vowing to kill him. They missed, however.

Thomason reached Liberty about ten o'clock that night and found the town considerably excited over the report that he'd been killed. When his posse had lost track of him, they returned to Liberty and circulated that report. Thomason's story was that when he realized he couldn't hit the robbers from a running horse, he dismounted to get one well-aimed shot.

The James's version later was that when they found only one man pursuing them, they turned on him and killed his horse, whereupon he plunged into the thicket. They were willing to allow his getaway, but they never dreamed he'd have the gall to help himself to a fresh horse from their stable.

Of course, the entire county turned out to catch the Jameses—without success. The robbery was perhaps the most remarkable of all in the Missouri bandits' repertoire partly because two men only were involved, and partly because of the utter wantonness of the slaying.

Jesse was so furious about the borrowed horse that he wrote Thomason a letter threatening to kill him if the animal was not returned at once, though he was reluctant to do such a thing since the ex-sheriff had been a soldier in the Confederacy. The captain promptly returned the horse, although he claimed he ought to be paid for the horse he had lost. Ironically enough, years later after Captain Thomason's death, Jesse met Scott Thomason on the Texas plains and upon learning who he was, paid him $125 for the horse he'd killed.

Many years ago this author talked with Thomas Lewis and recorded his account of the Gallatin raid:

Captain John Sheets was killed by the James boys at twelve o'clock noon on December 7, 1869. I was just across the street—eighteen years old at the time.

James McDowell ran out and said, "Sheets has been killed." Captain Sheets was my brother-in-law.

I forgot the shooting and ran into the bank where he had been killed. There was a man in there, pulling the body from under the counter, where it had fallen after he was shot. While I was in the bank, this man had gone back into the alley. As he attempted to mount, his horse threw him and jerked loose in front of the bank. I heard the crowd holler, "Catch him!"

I darted out the door. The crowd was behind the bank. This man had gotten up on his feet; he saw me and drew a revolver. I rushed toward him; he pointed the gun at me and drove me back. I backed away and watched until I got out of sight around a corner of the bank building.

I then ran across the street to the Post Office, and Chris Gillihan handed (me) a revolver across the counter. I reached for it, but E. Barnum grabbed it.

We ran back to the door of the Post Office. The two men were trying to get on one horse. They left town, both on this one horse.

Two or three citizens after them on horses got close enough to shoot, but their guns were rusty or failed to operate, and the robbers got away.

They went south and met Preacher Helm. Told him that if he did not take them to a certain red barn, near Kidder, a small town, they'd kill him.

Now Preacher Helm didn't know anything about a red barn, but luckily for him he struck it just right, and they released him unharmed.

RETREAT

Since the murder of John Sheets was making things too hot for them, the Jameses decided to hide out for a while. They traveled to Matamoras, Mexico, just in time for a public fandango. Naturally Jesse and Frank were unprepared to execute the graceful steps of the Mexican young bloods, but they tried. Their attempts were so amusing to the audience that soon the Mexicans began to mimic and poke fun at them.

This was too much for Frank; he simply knocked down the Mexican who had been laughing loudest. His response caused a near disaster. A large raw-boned Mexican reached out and struck Frank full in the face, knocking him into a group of onlookers. Jesse seldom fought with his fists. Up came his revolver and the swarthy Mexican fell dead with a bullet in his brain.

Jesse and Frank rushed for the door, but a dozen belligerent Mexicans blocked it. There was nothing to do but shoot their way through. Four Mexicans fell dead; others struck at Jesse and Frank with their needlepoint stilettos. Jesse's right arm was pierced, and Frank was wounded in the shoulder. Fortunately, the hidalgos had no firearms, or their careers would have ended then and there.

Safety lay in flight, so the Jameses mounted their horses and sped toward the Rio Grande. So many Mexicans were swarming around now that their only avenue of escape was the river. Putting spurs to their mounts they plunged into the Rio Grande and swam to the other side. They stopped in Conception, Texas, and remained under the care of a physician there for a time.

Meanwhile, Jesse was suffering from a chronic discharge in his right chest, the result of earlier gunshot wounds. He became more and more thin and feeble. When he and Frank returned North from Mexico, they avoided Missouri and holed up at their uncle's (Major George B. Hite) home near Adairville, Kentucky. It was here that Jesse attempted suicide. The attempt is correlated partly to his poor state of health and party to his bitter opposition to his sister Susan's prospective marriage to the ex-Quantrillian, Allen Parmer.

It was in early January, 1870, when Jesse rode into town and procured sixteen grains of morphine; he used morphine sometimes to mitigate the pain from his lung wounds. He may have already established a degree of tolerance for it. When he returned to his

The Hite home, located among the trees, near Adairville, Kentucky, was a hideout for outlaws. Jesse tried to commit suicide here.

Reprinted with permission of the Courier-Journal

uncle's, he swallowed all sixteen grains in one dose. Later that day he felt the drug beginning to take hold and believed it was too late for any remedial efforts to prove effective. He therefore called Frank and Susan, advised them of his condition, and gave directions regarding messages he wanted them to deliver for him. Frank immediately sent for Dr. D.G. Simmons. It was 7 p.m. when the doctor arrived. He found Jesse in a profound stupor and insensible to his surroundings, apparently dying. His pulse was slow and forced, and his respiration was heavy and stertorous, characteristic of opium poisoning.

Frank and Susan assisted in every possible way. In addition to giving Jesse the usual evacuant and antidotal remedies, they tried to counteract the narcotic's toxicity with mental and physical excitement. When

Front door of the Hite home, Adairville, Kentucky

Courtesy of R.N. Holman

vocal appeals and circumambulatory stimulants had been tried for a while and Jesse failed to respond, Frank tried to think of something else to arouse his brother. It was vital that Jesse be kept alive until the drug had at least partially left his system.

Then force of habit manifested itself in a striking manner. Jesse evinced a powerful reaction when Frank whispered to him certain warning words, perhaps in code. It was as if they were in a precarious situation where they had to escape or defend themselves to the death. Each time Jesse started to sink back into the narcotic-induced coma, Frank's cabalistics brought him back to his feet. He called for his pistols (which had been emptied) and flourished them. Frank and Susan propelled him around the room. Every few seconds he lapsed into profound slumber even when they forced him to continue walking. Frank aroused him over and over using the same talisman, but Jesse's eyelids seemed to have millstones suspended from them.

About 4 a.m. all efforts to keep him awake proved futile. His pulse was reduced to a mere thread, his breathing was feeble and very slow, and it seemed that the angel of death was hovering over him. Dr. Simmons suggested they allow him to rest. He would probably die, but a rest might prove an advantage. His sister mourned over the bed. Frank sat motionless, in mute and stern despair. His eyes were fixed vacantly on the floor and his arms were folded across his chest. His jaw remained rigid and his lips sternly compressed.

Within half an hour, Jesse's pulse began to show signs of improvement. His breathing also became more natural. Soon there could be no doubt of his survival. By 6 a.m. he was awake and recognized the family, and by breakfast he was feeling hungry. When he was fully conscious he expressed considerable emotion, joyful that he had failed to kill himself. He thanked Mrs. Hite and the others profusely for their

Susan James Parmer

Allen Parmer married Susan James, sister of the outlaw Jesse James.

Courtesy of R.F. James

The safe of the Ocobock Brothers Bank, Corydon, Iowa was robbed by Jesse James on June 3, 1871. The safe is now in the Wayne County Museum.

efforts throughout the night to revive him. He showed both shame and contrition.

The following November 24th, his sister Susan married Parmer just the same.

CORYDON, IOWA

After a period of idleness, plotting, and recuperation, the reorganized band, consisting of the Jameses, Cole and Jim Younger, McClelland "Clell" Miller, Jim White and one other—probably Jim Koughman—decided to rob the Corydon County treasurer's office in Corydon, Iowa.

The bandits took over the office in their usual efficient manner, but the frightened clerk was unable to open the time lock safe. When he finally convinced the outlaws he was telling the truth about the lock, they proceeded down the street to the Ocobock Brothers Bank.

It was noon on June 3, 1871, when three of the outlaws entered the bank; the other four remained outside. The bank cashier was startled by three revolvers aimed at his head. All alone in the bank and perhaps remembering the fates of other cashiers, the unfortunate man handed over the keys. The robbers emptied the safe of its contents, about $6,000.[6]

To add insult to injury, the men donned masks and appeared at a political meeting being addressed by Henry Clay Dean. In his customary brash manner, Jesse called out, "You-all been having fun, so have we. We just robbed your bank of its last dollar. If you want to arrest us, just follow and we'll oblige."

As soon as a holdup was accomplished, the robbers split up and rode in different directions. They did just this after riding southward out of Corydon. Jesse rode off alone and in a few hours two pursuers caught up with him, but he had clothed himself in the garb of a farmer.[7] Without giving the posse a chance to question him,

[6]Some reports claim that $40,000 was taken.

[7]Jesse always carried farmer's garb in his saddle roll for such emergencies.

he enlisted their aid in a search for several men he said had stolen some of his horses. In order to divert their suspicion even further, Jesse rode part of the way with them, and then on some pretext took another route. The robbers were fortunate to have thought of masks when they rode out of Corydon.

The *Osceola Republican* gave a stirring account of the robbery, as well as descriptions of several of the outlaws. One was described as about twenty-five years old, wearing false whiskers, about five feet eight inches tall, no necktie, and dressed in a dark barred muslin coat, barred pants, black slouch hat, and linen duster. This was probably Jesse James.

Descriptions of the brothers were often given in reverse, however. Frank stated later in his 1912 writings that they planned this. Sometimes he would look like a tall man; at other times he would remove the heels from his boots and wear a flat cap. Jesse would merely reverse this: sometimes he would be wearing heels and a high hat, giving the impression of being taller than Frank, and at other times he would be shorter.

Chapter Six

Robberies Continue

COLUMBIA, KENTUCKY

Columbia is a thriving community in Adair County, the south central part of Kentucky. It had a population of about one thousand on the day of the famous bank robbery and murder, April 29, 1872.

Several days before the event, five strangers, all riding exceptionally fine horses, rode into Columbia and secured quarters for themselves and their mounts at the residence of Mr. Green Acrees. They represented themselves as livestock buyers and were most agreeable to Mr. Acrees and his family.

Of course, their riding about the country, ostensibly looking for stock to purchase, was in reality an excuse to acquaint themselves with the terrain and plan their manner of escape. No suspicion at that time or ever afterward was attached to the amiable Mr. Acrees, for he, as well as other persons in the locality, was obviously duped. Mr. Acrees was dumbfounded when he later discovered that he had been host to five members of the James-Younger gang. It is difficult at this late date to determine exactly who these five bandits were, but

BOB YOUNGER.

JIM YOUNGER AS A BOY.

Bob Younger, Jim Younger
Courtesy of Harry Y. Hall

Cole Younger during the Civil War.

village talk implicates Frank and Jesse James, with Cole, Jim, and Bob Younger.[1]

On the morning of the robbery of the Bank of Columbia, sometimes referred to as the Kentucky Deposit Bank, the five strangers rode into town and up to the bank, which was located just off the square

[1]Joe Williams, a small boy in 1872, said he was in Simon Spring when five mounted men came along and asked him the way to town. When he started to reply one of the men reached down and pulled him into the saddle with him, and the boy thus indicated the way to Columbia. Later Williams was a guard at Stillwater Prison when Cole Younger was a prisoner there. He identified himself to Younger, who remembered him from that day outside Columbia.

on Burkesville Street. Three of them dismounted, cast unconcerned glances up and down the street, and then filed into the bank. The other two remained outside, taking positions from where they could command the street. They drew heavy Colt revolvers and with a hearty yell, began shooting and telling everyone to get into their houses. Naturally, the surprised citizens hunted cover.

Inside the bank, talking in front of the fireplace, were R.A.C. Martin (the cashier), James T. Page (circuit clerk of the country), Judge James Garnett (lawyer and bank director), and Major Thomas Claburn Winfrey. The cashier was busy at his unrailed desk, and the other men were seated at a table engaged in discussion.

At that time William H. Hudson entered the bank. As he did so, he recognized one of the outlaws as the man who had been a dinner guest in his home the day before. The men in the bank were caught unaware as the bandits drew their guns and one of them gruffly ordered, "Get your hands up, and keep 'em up, and you won't get hurt."

The third man, reportedly Jesse James, said to Mr. Martin as he covered him with a heavy Dragoon revolver, "This is a holdup, and if you don't wanna get your damned head shot off, don't start nothin'. We mean business, no damned fool tricks outta ya, or I'll drill you."

Judge Garnett started to rise from his chair and yell, "Robbers! Robbers! The bank is being robbed!"

"Shut your damned big mouth or I'll blow your head off," one of the bandits snarled, and then struck the judge with the barrel of his pistol.

Mr. Hudson grabbed a chair and swung at the robber who was menacing the judge. The robber dodged; his trigger finger nerved, and the revolver fired. The judge was shot in the hand, to such an extent that amputation was later necessary. The two bandits up front were thus kept pretty well occupied. The third was shoving the heavy revolver into the brave cashier's face, "Open up that safe; be quick about it too, or I'll spatter your damn brains all over Adair County." Mr. Martin however reached for a gun which lay in a nearby drawer. It was his last act, for a .45 calibre slug tore through his head and he dropped to the floor. James Page, who had been standing near Martin, later stated he thought the bandit meant only to frighten Martin into opening the safe. As Martin turned, the bandit swung the pistol in his direction and fired.

Momentarily distracted by the shot, the two robbers looked around, giving the other men a chance to escape to the street. Page and Winfrey found safety in an old tavern on the corner. After looting the bank of all the money in sight—between $1500 and $4000—the three bandits joined their two mounted companions and fled south out of town.

They turned up a creek and crossed a field where a gate opened into another road. As they galloped toward the gate, they noticed a man and a boy approaching from the opposite direction. The man was closing and fastening the gate when the bandits galloped up and reined in their horses.

"Open that gate!" one of them snapped.

Now the man to whom this demand was addressed was not accustomed to such un- friendliness. William Conover was a brave man and his response was understandable. "Who in the dod-blasted hell do you think you all are, ordering people around like that. If you want the gate opened, open it yourself!"

Several of the men guffawed—not the man who had given the order. Face flush- ing, he drew his revolver and leveled it at Conover's head barking, "I said open it and that's what I meant. Now open it, and damned quick, or I'll blow your empty head off your shoulders."

Conover wasn't about to argue with the .45 so he opened the gate saying. "Why

shore, shore, gentlemen, I was only fooling. No hard feelings."

From that day on Conover was known as Open the Gate Bill Conover. Both he and the boy later affirmed that the angry man had been Jesse James, judging by his re- semblance to the man killed in St. Joseph.

Columbia's citizens formed a posse and named Captain J.R. Hindsman (later a lieu- tenant governor) in charge. Mr. Alexander, president of the bank, offered a reward of $2500 for the bandits' apprehension, and cashier Martin's body was taken to Shelby- ville, Kentucky for burial.[2] The bandits made a clean getaway, apparently riding north through Taylor and Marion Counties to their hideout in Nelson County.

Some years afterward, a tent show visited Columbia. One old fellow stepped out to the front platform shouting, "I am the original and only Jesse James!" Here was another pseudo Jesse, trying to gain pub- licity. Marshal Evan Atkin was then the principal law enforcement agent in Colum- bia. With a grin on his face he retired to the courthouse and hunted up the bench warrant issued when the real Jesse James and his gang paid a visit to Columbia. When Marshal Atkin returned to the carni- val grounds, the man who said he was Jesse James was still holding the crowd spell- bound as he recounted his astounding ad- ventures and escapes from the long arm of the law. Marshal Atkin stepped forward and asked, "Is this man really and truly Jesse James?"

"Why, my dear sir, there is absolutely no doubt of it—this is Jesse James!" the barker continued.

The old man interrupted and drawled, "Why shore, I am Jesse James."

---

[2]Major Winfrey's son, Dr. Frank Winfrey, said he once worked for Frank James in Kansas City, and that Frank admitted privately he had fired only to frighten Martin. He hadn't thought Martin would dodge into the line of fire. Also S.F. Coffey, of Columbia, mentioned meeting Frank James in 1901 when he admitted being in Columbia and that an unfortunate thing had happened there.

The marshal revealed his badge and commented, "Well, I have a warrant right here in my pocket for the arrest of Jesse James on charges of murder and bank robbery. So if you are not out of town in thirty minutes, I'll serve this warrant on you."

The carnival departed in a hurry.

KANSAS CITY FAIR

Jesse and Frank relied on variety and surprise in their escapades. "Who but Jesse and Frank would have thought to rob the Kansas City Fair?" people asked afterward.

The fair was held in September, 1872. At the peak of the evening events, at least twenty thousand people were watching the attractions. Overly romantic accounts say that two mounted men dashed up to the gate and robbed the cashier of his receipts.

Not so, claimed Frank James.[3] His version was that at about 6 o'clock on the evening of September 26, he and Jesse strolled into the fairgrounds to assess the situation. They spotted a man in a booth set off about fifty feet from the administration building. He was counting money. The man was locked in behind a small sliding window and there were no guards around. Jesse produced a large bill, tapped on the window and showed it. The window opened a little but the man said he was closed for the time being.

Jesse replied, "All I want is change."

The man looked Jesse and Frank over pretty closely. As they were dressed in fine clothing, he probably figured they were connected with the fair, so he opened the window and took the bill. When he looked up again he was staring into a cocked .45. Jesse ordered him to keep his mouth shut or he'd die, and to dump all the money into a bag on the counter. He complied and Jesse told him to sit still for ten minutes or he'd be back with a bullet for his head.

[3]Frank also claimed that he and Jesse alone were involved in the Kansas City Fair robbery. Cole Younger was not, though the newspapers printed otherwise.

The safe of the Ste. Genevieve Bank.

The outlaws ran to their horses and escaped with about $8,000. Frank said it was the neatest robbery they'd ever pulled off. The papers blasted the two men the next day and demanded the high-priced Pinkertons do something to arrest them

STE. GENEVIEVE

The winter of 1872–73 was severe so when May rolled around the bandits were restless. Frank James and Jim Younger left for California hoping to obtain information on large gold shipments leaving San Francisco on the Union Pacific Railroad. Jim's uncle owned a large general store there and Frank's uncle operated the Paso Robles Hot Sulphur Springs in San Luis Obispo County.

Jesse decided the five members still hiding in Jackson County should go into action. These included Cole and Bob Younger, Clell Miller, Bill Chadwell (alias Bill Stiles), and himself. They would ride to Ste. Genevieve, Missouri, and plunder the bank.

On May 1, 1873, the five departed Jackson County and stopped at a country place a few miles south of Springfield. From there they proceeded to Bismarck along the Iron Mountain Railroad, remaining there just a day. Shortly after nine o'clock, the morning of May 27, three entered Ste. Genevieve from the south of town and two from the north.

No one was inside the bank except the cashier, O.D. Harris, and the son of State Senator Firman A. Rozier, the president of the bank. The robbers leveled their pistols and ordered him to open the safe. Young Rozier began to speak but was cut short.

"You keep still, you damned little rat, if you don't want to die!"

"For what?"

"For another word."

Driven by an overpowering urge, Rozier junior leapt down the steps near the landing and raced from the building. The two bandits standing guard outside fired three times at the boy, one bullet passing through his coat. Mr. Harris opted for the more sensible alternative and unlocked the safe, allowing the outlaws to help themselves to about $4,000, most of which was in silver.[4] Throwing it into a sack, they mounted their horses and sped away. Fortunately for the bank, about $100,000 in cash had been transferred to the Merchants Bank in St. Louis the day before.

Outside of Ste. Genevieve, the robbers met a farmer traveling toward town. They informed him that he would find some things of value along the road ahead that belonged to the bank. Accordingly, the farmer found an empty coin box and lots of papers scattered about. The bandits had lifted a number of the bank's important documents, but perceiving they were useless to them, had discarded them.

An impromptu posse pursued the robbers, halting from time to time to retrieve the scraps of paper. They read some of the messages:

> Married Men Turn Around and Go Home
> Single Men Follow.
> We'll be in Hermann on May 30—come and
> have dinner with us.

The bold desperadoes were true to their word. On May 30, the band rode into Hermann, Missouri, stopped for dinner,

---

[4]This safe still stands in the museum at Ste. Genevieve.

and identified themselves. No law enforcement officers were there to greet them.

Evidence connecting Jesse and Frank James with the Ste. Genevieve robbery was not entirely firm, however. We know that Frank was still on the West Coast. Men and women in the Midwest had long since taken sides. People who were friends of the family, who shared Confederate hardships, or who bore an animus towards banks, railroads, or corporations were inclined to deny the boys' involvement. But, there were those whose opinions were neutral as well as against them.

General opinion in Ste. Genevieve following the robbery was that the gang was headed by Sam Hildebrand and Cullen Baker, a Texas gunman. These two names were bantered around through ignorance or as red herrings since both men had been dead for some time before the robbery. Cole Younger was also accused, but he came up with an alibi "proving" he was with a sick friend, Mr. Murphy, in St. Clair County.

In calmer years, when historians had time to weigh the evidence, students of Jamesiana generally believed that those named herein did enjoy life for a while on the spoils of the Ste. Genevieve robbery.

State Senator Rozier went to St. Louis on May 28 to see police authorities there. Theories as to the identity of the robbers were discussed and published, and plans were laid to capture them. Although they spent many days searching, all endeavors proved fruitless. Senator Rozier, despite his loss, must have smiled to himself knowing that most of the bank's assets were safe in St. Louis.

When the five outlaws reached Jackson County from Ste. Genevieve, they found Frank James and Jim Younger waiting. A new campaign was planned. Hitherto they had plundered banks but they were now to commence another line of business. Holding up a railway train was something new. The Missouri bandits were going to give the public something to gasp over.

Chapter Seven

Robberies on Wheels

ADAIR, IOWA

Initially, the plan was to rob a train on the Hannibal and St. Joe Railroad or some other road in Missouri. This idea was rejected after due deliberation. Jim Younger and Frank James had learned that a fortune in gold would be shipped over the Union Pacific Railroad, reaching Omaha, Nebraska, the morning of July 21 and then continuing into Iowa. The gang made preliminary plans and separated.

On July 14, the bandits met in Clay County for final arrangements. Then they separated into pairs. As usual, Frank and Jesse took the same route, Cole and his brother, Chadwell and Miller, and two other men took another.[1]

On July 20, the bandits neared the line of the Chicago, Rock Island, and Pacific Railroad, some eighty miles east of Council Bluffs, Iowa. They stayed at the home of Carrie Sisson, then a young girl living with her folks south of Adair, a small town in Adair County, Iowa. They had supper with section foreman Robert Grant and his wife, Mary, on the evening preceding the holdup. Grant's home was called the Section House; it was located on Depot Hill in Adair.

On the afternoon of the twenty-first, they agreed to wreck the evening passenger train. They selected a spot about a mile or so west of Adair, where there was a sharp curve in the road obscuring the rails sixty yards in advance of the engine. Tying their horses some distance from the tracks and out of sight of the train, the outlaws got a spike bar and loosened one of the rails. To the loose rail, they tied a rope leading several yards out into the grass where they concealed themselves. The train consisted of seven coaches, including two sleepers, and was due at the point of ambush at 8:30 p.m.

As the train puffed up the incline, engineer John Rafferty spied the rope from his cab. He understood the situation and threw the engine into reverse, but the distance was so short and the momentum of the train so great, that the engine plunged through the break in the tracks, crashed into the ditch, and toppled over on its side. By some miracle the cars remained upright. Rafferty, trapped in the engine, was scalded to death by the steam, and in the coaches men, women, and children screamed in fright.[2]

From the wrecked engine Dennis Foley,

---

[1] Some say that two of the robbers were Bob Moore and Comanche Tony, but this has never been substantiated.

[2] Engineer Rafferty, a real hero in the disaster, was about twenty-five years old, married, and the father of one child. Mrs. Rafferty told me a few years ago that her husband was the son of this brave engineer. She told me he was a hero, but is not usually given credit for sticking to his post at the cost of his life. I hope that one day full recognition will be granted him for his brave actions.

the fireman, got up and staggered forward, screaming in agony, his oil-soaked overalls in flames. Rolling desperately in the high grass, Foley was able to extinguish the flames, but he was badly burned. It was a heroic effort on the part of this young man in his twenties.

Undaunted by the results of their plan, the robbers quickly boarded the cars. Two entered the express car, while the others forced the demoralized passengers to deliver up all their money and valuables. John Burgess, the express messenger, was compelled to open the safe and give the bandits what money he had, but the amount was small—around $3,000. The bandits were bitterly disappointed, for they had expected not less than $50,000 in gold there. Burgess informed them that the gold shipment was due on the next train. When William A. Smith, the conductor, walked toward the express car, the bandits fired into the air, chasing him back into the coach.

With the entire booty of about $26,000 in the proverbial grain sack, the seven robbers shouted farewell to their victims and galloped away to the south. The first train robbery wasn't a complete success—it was twelve hours too soon.

The citizens' outrage was uncontrollable; hundreds of men volunteered to chase the robbers. The trail led straight through Missouri to the Missouri River, where unmistakable evidence proved the outlaws swam the river with their horses. Following the tracks on the other side, the band was hunted into Jackson County, where, as usual, every trace of them disappeared. A party of detectives went to Monegaw Springs and found two of the Younger brothers who promptly disarmed the possemen with an invitation to coffee. Bob explained to the officers:

> You know that my brother Cole was accused of being in the band that robbed the Iowa railroad train which occurred July 21, 1873. At that time, my brothers and I were all down at the bottom at Monegaw Springs in St. Clair County, Missouri. The robbery was committed on Monday, and Sunday we attended preaching. This we (can) prove by a great many people of Greenton Valley, Lafayette County, Missouri, and the Reverend Mr. Smith, who was here in this very same hotel at the time on a visit.

On the day after the robbery, five of the suspected bandits ate dinner at the home of a farmer named Stuckeye, in Ringgold County, Iowa. He described the men as follows:

1. (Jesse James) Seemed to be the leader; five feet seven or eight inches tall; light hair, blue eyes, heavy sandy whiskers; broad shoulders; short nose a little turned up; high, broad forehead; looked to be well-educated, not used to work; age thirty-six to forty.

2. (Frank James) Tall and lithe; light complexion, high forehead, light brown hair, long, light whiskers, almost sandy; long, slender hands that certainly had not done much hard work; nose, a prominent Roman. He was very polite and talked little. Looked thirty-six years old.

3. (Clell Miller) Slender, five feet nine or ten inches tall; hair, cut and of light brown color; straight nose, uncouth and sarcastic in speech; brown eyes, and wearing a hard, dissipated countenance. Middle-aged, and wore dark clothes.

4. (Jim Younger) Dark complexion, dark hair, clean-shaven; five feet eight inches tall; heavy-set; straight black eyes, straight nose, good-looking but appeared dissipated. Middle-aged, and wore light pants, hat, vest, and dark coat.

5. (Cole Younger) Five feet ten inches tall; large, broad shoulders; straight blue eyes, reddish whiskers, Roman nose. Middle-aged and very pleasant in appearance.

What happened to the other two men remains a moot question. It is known definitely that the seven outlaws were together when they rode through Missouri.

One bit of keepsake evidence remains of the Adair train robbery. It is a gold signet ring that the robbers tossed in the Nodaway

River bottom as they rode away from the train wreck. It belongs to Elmer Johnson of Greenfield, Iowa, and has been kept proudly in his family for three generations.

It seems that Elmer's father, then about ten, was returning home with his father, John Johnson. As they rode across an unfarmed area in their wagon young Johnson spied something on the ground. It was a bunch of cheap rings. Mr. Johnson gave each of his children one of the rings and turned the rest over to the postmaster.

HOT SPRINGS, ARKANSAS

Stagecoach robberies were not beneath the dignity of the elusive bandits, especially when the stage was on a run patronized by well-to-do passengers. A coach service connected Malvern, Arkansas, a railroad point, with fashionable Hot Springs, Arkansas, at that time without a railroad.

The Jameses, along with the Youngers and Clell Miller are supposed to have waylaid this coach and robbed the passengers on January 15, 1874.[3] They hauled in nearly $3500—and further increased the perennial apocrypha about the courtesy and lifelong Confederate sympathies of the James boys.

The legend goes that George R. Crump, a passenger from Memphis had his watch and money returned to him because the holdup artists learned he was an ex-Confederate soldier. First, though, Crump had to furnish the name of his company, his commanding officer, and some of the battles in which he had fought.

Once again, Cole Younger filed affidavits to the effect that he had been in Carroll Parish, Louisiana—far away at the time of the holdup.

A second train robbery attributed to the James boys and their allies was at Gads Hill, on the line between St. Louis, Missouri, and Little Rock, Arkansas. The passenger-express train of the St. Louis, Iron Moun-

tain, and Southern Railroad left the Plum Street depot in St. Louis at 9:30 a.m. on January 31, 1874, bound for Texas.

At 5:30 p.m. the train approached Gads Hill, a little hamlet named after Sir John Falstaff. As the train drew near the station, the engineer spotted the red flag and the semaphore signal set on STOP, so he signaled the brakemen to stop the train.

Had the engineer been aware of what had occurred at 3:00 p.m. that afternoon he might have sped by, even though the train was greatly slowed down by the steep grade. He did not know that seven heavily-armed horsemen had arrived at the station, taken the agent into custody, and seized the blacksmith, some of the citizens, and several passengers awaiting the incoming train.

The prisoners were confined to the small station house, under guard of one of the robbers. Fortunately, the engineer was unaware of all this, for one of the robbers had opened the end of the switch, so that if one train tried to pass the station it would derail. The bandits also set the signal flag on the track, and then waited under cover for their quarry.

As the train slowed to a halt, conductor C.A. Alford stepped down to the little platform. He was instantly greeted by the gaping muzzle of a heavy revolver and robbed of his gold watch and wallet.

Meanwhile, one robber had covered the engineer with his gun and forced him out of the cab. Others occupied the platforms of the passenger coaches. Still two more advanced through the cars demanding the passengers' money. Seeing guns, the passengers were defenseless.

John H. Morley, chief engineer of the St. Louis, Iron Mountain, and Southern Railroad, was among the passengers; he too was forced to surrender his possessions. The bandits made a clean sweep, taking all the money and jewelry available. Having stripped the passengers, the robbers broke open the safe in the express car and cleaned it out. Lastly, they cut open the mail bags

---

[3]Clell was later implicated with Jesse and Frank at the Northfield Bank (Minnesota) robbery.

and rifled their contents. Total booty—about $10,000.

Before they left, one of the bandits stepped up to Alford saying, "Since you are the conductor of this damned train, you'll probably need your watch," and he handed back the astonished conductor's watch.

They also gave conductor Alford an envelope saying, "This contains an exact account of the robbery. We prefer this to be published in the newspapers rather than the grossly exaggerated accounts that usually appear after one of our jobs."

Oddly enough, the papers carried the item:

> The most daring on record—the southbound train on the Iron Mountain was robbed this evening by seven heavily armed men, and robbed of _____ dollars. The robbers arrived at the station some time before the arrival of the train, and arrested the station agent and put him under guard, then threw the train on the switch. The robbers were all large men, none of them under six feet tall. They were all masked and started in a southernly direction after they had robbed the train. They were all mounted on fine blooded horses. There is (one) hell of an excitement in this part of the country.

Finally, the bandits released the engineer and told him to head for Piedmont (Missouri).

At Piedmont, the news was quickly telegraphed to St. Louis and Little Rock. The lawmen formed the usual posse but the outlaws had sixty miles on them before they got started. On the morning after the robbery, the bandits called on a Mrs. Cook to prepare breakfast for them. Mrs. Cook lived about a mile from Carpentersville on the Current River. She later stated that only five men came to her home, each armed with a pair of revolvers and a repeating rifle.

The bandits next stopped at the home of Mr. Mason where they demanded food and stayed all night, proceeding westward the next morning.[4] The posse tracked the out-

[4]Mr. Mason was state representative and was not at home when the robbers came to his home.

John Younger was slain by officers near Osceola, Missouri after the Gads Hill train robbery.

laws as far as Mrs. Cook's, but then, after losing the trail, returned empty-handed to Piedmont.

As a result of the Gads Hill robbery, the railroad trust engaged the famous Pinkerton Detective Agency to track down the outlaws in Missouri. Allan Pinkerton assigned John W. Whicher, one of his shrewdest operatives, to capture Frank and Jesse James.

The detectives quickly gathered clues from Mrs. Cook and Mr. Mason's family, leading them to believe that the two Jameses, the Younger brothers, and perhaps George Shepherd and several Texas gunmen took part in the Gads Hill robbery. Some people even thought that John Wesley Hardin or Jim Reed might have been involved.

The case attracted intense investigation for several reasons: rewards were offered by both Governor Woodson of Missouri, and

Allan Pinkerton gave Jesse and his men a merry chase.

Governor Baxter of Arkansas, as well as by the railroads. Then, too, the Pinkerton Agency longed to claim fame as having eradicated the James gang.

Meanwhile, Frank and Jesse were living in the vicinity of Kearney near their mother's home. On March 9, Jesse even had the nerve to spend a few hours in Kearney, and to have several horses shod by a local blacksmith.

On Wednesday, March 10, 1874, Whicher arrived from Kansas City and took a room at Liberty. Whicher was a daring and vigorous young man, twenty-six years old and recently married to a beautiful young woman from Iowa City. Apparently,

Allan Pinkerton and young Whicher were unaware of the ingenuity of the Jameses, their lines of communication, or their many friends in Clay County and elsewhere.

Whicher next called on Mr. Adkins, president of the Clay County Savings Association Bank, to inform him of his purpose. Adkins was unable to supply the detective with enough information, so he referred him to Colonel O.P. Moss, ex-sheriff of Clay County.

Colonel Moss tried in earnest to persuade Whicher to abandon his mission. He warned him that the Jameses were never caught unaware, and that his presence probably was already known to them, but to no avail.[5] Whicher had obtained what he regarded as positive evidence that the James boys had planned the Gads Hill affair, and nothing could dissuade him.

Whicher must not have known the meaning of fear, or he would have waited for help. He decided to leave that very evening for the Samuel house. Disguised as a farm laborer and swinging an old carpetbag on a stick, Whicher took the evening train for Kearney, and there made inquiries for work on a farm. He left the station before long and set out for the Samuel place. His fate had already been settled by those whom he hoped to capture and bring to trial.

When Whicher arrived in Kearney, the Jameses were ready for him. In the evening, Jim Anderson, Jesse James, and Bradley Collins waited on the roadside, about a half mile from the Samuel home. Whicher soon came along. He was carrying the carpetbag and dressed as a farmhand. Jesse emerged from their concealment and met Whicher in the road.

Whicher knew he was looking at Jesse James, and that most likely he probably was covered by hidden guns. He wanted desperately to reach for his pistol, but the outlaw had him at a disadvantage.

"What were you doing in Liberty today? Why did you go to the bank to talk with Adkins, and why did you talk to Colonel Moss? Where are the clothes you wore into town? Plotting to capture the James boys, eh?" Jesse then laughed outright.

Anderson and Bill Fox (who had joined the men in hiding) came forward, pistols in hand. Whicher now saw that his case was hopeless; the outlaws had known his plan all along. He had underestimated the Jameses; now he would pay with his life.

Whicher thrust his hand into his pocket, but it was too late. Fox and Anderson sprang upon him, while Jesse placed the muzzle of his pistol against the detective's head. In an instant the outlaws had relived him of his Smith & Wesson. Whicher felt either Adkins or Moss had betrayed him. He was never to learn the truth.

The outlaws bound and gagged him and then put him on a horse, both legs bound under the animal's belly and his arms tied to the saddle horn. About 3:00 a.m. on March 11, the drowsy ferryman at Blue Mills, on the Missouri River, was roused by shouts of men on the north side signifying their wish to cross the river. Jesse yelled that they were in a hurry—they were after horse thieves.

Thus summoned, the ferryman lost no time getting his boat across to them. When the outlaws came down, one said, "We have caught one thief, and if you want to keep your head on your shoulders, you had better get us across the river fast." The ferryman could see that one man was bound and gagged—he could do nothing but stand and scratch his head as the strange group moved off on the Independence Road.

Later that morning an early traveler, halfway between Independence and Blue Mills, came upon Whicher's body in a lonely spot.[6] There was a bullet hole through his heart and another through his head. He had not been tortured as some lurid recorders would have us believe.

Like many other crimes of which Jesse was accused, Whicher's murder was never successfully laid at his feet. Some people claimed the guilty man in this case was a Texan still alive as late as 1898. Cole Younger said years later that he believed Jesse had done the killing. He added, though, that he and Jesse were on bad terms

---

[5]The very day Whicher arrived in Liberty, a man named Jim Latche observed him visit Mr. Adkins and from there traced him to Colonel Moss's home. He immediately concluded that the man was looking for the James boys. Latche had ridden with Jesse and Frank on one of their raids and was now staying with them near Kearney. When he saw the detective in farmhand disguise, he felt certain of his guess. He hastily reported everything to Jesse.

[6]John Whicher's body was first buried at Independence, Missouri, on March 12, 1874. On March 21, the body was removed to Chicago, Illinois by L.L. Angell, a relative of the deceased and also a Pinkerton agent.

at the time, so Jesse probably carried the body to Jackson County to make it look like the Youngers in that county were responsible. This is supposition at a gallop. It shouldn't be taken as anything like proof that Jesse had killed the Pinkerton man. In his own writings of 1912, Frank James claimed he killed Whicher when the detective pulled a pistol on him.

Chapter Eight

Jim Reed's Murder

Without doubt Jesse and Frank James were accused of many more crimes than they committed. Occasionally, in their hey-day, robberies hundreds of miles apart were perpetrated at the same time. The public was so pre-conditioned by the notoriety of the Jameses that on such occasions, people were positive they'd accomplished both holdups. Some authorities felt that, though Frank and Jesse might not have been at the scene of the crimes, they could have planned them and assigned members of their band to carry them out.

SAN ANTONIO STAGE

At seven o'clock in the evening, on April 7, 1874, the regular mail stage running between Austin and San Antonio, Texas, was stopped about thirty miles southwest of Austin. Several prominent persons were on board: C. Breckenridge, president of the First National Bank of San Antonio, and Bishop Gregg, as well as several ladies. All passengers were relieved of their valuables. Mr. Breckenridge was the heaviest loser, since he had to part with $1,000 in cash. Courteous to the ladies throughout, the bandits ordered them to throw all their jewelry and money into the grain sack or they would be searched. The ladies quickly complied.

Inasmuch as the robbery took place so close to Austin, the robbers cut loose several of the horses, thus delaying the stage's arrival by a number of hours. In fact, it did not reach the city until nearly daylight. The five bandits were said to be Jesse and Frank James, Arthur McCoy, Jim Greenwood, and Jim Reed.

Some accounts relate that Jim Reed, later fatally wounded by Texas Rangers in a fight, confessed on his deathbed that he participated in the Gads Hill and Austin-San Antonio Stage robberies. As a matter of fact, Reed was not killed by officers of the law and he made no deathbed statement of any kind. He was Belle Starr's husband and was killed the same way Jesse James was—by treachery. Belle commented, "One of the most treacherous deeds ever perpetrated in the annals of infamy was the murder of Jim Reed, the desperado."

Here is a brief account of that affair:

Shortly after the stage holdup, Reed drifted to Paris, Texas, where he met John Morris. Reed, always willing and usually able to help a friend, loaned Morris $600 because Morris had lost all his cash in a high-stake poker game.

Several days later, Morris and Reed stopped near Bois d'Arc Creek (Greene County, Missouri) where they had breakfast with a mutual friend, Charles Lee.

Before entering the house, however, Morris suggested they leave their pistols in the saddlebags so as not to appear discourteous or suspicious. Reed took off his six-gun and put it in the bag with his friend's weapon. Morris finished his meal first and then walked to the back door and then walked to the back door where he suggested to their host that they kill Reed and share the reward. The two men shook hands on the deal. Morris went outside, got both guns from the saddlebag, and came back into the house just as Reed was finishing his meal. With menacing guns Morris called on him to surrender. Reed jumped up, just in time to stop a bullet in the right chest. Quickly he caught the heavy table in his grasp and, raising it for a shield, pursued Morris to the door while Morris kept discharging his pistol through the up-ended table. One bullet struck Reed close to the heart and he died without further struggle.[1]

Morris claimed $1700 in rewards, but the money did him little good. He was killed shortly afterward on his ranch near Fort Worth, Texas. It is also said that Morris was not killed in Texas, but lived until 1933 in Lindsay, Oklahoma, where he ran a nursery.

Charles Lee received $300 for his role in the assassination.

[1]Some writers say that Morris sneaked up from behind and shot Reed in the back, but both Belle Starr and Mrs. Shirley verified the first report. News of Reed's death reached Belle in Dallas the next morning and she swore to avenge him. Nothing, however, has surfaced of any action she might have taken.

Chapter Nine

The James Boys' Private Lives

Jesse and Frank, in their financially flush periods between robberies, weren't always hiding out in Missouri caves or in the barns and attics of relatives and friends. Photographs of the two outlaws were rare and the official WANTED photos were nonexistent. Neither was fingerprinting known, or the rapid means of communication and ingenious criminal-catching techniques of today. Thus, by simply changing their names, Frank and Jesse were able to travel about the country with a good deal of freedom when they had the money.

At one time, Jesse posed as William Campbell, a wealthy Kansas cattleman. On another occasion he lived in New York City under the name of Charles Lawson, of Nottingham, England. Curiously, Nottingham is the name of a city associated with Robin Hood.

Jesse and Frank both spent time at one of the most fashionable eastern spas of the day—Saratoga Springs, New York. Long Branch, New Jersey, was another of their favorite resorts. New York City had a special attraction for Frank because of its theaters, which he attended frequently while Jesse gambled or played the horses at Long Branch.

Whether they were in sophisticated eastern cities or in the more rural midwest towns, the James boys had poise and they took pains to be amiable. They had a reputation for indiscriminate *noblesse*

Jesse James, dressed for the gaming tables at Long Branch, New Jersey, wrote numerous letters during his gambling days.

oblige—charming and wealthy easterners one month and the next month paying a neighbor's overdue doctor bill with the proceeds of armed robbery.

They are credited, for example, with trying to help establish a school for black children in Missouri. J. Milton Turner, a noted black educator, was sitting on his porch with a friend one day. They were discussing ways to finance a school. Two riders appeared suddenly, threw a sack on the porch and left just as quickly shouting, "Use the gold to start your school." Turner's friend believed that one of the men was Jesse.

Turner handed the gold over to authorities. The search for the owners was ineffectual and prolonged. Somehow, the money that had appeared so dramatically leaked away while in official custody. Turner later said he wished he'd kept it and gotten the school started, instead of struggling for years to finance his project more conventionally.

If the would-be benefactors really were Jesse and Frank, it would seem that Frank was the more interested in the school. He was fond of Shakespeare and had a speaking knowledge of German and Spanish.

On April 24, 1874, Jesse married his double-first cousin, Zerelda Amanda Mims, who had nursed him after the wear. Apparently Zee's father died in April of 1869 and for some reason Zee went to live with her sister, Mrs. Charles McBride. Zee's mother, Mary Mims, was living on Sixth Street, between Grand and Walnut Avenues, in Kansas City, in 1862. Zee's sister refused to consent to the marriage until Zee threatened to elope.

The wedding took place at the home of the bride's older sister, Mrs. W. B. (Lucy) Browder, of Kearney. Reverend William James, a brother of the groom's father, reluctantly officiated at the marriage of his nephew and niece.

Zee's mother suffered deeply over her daughter's marriage. By 1877 she was living alone at 1005 Grand Avenue, Kansas City. She died on July 23 of that year—fortun-

Jesse James, 1875

Zerelda Mims James, wife of Jesse James

ately before news of Jesse's murder and Zee's subsequent suffering made the headlines. Mrs. Mims was buried in Union Cemetery, Kansas City.

Jesse and Zee had their first child, Jesse Edwards James, on August 31, 1875, on 606 Boscobel Street East, in Nashville. Dr. J. Vertrees attended. The child was named after General Jo Shelby's fiery aide-de-camp, Major John Newman Edwards of Sedalia, Missouri.[1]

Twin sons arrived next in August of 1877, in Humphreys County, near Waverly, Tennessee. They were named Gould and Montgomery after the doctors who attended Zee. Both infants died after only five days. Jesse carved two headstones and buried the twins on the farm of Banks Link from whom he had rented some acreage. The area today is on the edge of water from the Tennessee Valley Authority called Big Bottom.

[1]Jesse Edwards James later married Stella McGown. They had four daughters: Lucille, Jo Frances, Estelle, and Ethelrose. Jesse Edwards died on March 26, 1951, and was buried in the Forest Lawn Cemetery, Los Angeles. Stella was born February 27, 1882, and died on April 1, 1971.

Mary James was born to Jesse and Zee on July 17, 1879. She married Henry Barr, had three sons, and died on October 11, 1935. A fifth child was expected when Jesse was killed in St. Joe, but as a result of the shock and ordeal, Zee had a miscarriage. Thus only two of their children reached maturity. When Zee died on November 30, 1900, her last request was to have Jesse's remains moved from the Samuel homestead and reburied in Kearney Cemetery. Her request was honored in 1902.

Frank James married Annie Ralston, of Independence, Missouri, in June of 1874. The marriage took place in Leavenworth, Kansas, when Frank was thirty and his bride was twenty-two years old. At first the prominent Ralston family refused to recognize the marriage—even going so far as to disown Annie—but in later years they were reconciled. Frank and Annie had one child, Robert Franklin, born on February 6, 1878. Robert married May Sullivan, who died young, and then Mae Sanborn. There were no children from either marriage. Robert died on November 18, 1959 and his wife on April 19, 1974.

In this little cabin near Noel, Missouri, Jesse and his bride Zee spent the first few days of their honeymoon.

Front view of Jesse James's home at 606 Boscobel Street, East, Nashville, Tennessee.

Jesse Edwards James

John Newman Edwards was a famous newspaper editor and friend of the James family.

Mary James (left) and Jesse Edwards James

Mary James, daughter of Jesse James

Home of Jesse James near
Nashville on the Pike.

Frank James, age 33

Annie Ralston James, wife of Frank James
Courtesy of Robert James

Robert Franklin James, son of Frank James

These two stones, one face down and one leaning, were hand-carved by Jesse James to place on the graves of his twin sons who died in infancy in Humphrees County, Tennessee.

The wedding photos of Robert Franklin James and Mae James were taken on December 26, 1901, at the F.W. Guerin Studios, St. Louis. They resided at 4726 Delmar, St. Louis.

Chapter Ten

Jesse's Home Is Assaulted

Many respectable Clay County citizens finally agreed that Jesse and Frank James were nothing more than outlaws and murderers. They had no more sympathy for their troubles during the Civil War and its aftermath. Some of them living closest to the James-Samuel farm plotted with the Pinkertons to end the matter once and for all. William Pinkerton, Allan's brother, arrived in Kansas City to direct the effort. He communicated with his allies in the vicinity of Castle James, as the Pinkertons dubbed Jesse's home.

Toward the end of January, 1875, William Pinkerton received information that Jesse and Frank had been seen around their home and that the opportune moment had arrived. Pinkerton exercised every precaution. No strangers were permitted to loiter in the Liberty area—nothing was to arouse the outlaws' suspicion. The boys had friends more shrewd than the officers—friends shrewd enough to notice every little incident. They detected coded messages sent by a Clay County resident, so the outlaws were doubly watchful.

On the afternoon of January 24, several small bands of men arrived in Clay County and came into Liberty after nightfall. They were secreted in many places, and the citizens were unaware of their presence. Late on the evening of the twenty-fifth, a special train came up from Kearney carrying a detachment of Pinkerton agents from Kansas City. Citizens well acquainted with the locality led them to the rendezvous.

Just past midnight Pinkerton detectives stationed themselves at strategic points around the Samuel home. Two men approached the house from the rear, carrying turpentine balls to light up the inside of the house. When they tried to open the shutters they awoke a black servant who spread the alarm. Dr. and Mrs. Samuel and the young children stumbled around in the dark. A lighted turpentine ball thrown into the kitchen started the fire raging. Mrs. Samuel quickly recovered her presence of mind enough to try to subdue the flames. She was permitted only a moment to engage in this task before another object was thrown in the kitchen. Dr. Samuel assumed it was another ignited turpentine ball and tried to kick it into the fireplace. Finally he grabbed an old broom and managed to push it into the hot coals. Before long it exploded.

In the house were the black woman and her four-year-old son Perry, Dr. Samuel and Mrs. Samuel, plus Archie, Fannie, and John Samuel. As the object exploded, a piece of it struck Archie, then eight years old, in the chest. He died before dawn.[1]

Another piece of the object hit Mrs. Samuel in the right arm, between the hand

[1]On January 28, Archie was buried in the Kearney Cemetery, Clergyman Thomas H. Graves officiating. Mrs. Samuel was too grief-stricken to attend the funeral.

James farm (August, 1988 photo).

and the elbow. Later, her arm had to be amputated at the elbow. She would have bled to death if Dr. Samuel hadn't been there to treat her. The little black boy also received a slight injury.

The object has always been referred to as a bomb; actually, it was a pot flare, one such as those used on a road or a railroad track to indicate repair work was going on. It was filled with coal oil and the wicks lighted. The detectives evidently thought it would light up the kitchen so they could see the occupants. The top of the thing blew up, but not the heavy cast iron bottom, which was hemispherical and made of cast iron. The bottom has been preserved by the James family to this day. It seems

that the whole thing was made of such metal. The top was made of heavy brass with two tubes about six inches long to carry the wicks. The heavy bottom kept the flare from tipping over in the wind.

In writings of 1912, Frank James said it was not a bomb as such. The heavy brass portion of the object, being the least resistant, expanded and flew into bits from the heat of the fireplace.

Even so, the object had all the characteristics of a bomb. Ralph Dudley, one time general manager of the Pinkertons, said it was a road flare as described by Frank James.[2] Anyone who has seen the old cabin

[2]Frank also reported this information to the author's grandmother who knew him well.

Jesse was born in this house. This is also the house alleged to have been bombed in 1875. It has long since been renovated and is still open to the public. This photo is of the front part of the building which was added to the original log cabin where Jesse was born. (This is the same house seen in the Chapter I photo with Mrs. James and Mary in the yard.)
Courtesy of Pinkertons National Detective Agency, Inc.

probably realizes that if the object was a grenade of a thirty-two bomb (as some have suggested), it would have blown the cabin to bits and probably killed everyone inside.

Some writers claim that Jesse and Frank were not in the cabin at the time of the raid; some say that the upper floor of the added "T" part of the house would not hold people. They are correct in the sense that the present-day weatherboard "T" section has a very low upstairs, but photos prove that the original addition did have enough room. The present "T" section was built with the money Mrs. Samuel got for the original section. Ironically, the original section's lumber got no farther than the depot—the Fair people never called for it. It eventually went into Bob Ford's home near Excelsior Springs.

Contemporary records definitely establish that not only were the James boys in the upper room at the time, but also that Clell Miller, Dora and Bill Fox followed them out the window and down a nearby tree when the commotion began. Research indicates that Jack Ladd, a member of the attacking force, was wounded by the outlaws and later died en route to Chicago. Ladd had been a Pinkerton lookout agent on the Dan Askew farm for nearly two years.

Reporters and officials who visited the Samuel home the day after the blast found evidence of a desperate fight on the premises. Somebody had been shot since bloodstains were found on the ground. The investigators weren't all sure of the time of the shooting, but most agreed it occurred after the explosion. They estimated the number of shots to be between four and twenty. There were seven bullet holes in the fence at the northeast corner of the yard as well as bullet holes in the fence separating the yard from the house lot. This indicated they were fired from the ice house. Then, there were numerous footprints behind the ice house and behind the barn. Apparently, the detectives had attacked in three squads: from behind the ice house, the barn, and from against the kitchen at the northwest corner of the cabin.

Jesse and Frank must have succeeded in

getting their horses from the barn because the investigators saw clear marks of horse hooves moving at great speed at the barn door. The marks led to the east gate in the pasture lot, suddenly veering toward the bars of the gate, and then disappearing. The horses could easily have jumped this fence.

The Pinkertons left a clear trail over the wheatfield west of the barn, showing plainly they were in a hurry. There were drops of blood near the stable as well as in the pasture lot south of the house.

E. Price Hall, just a boy when the raid occurred, lived on the adjoining Hall farm. Hearing the explosion, he hurried to investigate. When he trailed the Pinkertons to the depot nearby, he found a revolver stamped with the Pinkerton markings. It was a valuable possession to him until it disappeared and was never again found. Hall also stated it was the black boy, Ambrose, who had run from the house and fired the shotgun wounding Jack Ladd. Ambrose had been in another part of the house and arrived in the kitchen just after the explosion.

Further proof that Jesse was there at the time of the Pinkerton visit lies in the fact that his favorite sorrel horse was roaming on the farm the next day. Investigators never learned why he left it behind. It's possible he grabbed the first mount in sight or thought the sorrel too visible an identification. At any rate he used another horse in its place.

Dr. Scruggs, who was called in from Kearney to treat Mrs. Samuel and to do for Archie what he could, had left his horse in front of the house. He never did see it again.

The inquest verdict concerning Archie's murder read:

> We, the jury, find that the deceased, Archie Peyton Samuel, came to his death as a result of a torpedo thrown through the window of the Samuel residence, by person or persons unknown.

Archie Samuel was killed by the Pinkerton bomb-flare. He was the half-brother of Frank and Jesse.

This report, coupled with that of the Adjutant-General, gave birth to the idea that the pot flare was a bomb.

The official report of the Adjutant-General of Missouri, which appeared in the *Liberty Advance,* February 11, 1875, read:

> To His Excellency, Chas. H. Hardin,
> Governor of Missouri.
> Dear Sir:
>   In pursuance of instructions received from you on Friday last, I proceeded without delay to Clay County, to ascertain as far as possible the fact relating to the recent outrage perpetrated in said county upon the family of Dr. Samuel, the stepfather of the notorious James brothers. Mr. Samuel resides about two-and-a-half miles east of Kearney, a small town nine miles north of Liberty . . . On the night of January 26th, between midnight and two o'clock, the residence of Mr. Samuel was approached by a party of men . . . The party which approached the rear and west portion of the building and set fire to the weather-boarding of the kitchen in three or four places, also threw into the house by a window thereof, a hand grenade.

This instrument was composed of cast and wrought or malleable iron, strongly secured together and covered with a wrapping saturated with turpentine or oil. As it passed through the window and as also it lay upon the floor it made a very brilliant light alarming the family who supposed the kitchen to be on fire and rushed in to extinguish the flames. Mr. Samuel mistook it for a turpentine ball and attempted to kick it into the fireplace . . . It then exploded with a report which was heard a distance of two or three miles. The part composed of cast iron broke into fragments and flew out with great force. One of the fragments shattered the right arm below the elbow of Mrs. Samuel, the mother of the James boys, to an extent which made amputation necessary. Another entered the body of her little son, Archie, wounding him mortally and causing his death in about four hours.

Mrs. Samuel succeeded in putting out the fire in the weather-boarding and aroused the neighbors with the cry of murder . . . Four pistol reports were heard by the neighbors . . . but . . . the parties perpetrating the outrage had disappeared.

On Monday, January 26, about half-past seven o'clock in the evening an engine with only a caboose attached came down the road from the north and stopped in the woods about two miles north of Kearney. Several unknown men the got out of the caboose, which then continued south in the direction of Kansas City. About two or three o'clock in the morning, Tuesday, the same or a similar engine and caboose came from the direction of Kansas City and stopped for a considerable time at the place where the unknown men had been left. The tracks of the persons who were stationed behind the house and of those who set fire and threw the grenade into the kitchen, were made by boots of superior quality, quite different from those usually worn by the farmers . . . in the surrounding country. In following the trail of the parties on their retreat, a pistol was found which is now in my possession. This pistols has marks upon it which . . . are identically such as are known to be on the pistols of a well-known band of detectives.

The parties who perpetrated the outrage doubtless approached the house under the belief that the James brothers were there . . . on discovering that they had murdered an innocent lad and mutilated his mother, they deemed it prudent to retire and leave as little evidence . . . as possible. There are no details concerning the signs of the struggle which took place near the barn and elsewhere on the premises . . .
Respectfully,
G.C. Bingham, Adjt. General

Public sentiment rose to a high pitch in favor of the Jameses and Youngers after this wanton and senseless attack. In March, General Jeff Jones, of Callaway County, introduced a resolution in the Missouri House of Representatives offering amnesty to the five boys for Civil War crimes if they would surrender and stand trail for crimes they allegedly committed after the war. Zeal and eloquence went into this proposed legislation; men of prominence and political influence publicly expressed the opinion that the crimes of which Jesse and Frank were being accused resulted from the Civil War's bitter passions. Many agreed that if amnesty were granted them and their former guerrilla companions, a climate of reconciliation between the Jameses and the representatives of the law could be established.

This proposed legislation, though it did not become law, did arouse much interest. The Jameses themselves apparently wished to pass it, and they communicated with Missouri's Governor Hardin and Attorney General Hockaday about it.

The proposal may have caused the death of their neighbor, Daniel H. Askew. Askew was reported to be a spy for federal forces. Rumor had it that he was one of the principal Pinkerton agents in the raid of the Samuel home. On the night of April 12, 1875, while returning to his house with a bucket of water from the spring, he was shot and killed by unknown men hiding behind a pile of cordwood.

Gossipers accused Frank and Jesse of this also. One group reported that Jesse killed Askew because of a heated dispute his mother had with Askew over a fence line. Not too many years ago, a man in Kansas City said this was true, yet it surely was an inopportune time to commit murder. Jesse, Frank, and their relatives retorted that their

Warrant for the arrest of Jesse James from the State of Kansas. Many people claimed no such warrants were issued against the Missouri robber.

Warrant for the arrest of Jesse James issued by the State of Missouri.

enemies had killed Askew to prevent the amnesty measure from going through. Regardless of the motive or the killers, the murder did revive strong feelings against the outlaws. The amnesty proposal was defeated.

From what we can determine, Jesse's comment to James Vaughn in Arkansas, an ex-Quantrillian and later pallbearer for him, was in the form of a letter. Typically, Jesse's writing is no example of literary elegance, but it is vigorous, clear, and to the point.

> Commanche, Texas
> June 10th, 1876
> Dear Jim
> I hear they are making a great fuss about old Dan Askew, and say the James Boys did the killing. It's one of old Pink's lies, circulated by his sneaks. I can prove that I was in Texas, at Dallas, on the 12th of May, when the killing was done. Several persons of the highest respectability know that I could not have been in Clay County, Missouri, at the time. I might name a number who could swear to this, whose words would be taken anywhere. It's my opinion Askew was killed by Jack Ladd and some of Pinkerton's men. But no meanness is every done now but the James boys must bear the blame for it. This is like the balance of the lies the Kansas City papers have printed about the shooting of old Askew, and oblige,
> Yours faithfully
> Jesse

Of course the Askew slaying occurred on April 12, not May 12 as the letter indicates. Perhaps the legislators should have stalled for a while. For even if only by coincidence, robberies were at a low ebb in Missouri and surrounding states while the measure was under consideration.

Chapter Eleven

Jesse Claims Innocence

HUNTINGTON, WEST VIRGINIA

The next robbery attributed to Jesse, Frank, and their companions was the looting of the bank at Huntington, West Virginia. The names finally narrowed down to Frank James, Cole Younger, Tomlinson (Tom) McDaniels, and Tom Webb (also known as Jack Keene). The raiders claimed Jesse was not present. His wife had had a son on August 31 in Nashville and Jesse had refused to leave his family at the time.

On Monday, September 6, 1875, the quartet rode into Huntington, each man wearing a long linen duster over a heavy winter coat. Two dismounted and went with drawn pistols into the bank. At the same time, the two still on horses opened a fusillade with their guns, driving everyone on the streets indoors.

John H. Russell, president of the bank, was at lunch at the time. The cashier, R.T. Oney, was the only person in the bank. Both robbers leaped over the counter and grabbed the revolver that Oney was trying to reach. They told him to put up his hands and open the vault. Oney replied that the safe was open, but the outlaws ordered him to get the key for the inner drawer. He refused.

"If you don't get the key and open the drawer, we'll kill you!"

"All right then, do that, and you'll never get the money," responded the cashier.

Oney saw that the men meant business,

so he produced the key and opened the money drawer. He produced two packets, gently pushing back a third. The robbers demanded the third package too—and got it. Oney later stated that they seemed disappointed there was no more money in the vault.

"Any of this money yours?" asked the robber.

"Yes, I have a balance of seven dollars in the bank," Oney replied.

"Well, we don't want this little scrape to cost you anything," said the big robber, and counted out his seven dollars. Then they told the cashier he was the coolest man they'd ever come across.

By that time, the firing in the street had subsided and the bandits turned to leave. At that very moment, a black messenger named Jim entered the bank with the mail. The bandits asked him whether there was any money in the packages. Jim said he didn't know.

After a thorough search, the robbers marched Oney and Jim across the street to their horses. Russell, in company of Ben Davis, was cautiously turning the corner at that time. As soon as Oney realized only one robber was pointing a pistol at him, he yelled and tried to jump to safety. The robbers meanwhile mounted their horses and dashed from town.

Russell aroused Sheriff Smith and a general alarm was given. Russell mounted his fleet gray horse, armed with a shotgun, and in short order he and the sheriff were in swift pursuit of the bandits. Soon others followed, among them the Reverend Gibson, J. Emmens, A. Pollard, F. Donnell, W. Stuart, T. Noble, and J. Elkins. The sheriff and Russell came so close to the bandits that they saw them drop a money sack. It contained thirty dollars in nickels and a $5,000 deposit certificate. A man who was taken by the robbers and compelled to go with them later said the pursuers were so close that the bandits debated whether to wait for them and kill them. Two were in favor but the other two said it would do no good, so they continued on.

With the pursuit in progress, urgent telegrams were sent to every station between Catlettsburg and Louisa, as well as Charleston, Barboursville, and other strategic points. George F. Miller organized a party from Barboursville to try and head the outlaws off, but got behind them. Some of the posse rode twenty miles to Cracker's Neck, Kentucky, not returning to Huntington until Tuesday night. Even then, Miller continued the pursuit.

Returning to the bank, Russell and Oney determined that nearly $20,000 in valuables and currency had been taken. That didn't stop the bank from doing business, however, for Erskine Miller, a stockholder, arrived the next day with a supply of currency. Other funds were sent in from Charleston.

The chase went on, and on Saturday evening, Russell received a telegram.

Willard, Ky., Sept. 10, 1875
To John H. Russell, President, Huntington Bank
We are at West Liberty. Have fifteen fresh men and horses after the parties. Think they will overhaul them. They have gone toward Cumberland Gap. Will stay until we hear.
G.F. Miller

On Friday Oney received a letter from the chief of police of Louisville, enclosing a photograph and a description of the sus-

pected leader of the band. He took the picture to Mr. Crump's home, where the bandits had stayed the Saturday night prior to the holdup. They didn't tell Crump who the man in the picture was; they simply asked him whether he had ever seen him. Without hesitation Crump and his son said, "Yes, he is one of the men who stayed here Saturday night." The photograph was one of the Younger brothers.

The pursuit was one of the best ever put up against the boys, and they were rather hard pressed. The general route of the getaway was to the southwest, through the mountains of West Virginia, and across the state line into southeastern Kentucky.

A few days after the robbery two young brothers named Dillon, living on a farm near Pine Hill in Rockcastle County, read accounts in their local papers that stressed the possibility of the fugitives hiding out somewhere in southeastern Kentucky. The young men concluded the robbers just might come near their home, so they loaded up two old army muskets with slugs and kept a sharp lookout for any suspicious characters in the neighborhood.

On the night of the fourteenth, the Dillons saw four figures moving on foot through the woods about fifty yards south of their home. Near the road the men stopped to talk for a moment. Then two came down the road, while the other two headed toward the brothers. They were all tall men, wearing linen dusters and armed with pistols, the handles of which protruded from the front of their coats.

"Halt! Throw up your hands!" commanded the brothers.

Instead of doing so the bandits opened fire. The Dillon boys returned with a thunderous roar from their old muzzle-loaders. The robbers escaped in the dark and the boys returned home, not knowing whether their bullets had struck their mark or not.

Next morning they returned to the scene of the fight and saw bloodstains on the ground. They followed the stains for a short distance to a corn field and found Tom McDaniels suffering from his wounds. They took him home and called the doctor, but nothing could be done. After his death, a photograph was found on his person and cashier Oney positively identified him as one of the robbers.

The day after McDaniels' death, September 19, three men came to the Dillons and asked to see the body. Only Mrs. Dillon and some other women were home at the time. They became frightened, believing the three men to be the surviving Huntington robbers. Mrs. Dillon refused, saying the coffin had already been screwed shut.

One man spoke in a firm voice. "Madam, we are sorry that circumstances require us to appear rude; we came to see the dead body, and therefore we ask again that you show us the body."

Mrs. Dillon, frightened, conducted the three strangers into another room where the coffin rested on two chairs. A screwdriver lay on the window sill, and with this the lid was readily removed. The trio looked long and sorrowfully at the dead man's face. The largest man betrayed great emotion as tears streamed down his cheeks. After a long speechless gaze, the men asked whether the person who did the killing was about. Informed that he was not, they courteously bade Mrs. Dillon goodbye and left.

W.R. Dillon, one of the brothers who had fired on the bandits, later made this statement:

> One night while McDaniels' body was still at our house three men came and asked to see the corpse. Luckily, I guess, I was not at home. At the time the three men asked to see the body, only Mrs. Dillon and one or two neighbor women were present. No men being present, they refused at first to allow the visitors to view the body, stating the coffin lid had already been screwed into place. The men insisted, however, and were allowed to see the remains. One of the men was crying. They asked for me and went into the cornfield.
> W.R. Dillon

The three surviving bandits remained hidden for a time. Frank James and Cole Younger eventually escaped. Tom Webb (alias Jack Keene), however, was wounded and captured in Fentress County, Tennessee. He was taken back to Huntington and identified as one of the robbers. He had about $4,000 in his clothes and admitted his part in the affair.

At his trial Webb was found guilty and sentenced to twelve years in the West Virginia Penitentiary at Moundsville. He was received at the prison on December 8, 1875, as prisoner #457. The 1880 census records show Webb working in the wagon shop of the prison. On February 8, 1885, West Virginia Governor Beeson Jackson wrote a pardon for Webb, releasing him so that he could return to his home in Pike County, Illinois.[1]

Detective Bligh of Louisville at first boasted that Jesse James was captured when Webb was arrested. Statements subsequently made by the convicted robber left no doubt that Frank James had been with him and probably Cole Younger. At any rate, the leaders of the Huntington raid escaped, carrying the bulk of the bank's funds with them.

ROCKY CUT, MISSOURI

The robbers next planned to hold up the Missouri-Pacific train at a lonely little place called Rocky Cut, at the Lamine bridge near Otterville, Missouri. The date was July 7, 1876.

On July 1, Frank and Jesse James, Cole and Bob Younger, Clell Miller, Charlie Pitts, Bill Chadwell, and a new recruit, Hobbs Kerry, converged on a small farm-

---

[1] In trying to find more information about Webb, the author was told by prison officials that they could find no record of his release. Some said he died there. The author is indebted to the untiring efforts by the Research Committee of the Wheeling Area Historical Society and the work of Colonel Tom Foulk, Jr., James C. Dunklin, and Mr. Pyles in uncovering what really happened to Tom Webb.

house in the lead-mining district of south-west Missouri. The eight men were rough-looking and well-armed.

The bandits' strategy was to conceal their presence, even from friends, just before a robbery. This would make the holdup such a surprise that people would be too confused for an immediate or intelligent pursuit.

On reaching Rocky Cut, the bandits took into tow the watchman, a Swiss immigrant named Henry Chateau. Holding their captive under guard, the gang piled ties on the track. There was no spur there and no way of being sure the engineer might not take alarm and try to run past the robbers. One bandit loosened a rail to make certain the train wouldn't get by.

Six of the gang went down to the tracks, leaving Miller and Kerry with the horses. They forced the watchman to wave down the train with his red lantern. Engineer John Standthorpe saw the red light and brought his metal monster to a halt, right in front of the pile of ties on the track.

The Missouri-Pacific train had left Kansas City at 4:45 p.m. with two new Pullman sleeping cars, a smoker, and a combination express and baggage car. At Sedalia, it took on a Missouri-Kansas, Texas express locked car, without any special express messenger aboard. John B. Bushnell, in charge of two safes, occupied the Missouri-Pacific baggage and express car. Bushnell was a United States express messenger, in charge mainly of the express company's own safe. The other safe belonged to the Adams Express Company. With Bushnell was Louis P. Conklin, of St. Louis, baggage master for the railroad company.

Conklin was sitting peacefully in a chair by the open door of the baggage car, watching the moonlight flick through the scenery and catching the cool breeze.

Suddenly a bullet struck the door near his chair, interrupting his meditations. Three men, with bandannas over their faces, climbed in through the open side

door. Bushnell, farther back in the car, instantly realized something was amiss. He slipped through the rear door, ran through the train and handed the express safe key to the brakeman who tucked the key in his shoe. Bushnell tried to lose himself among the passengers.

Pete Conklin always believed that the man just outside the car was Frank James and that the other two who came inside were Jesse James and Cole Younger. Soon the engineer and fireman were pushed into the baggage car and lined up against the wall with Conklin. When the robbers found the safe key missing, they marched Conklin back through the coaches and forced him to point out Bushnell, who, in turn was forced to point out the brakeman. No one dared resist, and the key was turned over to the robbers.

The robbers returned to the express car. They opened the express safe easily with the key and threw the cash in a wheat sack. Then the apparent leader of the group turned to the Adams Express safe. Blue and blinky eyes flashed above the mask covering this outlaw—probably Jesse James. Convinced there was no key to the safe, Bob Younger got a pick from the engine tender and brought it back to the express car. He tried to break the hinges of the door with the pick but to no avail. Neither did several sharp blows to the door of the sheet-iron safe open it.

The biggest of the bandits, no doubt Cole Younger, seized the pick and dealt a series of smashing blows in a circle. He knocked out a piece of the metal, but the opening was too small for the man's large hands. Another robber, a small man wearing skin-tight silk gloves, managed to fit his hands inside, slit the leather pouch and remove the currency in handfuls. This they tossed in the sack with the other currency. No doubt the small man was Jesse, since he also appeared to be the leader of the mob.

As soon as the train reached Tipton, Missouri, Conductor Tebbets wired the news to St. Louis, Sedalia, and Kansas City. Posses rushed to central Missouri, but the robbers had already split the loot and scattered. Before doing this, though, they had ridden over twenty miles to a secluded spot. They counted a total of $17,000 from the two safes; the amount taken from the passengers was never ascertained.

Hobbs Kerry, the silly greenhorn, was given $1200 for his part in the Rocky Cut robbery. He hid his saddle in the brush and turned his mount loose near Montrose. Then he boarded a Missouri-Kansas, Texas train and went to Fort Scott, Kansas. There he outfitted himself with new clothes and boldly ate supper in a hotel. After that, he took a train for Parsons where he stayed overnight before proceeding to Vinita and to Granby, Missouri, a lead-mining center. He reached Joplin, Missouri, on July 18 and continued to Eufala, Indian Territory, where he was foolish enough to display too much money.

Several weeks after the robbery, Detective Sergeant Morgan Boland of the St. Louis Police Department asked permission of Chief James McDonough to do a little quiet investigating in southwestern Missouri. Boland soon learned from the lead miners that Hobbs Kerry was living "high off the hog." Kerry had returned to Joplin, Missouri by that time so Boland found him and became friendly. The simple-minded Kerry, impressed with his greatness as a bandit, boasted of having been in the train holdup with Jesse James.

Kerry was arrested and taken to Boonville, Cooper County, where he made a full confession, telling the whole story and naming the participants as far as he knew them. For turning state's evidence, Kerry got off with a two-year sentence in the state penitentiary.

Once more, Jesse was careful about his public relations. A few days after Kerry's arrest, a stranger rode up to the *Kansas City Times* reporter and handed him a letter which afterward appeared in the paper.

> Oak Grove, Kansas, August, 14, 1876
> Dear Sir:
> You have published Hobbs Kerry's confession, which makes it appear that the Jameses and the Youngers were the Rocky Cut robbers. If there was only one side to be told, it would probably be believed by a good many people that Kerry has told the truth. But his so-called confession is a well-built pack of lies from beginning to end. I never heard of Hobbs Kerry, Charlie Pitts and William Chadwell until Kerry's arrest. I can prove my innocence by eight good, well-known men of Jackson County, and show conclusively that I was not at the train robbery. But at present I will only give the names of two of those gentlemen to whom I will refer for proof.
> Early on the morning after the train robbery east of Sedalia, I saw the Honorable D. Gregg, of Jackson County, and talked with him for thirty or forty minutes. I also saw and talked to Thomas Pitcher, of Jackson County, the morning after the robbery. Those two good men's oaths cannot be impeached, so I refer the grand jury of Cooper County, Mo., and Governor Hardin to those men before they act so rashly on the oath of a liar, thief and robber.
> Kerry knows that the Jameses and Youngers can't be taken alive, and that is why he has put it on us. I have referred to Messrs. Pitcher and Gregg because they are prominent men, and they know I am innocent, and their word can't be disputed. I will write a long article to you for the *Times* and send it to you in a few days, showing fully how Hobbs Kerry lied. Hoping the *Times* will give me a chance for a fair hearing and to vindicate myself through its columns, I will close.
> Respectfully,
> J. James

As he promised, Jesse did write another letter to the editor of the *Kansas City Times* a few days later.[2]

> Safe Retreat, Texas
> August 18, 1876
> Dear Sir:
> I have written a great many letters vindi-

---

[2]The construction and clarity of Jesse's letters leads one to believe they were written either by Frank James or Major John Newman Edwards.

cating myself of the false charges that have been brought against me. Detectives have been trying for years to get positive proof against me for some criminal offense, so that they could get a large reward offered for me, dead or alive; and the same of Frank James and the Younger boys, but they have been foiled on every turn, and they are fully convinced that we will never be taken alive, and now they have (fallen) on the deep-laid scheme to get Hobbs Kerry to tell a pack of base lies. But, thank God, I am yet a free man, and have got the power to defend myself against the charge brought against me by Kerry, a notorious liar and poltroon. I will give a full statement and prove his confessions false.

Lie No. 1. He said a plot was laid by the Jameses and Youngers to rob the Granby bank. I am reliably informed that there never was a bank at Granby.

Lie No. 2. He said he met with Cole Younger and me at a Mr. Tyler's. If there is a man in Jackson County by that name, I am sure that I am not acquainted with him.

Lie No. 3. He said Frank James was at Mr. Butler's, in Cass County. I and Frank don't know any man in Cass County by that name. I can prove my innocence by eight good citizens of Jackson County, Mo., but I do not propose to give their names at present. If I did, those cutthroat detectives would find out where I am.

My opinion is that Bacon Montgomery, the scoundrel who murdered A.J. Clements, December 13, 1866, is the instigator of all this Missouri-Pacific affair. I believe he planned the robbery and got his share of the money, but when he went out to look for the robbers he led the pursuers off the robbers' trail. If the truth was half told about Montgomery, it would make the world believe that Montgomery had no equal, only the Bender family and the midnight assassins who murdered my poor, helpless and innocent eight-year-old brother, and who blew my mother's arm off; and I am of the opinion he had a hand in that dirty, cowardly work. The detectives are a brave lot of boys—charge houses, break down doors and make the grey hairs stand up on the heads of unarmed victims. Why doesn't President Grant have the soldiers called in and send the detectives out on special trains after the hostile Indians? A.M. Pinkerton's force, with hand-grenades, and will they kill all the women and children, and as soon as the women and children are killed it will stop the breed, and the warriors

will die out in a few years. I believe the railroad robbers will yet be sifted down to someone at St. Louis or Sedalia putting up the job and then trying to have it put on innocent men, as Kerry has done.

Hoping the *Times* will publish just as I have written, I will close.
Jesse James

About a year before Jesse wrote these letters to the *Kansas City Times,* he had written a more general defense of himself to the Nashville, Tennessee *Banner.* It was published in that paper's July 10, 1875, issue.

Ray Town, Mo., July 5th, 1875
Gentlemen:

As my attention has been called, recently, to the notice of several sensational pieces from the *Nashville Union* and *American,* stating that the Jameses and Youngers are in Kentucky, I ask space in your valuable paper to say a few words in my defense. I would treat these reports with silent contempt, but I have many friends in Kentucky and Nashville that I wish to know that these reports are false and without foundation. I have never been out of Missouri since the Amnesty Bill was introduced into the Missouri Legislature, last March, asking for pardon for the James and Younger boys. I am in constant communication with Governor Hardin, Sheriff Groom, of Clay County, Mo., and several other honorable county and state officials, and there are hundreds of persons in Missouri who will swear that I have not been in Kentucky. There are desperadoes roving round in Kentucky, and it is probably very important for the officials of Kentucky to be vigilant. If a robbery is committed in Kentucky today, Detective Bligh, of Louisville, would telegraph all over the United States that the James and Younger boys did it, just as he did when the Columbia, Kentucky, bank was robbed, April 29, 1872. Old Bly, the Sherman bummer, who is keeping up all the sensational reports in Kentucky, and if the truth was known, I am satisfied some of the informers are concerned in many robberies charged to the James and Younger boys for ten years. The radical papers in Missouri and other states have charged nearly every daring robbery in America to the James and Younger boys. It is enough for the northern papers to persecute us without the south, the land we fought for four years, to save from the Northern Tyranny, to be persecuted by papers claiming to be Democratic, is against reason. The people of the south have only heard one side of this report. I will give a true story of the lives of the James and Younger boys to the *Banner* in the future; or rather a sketch of our lives. We have not only been persecuted, but on the night of January 25th, 1875, at the midnight hour, nine Chicago assassins and Sherman Bummers, led by Billy Pinkerton, Jr., crept up to my mother's house and burled a missile of war in a room among innocent women and children, murdering my eight-year-old brother and tearing my mother's right arm off, and wounding several others of the family, and then firing the house in seven places. The radical papers here in Missouri have repeatedly charged the Russellville, Kentucky, bank robbery to the James and Younger boys, while it is well known, that on the day of the robbery, March 20th, 1869, I was at the Chaplin Hotel, in Chaplin, Nelson County, Kentucky, which I can prove by Mr. Tom Marshall, the proprietor, and fifty others; and on that day my brother Frank was at work on the Laponsu [sic] Ranch in San Luis Obispo County, California, for J.D.P.

Thompson, which can be proven by the sheriff of San Luis Obispo County and many others. Frank was in Kentucky the winter previous to the robbery, but he left Alexander Sayers, in Nelson County, January 25th, 1868, and sailed from New York City, January the 16th, which the books of the United States mail line of the steamers will show. Probably I have written too much, and probably not enough, but I hope to write much more to the *Banner* in the future. I will close by sending kindest regards to Dr. Eve, and many thanks to him for kindness to me when I was wounded and under his care.

Yours respectfully,

Jesse James

It is regrettable that Jesse's intention to write sketches of his, Frank's and the Younger brothers' lives was never carried out. Or, if it was, that the newspapers did not print them. At any rate, they have never been discovered in the newspaper files or among the documents now in possession of the James descendants.

Chapter Twelve

Disaster at Northfield

The robbery that more than anything else crippled the James boys' entourage and made effective recruitment for their band increasingly difficult, was the raid on the bank at Northfield, Minnesota, on the morning of September 7, 1876. It was accompanied by gunplay, violence, and drama on a larger scale than any of the other bank robberies in which the James and Younger boys were said to participate. The gang was thoroughly shot up, and three of its members captured and put behind the bars of the Minnesota Penitentiary at Stillwater.

The author spent many years investigating the Northfield raid story and believes this account will most definitively cover all points of the affair, as well as prove that the James brothers participated in it. A great deal of his information comes from family members, sons of Jesse and Frank James, Harry Hoffman, and Bill Stigers' family (who were confidantes of the James family).

The best and most reliable data of the Northfield story comes from Jim Younger himself, as he wrote it to Cora Lee McNeill, the girl he was supposed to marry just prior to the ride into Minnesota.

Cole and Jim Younger planned a double wedding in the early spring of 1876. Then they would go to Texas, find a few thousand acres of good rangeland, and run a sturdy breed of cattle that could make the drive to the nearest rail shipping head and still bring a good price at the point of delivery. Jim Younger had built up a nice business buying and selling horses. He agreed to sell the business before he traveled to Texas.

Previous to all this planning, Cole and Jim visited their uncle, Thomas Jefferson Younger, in California. Their uncle operated a general mercantile business and agreed to help finance the Texas venture. So in July, 1876, Jim sold his horse business and again traveled to his uncle's home on the west coast. He and Cole agreed to meet at Monegaw Springs, St. Clair County, Missouri, on his return trip.

In Los Angeles, Jim gave his uncle a detailed account of their plans, including his engagement to Cora Lee McNeill and Cole's to Lizzie Daniels. Jim then asked his uncle for an unsecured loan to help finance the venture. Uncle T.J. (as he was affectionately called) agreed, and advanced Jim a thousand dollars with the balance to be sent when needed.

A few hours before Jim was to leave Los Angeles, he received a letter from Cole, mailed from Osceola, Missouri. This surprised him; he thought Cole and Bob were in Louisiana. In the letter, Jim was further surprised that Cole signed the letter "Bud" since this was the nickname he had been known by as a young man. Cole also mentioned their brother Bob, referring to him as "Robert." This disturbed Jim because he knew Cole seldom referred to their younger brother by any name other than Bob.

Uncle T.J. read Cole's letter and also sensed that something was amiss. He said to Jim, "You hightail it back to Missouri and put a tight check on that bit in his [Cole's] teeth, yonker, before he gets too big for his pantaloons."

When Jim arrived in Monegaw Springs, he asked Cole why they had left Louisiana. Cole appeared troubled, but when he and Jim were alone in his room, he gave Jim some amazing information.

Shortly after Cole returned from Louisiana, he noticed that Bob was restless. Bob was often mentioning their younger brother, John, who had been killed at Osceola by detectives some time before. Cole sensed that since Bob and John had been very close as boys, John's death affected Bob more than they had realized.

Cole further related to Jim that Bob had met Jesse James on the street the day after Cole left for Monegaw Springs. Bob knew Jesse and Frank, but was never closely associated with either. Jesse persuaded Bob to come with him to his hotel and meet Frank. Jesse asked whether Cole was in town and Bob had replied that he was not.

At this point, Bob came into the room, and Jim listened in amazement as Cole and Bob related Jesse's plan for the Northfield raid. As Jim listened to the bizarre plan, he was shocked and furious for the first time in his life. He had a strong desire to do bodily harm—something he had never experienced. At that moment, Jesse would have been his victim.

Cole asked, "What does Jesse think is a sure thing?"

Bob replied, "Well, Jesse seems to have a plan where we can get $75,000 with little or no trouble. He intends to rob the bank at Northfield, Minnesota, when the vaults are bulging with grain money. Benjamin Butler and his son-in-law, General Adelbert

Ames, are both big stockholders in that bank. You remember how those two Union generals beat into the ground the Southern people of Louisiana during the Reconstruction days."

"Who else in involved?" asked Cole.

"Well, Jesse said that he and Frank would be there, me, and Charlie Pitts, Clell Miller, and Bill Stiles. I don't know any of them, but maybe you do. Jesse said he'd be known as 'Mr. Howard' and they'd be calling Frank 'Mr. Woods.' "

"What did Frank have to say to all this?" Cole wanted to know.

"Frank never said a word; he let Jesse do all the talking. Jesse told me not to tell you anything about it because he said you don't like him, though he doesn't know why."

Cole tried to reason with Bob, but the young man was determined to go on the raid. He did promise not to give Jesse an answer, though, until Cole and Jim had talked it out. Cole wanted to visit Kansas City to have a showdown with Jesse, although he knew it would solve nothing. Besides, he had always been on friendly terms with Frank James.

Jim demanded, "Bud, have you lost your reason to even think or talk of letting Bob and yourself take part in such a plot? Hasn't Jesse done enough to you in the past, implicating you in his robberies? I know Jesse figures you'll go along to protect Bob. That's just what he wants."

Cole did not reply. Jim then talked it over with Bob.

"Robbery is not your way of life, Bob. Most of the false implications have been instigated by Jesse James. He is using you only to drag Cole into his scheme. He knows you wouldn't go without telling Cole."

Bob was not to be diverted. He was not interested in horses or a horse ranch in Texas and it seemed a good way to get a lot of money without working for it.

"I'm twenty-three years old now," he said. "And I can take care of myself. Jesse's idea looks good to me. After that I can go to Canada and live well." Then Bob stormed out of the room.

Cole and Jim discussed the matter at length. Against their better judgment they decided to go with Bob and somehow change his mind if at all possible. When Cole informed Jesse James of their intention to ride along with Bob on their unsavory mission, Jesse became furious. This brought on a mild attack of epilepsy to which he was subject after his long illness from earlier wounds.

He cried out, "You just want a greater share of the money! You'd be three Youngers against two Jameses!"

Jesse went into a tantrum. Cole threatened to force his younger brother Bob not to take part unless he and Jim could ride along. Jesse seemed about to draw his gun on Cole, but Frank intervened, knowing the outcome. Cole already had his pistol out and was tapping Jesse on the chest with the barrel.

"Stay healthy, boy. Leave it as it is," Frank cautioned Jesse.

After that they made plans. Jesse insisted that the three Youngers understand the deal was his idea. Later it was given out as having been Cole's idea first, and Jesse had railroaded the idea through. Jesse also insisted that he himself would issue orders, and Cole agreed to that for himself and his two brothers.

Later, Jim explained to Cora Lee McNeill that he had to go north. Cole made the same announcement to Lizzie Daniels. They both said they hoped to return by mid-October. Then the double wedding would take place. Cora gave Jim a small picture that he carried for the rest of his life.

The gang was to meet in July at the Samuel home near Kearney. Jim Younger said he left Kansas City on the Lexington Road, where he was to meet the others. Jim had refused to meet with the others for the final plans. He said he didn't have to be present.

Jim joined the rest of the gang near Independence. Frank James introduced Charlie Pitts (alias Sam Wells), Clell Miller, and Bill Chadwell (alias Bill Stiles). He added, "Of course, you know my brother Jesse." Jim acknowledged the fact, wondering how in the face of past events, he could forget Frank's brother. Frank suggested that Cole, Bob, Charlie Pitts, and himself should ride north together. This left Clell Miller, Bill Stiles, Jim Younger, and Jesse to take another route.

Near Parkville, Missouri, the band had to cross the Missouri River. The man who rowed them was Charlie Turner, a brother-in-law of Sam Wells. To avoid suspicion, one man at a time was rowed across, the horses of each one swimming alongside the boat. Then the entire party of eight rode across Missouri and Iowa, into southern Minnesota. When they reached Albert Lea, Minnesota, Jesse and Clell Miller stabled their horses, telling the liveryman that whatever arrangements Jim Younger made for fresh mounts was all right with them.

Posing as cattlemen, Jim Younger and Bill Stiles purchased four sturdy animals, turning in their own four as partial payment. Jesse selected a big-chested buckskin, an animal of speed and endurance. Jim chose a long-legged friendly black horse, a dependable animal.

After their last meeting in the woods near Owatonna, the group split up. Bob Younger and Sam Wells went to St. Paul by train; Cole Younger and Bill Stiles rode there on horseback. Frank and Jesse James, Clell Miller, and Jim Younger, the rest of the contingent, rode their horses to St. Paul, but by a different route.

On August 20, Sam and Bob visited the livery stable of Hall and McKinney and looked over the best long-range animals available. They went on to the William Judd Stables, where they bought a black and a bay.

Bob Younger and Sam Wells met Cole Younger and Bill Stiles at the Merchants

Hotel on Third Street and Jackson Avenue in Minneapolis, from which point they visited the gambling houses in the city.

Jesse and Frank James, Clell Miller, and Jim Younger arrived in St. Paul a short while after the others, but they decided to visit the bawdy house of Mollie Ellsworth rather than try their luck at the gaming tables. From Minneapolis, Cole and Sam took a train to St. Peter. Bob and Bill followed on another train, and the remaining four took the train to Red Wing. Under assumed names, these four registered at the National Hotel in Red Wing.

The time scheduled for the bank robbery was near. The outlaws had kept only one of the original horses ridden to Minnesota from Missouri. This was the splendid buckskin they stole from the Stewart stables in Kansas City. In Red Wing, Cole registered at the hotel as J.C. King, and Bill Chadwell signed the register as J. Ward, cattle buyer. At Madelia, Cole signed in at the Flanders Hotel as J.C. King and Bill Chadwell signed as Jack Ladd. At that hotel they became friendly with Colonel Thomas L. Vought, a man Cole would meet again under different circumstances.

The outlaws' final meeting place was the secluded farm of Joe Brown. They used their time training their animals not to be gun-shy.

They separated after leaving the Brown farm and met on September 2, 1876, near the town of Mankato, Minnesota. All eight bandits rode into town, visiting the saloons and playing poker. Two of them later stopped at the Gates Hotel, two at the Washington Hotel, and the rest spent Sunday night at the home of George Capps, in Kasota, five miles south of Mankato.

Apparently, their plan was to attack the bank at Mankato first, but a large group of citizens was watching the construction work being done on the bank building. These "sidewalk superintendents" were no more aware of the noted outlaw gang than were the children playing at the nearby Catholic school.

Not knowing whether this was a trap or not, the wily bandits rode off, leaving town by way of Main and Fifth Streets. They decided to ride in pairs toward Northfield, the scene of their next planned operation. As they approached Northfield, the outlaws banded into two groups.

On the night of September 6, Jim and Cole Younger, and three of the men stayed at Janesville. Bob Cole and the other two men stayed at Faribault.

Early on the morning of September 7, the robbers rode along in pairs again, and met in a wooded section near Northfield. At ten o'clock, Frank, Jesse, Bob Younger and one other had breakfast at Jeff's Restaurant. Weatherwise, it was a dreary day, and it suddenly turned cooler. Dark clouds built up, indicating possible rain.

Frank and Bob had breakfast on the west side of the Cannon River, which separated the town. They also stopped at John Tosney's saloon and purchased a quart of whiskey.

The fact that Frank James and Bob Younger were drunk at the time of the raid was later attested to by Cole Younger. "Frank admitted he had a quart of whiskey which he and Pitts and Bob drank before going into the bank. Frank thought they could get the cash and be ready to ride out by the time Cole and Miller arrived."

Prior to the drinking spree by Frank, Bob, and Pitts, the gang met several miles from Janesville to arrange their strategy. Frank drew a diagram of the main street of Northfield looking south of the bridge. Frank, Bob Younger, and Charlie Pitts, who were to enter the bank first, would ride slowly into town. They were to stop at the hitch rail rack near the outside stairway of the building, but they were not supposed to enter the bank until Cole Younger and Clell Miller (who would be about two blocks behind them) reached their own positions.

Jesse James, Jim Younger and Bill Chadwell were to remain at the bridge. Should trouble arise, Cole was to fire one shot, the

Bridge Square, Northfield, Minnesota.

Courtesy of Harry Y. Hall

signal for them to ride in. If the raid proved successful, Jesse, Jim, and Bill were to ride south and then east to Rochester, where the eight would meet. From there it would be easy to reach Iowa and escape to Missouri. Bill Chadwell, who had once lived in Rice County, Minnesota, was elected to lead the bandits out of the state after the robbery.

A bridge in the center of Northfield connected the east and west parts of the town and led into Bridge Square on the east side. At the corner of Division Street and Bridge Square there was a two-story building called the Scriver Block. The First National Bank stood at the south end of the block, near an alley that ran behind two hardware stores operated by J.S. Allen and A.R. Manning respectively. Opposite the Scriver Block was a group of three stores and a hotel called the Dampier House. There, young Henry W. Wheeler, home on

vacation from the medical college at Ann Arbor, Michigan, was passing the time of day with a friend.

From the start, the timing was poor. Bob Younger was fuzzy from drinking whiskey. Frank James had also been drinking, but he could hold his liquor better than Bob, although he was inclined to be a bit trigger-happy when in his cups. Pitts, too, was a bit under the weather from sipping the bottle.

Following their original plan, Frank James, Charlie Pitts, and Bob Younger dismounted in front of the bank and tossed their bridle reins over some hitching posts beside the street. They then walked to the corner and lounged on some wooden boxes in front of the Lee & Hitchcock Store, assuming the attitude of loafers. When they saw that Cole Younger and Clell Miller had started down Division Street toward the bank, they walked closer to the bank. They

The James-Younger gang crossed this bridge when entering the town of Northfield, Minnesota in 1876 prior to the bank raid.

This stone building was called the Scriver Block. The First National Bank occupied quarters at the southern end of the building with the front entrance on Division Street.

Courtesy of Harry Y. Hall

were supposed to wait until the two riders joined them to complete the party going inside the bank, but instead they entered at once.

When Cole and Miller saw this they hurried to the bank, following the trio already inside. Cole dismounted and pretended to tighten his saddle girth on his horse. Miller went to the bank door and looked in. He then closed the door and walked back and forth in front of it.

These actions aroused the suspicion of J.S. Allen, one of the hardware store proprietors. Allen started for the bank to see what was going on. When Miller ordered him away from the building, Allen left, but as he fled around the corner he shouted, "Get your guns, boys! They're robbing the bank!" Allen had no horse, but he got one quickly and did a fine Paul Revere job in Northfield.

The inhabitants of Northfield's minuteman defense of their town resembled the warfare they used against the Indians. They grimly took up their rifles and shotguns. One townsman, Elias Stacy, blasted his shotgun at Clell Miller as Miller was mounting his horse. Bird shot peppered his face, but he got away. A.R. Manning shot at Charlie Pitts with a breech-loading rifle, but succeeded only in killing the bandit's horse.

Cole Younger was ready to call off the robbery. He yelled to the robbers in the bank to come out for a getaway. Manning's breech-loader bullet hit him in the thigh and his calls were interrupted. Manning backed away to reload and saw Bill Chadwell waiting beside his horse about eighty yards away. Manning shot and Chadwell fell dead to the ground, a bullet through his heart. The horse ran to a livery stable around the corner.

After young Wheeler had aroused the town, he hastened to the drug store where he usually kept a gun. Then he remembered he'd left it at home that day. He raced through the store to get a weapon he'd seen at the hotel, but when he found the wea-

pon, it was an empty army carbine. Mr. Dampier, the owner of the hotel, luckily located three cartridges in another room and in short order Wheeler was stationed at a second-story window of the hotel.

Jim Younger was riding by just then and Wheeler took a quick shot at him. His aim was too high, though, and the bullet missed. In vain Jim looked around for the sharpshooter who by then had picked another target, Clell Miller. The bullet passed through Miller's body, severing the great artery and killing him almost instantly. Wheeler's third cartridge fell to the floor—the paper broke, rendering it useless, but Dampier reached him with a fresh supply of ammunition, and another shot by Wheeler hit Bob Younger in the right elbow as he ran out of the bank. Bob quickly executed the "border shift," throwing his revolver in his left hand, ready to fire.

There ensued a brief lull in the fighting, as each side waited for the other to show itself. Taking advantage of the lull, Bob Younger raced up Division Street, where he mounted behind Cole. Then the remainder of the outlaws fled.

The battle was as decisive as it was brief. Six robbers were in flight, two of them wounded. Chadwell was dead near the bridge. In front of the bank lay the dead horse, and the body of Clell Miller half a block away on the other side of the street. The defenders rushed to the bank to see what had happened.

They found out that the three robbers had entered and quickly held under their guns the teller, A.E. Bunker, and the assistant bookkeeper, Joseph L. Heywood, who was acting cashier at the time in the absence of G.M. Phillips.

Heywood had told the bandits that the safe had a time lock and could not be opened. Ironically, even though the safe door was closed and the bolts thrown, the combination dial had not been twirled. The bandits would only have had to turn the handle to open it. Also, the whiskey must have dulled the minds of the raiders, be-cause any sensible person would know that the time lock would not have been set to open at that time of day.

Seizing a chance to escape, A.E. Bunker had dashed behind the vault toward an exit door. Charlie Pitts took several shots at him, the second entering his shoulder. Frank James, last to leave the building, deliberately shot and killed Heywood for no reason at all. Perhaps he was frustrated at getting no money, or perhaps the whiskey made him trigger-happy.

Frank Wilcox, the clerk, said, "The door of the vault was open, but not that of the safe inside. Mr. Heywood was ordered to open the safe. As one of the robbers entered the vault, Heywood sprang forward and closed the door, shutting the robber in. Another man seized Heywood by the collar and dragged him away, releasing his partner. Almost immediately, those two robbers took alarm and somehow jumped over the counter, making their exit. The taller man was the last to go. He mounted a desk at the front end, and as he turned to leave, he fired a shot at Heywood, a shot that seemed to miss. Heywood dodged behind his desk and sank into the chair, but the robber leaned over the desk and placed the re-volver at Heywood's head and fired, shoot-ing him dead."

Jim Younger wrote that for some reason Cole Younger always protected Frank James in the matter of Heywood's murder. He said the killer was not Jesse James, as was frequently claimed, but he refused to name the real murderer except to say that he was the man who rode the dun horse at Northfield.

Jim continued, "Frank James was the last of those who entered the bank to come out. I heard the two shots in the bank after Pitts and Bob ran out. Frank admitted he fired at the man we later learned was Joseph Hey-wood because [Heywood] was aiming a small pistol at him. I was not in the bank at any time, nor was Cole. The man who rode

the buckskin out of town was the man who killed Heywood, and that man was Frank James. If Cole feels his allegiance to Mr. Howard and Mr. Woods is so deep as to prevent his disclosing their true identifies as Jesse and Frank James for as long as [Cole] lives, I have no such scruple of conscience. I have sinned against society; I am now paying the price demanded by that society. [That] is as it should be, but I owe no loyalty to Frank James, alive, I am told, or to the memory of Jesse James."

The usual accounts report that the six outlaws raced out of Northfield on the Dundas Road. According to Jim Younger, Jesse and Frank left town a few minutes before the remaining outlaws, by way of Faribault Road. Jesse was riding the bay and Frank the buckskin.

Jim reported,

It was perhaps a half mile out of town that we joined Frank and Jesse. A few miles farther on we met a farmer leading a broken-down work animal which Cole paid the man thirty dollars for. Cole and Pitts had ridden double out of town, so this horse was given to Pitts. He seemed grateful, saying it was better than walking.

We rode along with Jesse and Frank in the lead. Frank called out, asking where Chad-well was. At our first report of news we learned that he and Miller were killed in the street at Northfield. When we stopped we learned that Cole had been shot in the hip while at the bank door urging the boys to come out. Neither Jesse, Frank, nor Pitts had been hit during the shooting.

Cole questioned Frank as to why he and the two boys did not wait until he [Cole] and Miller arrived, as planned, before they entered the bank.

Frank then admitted he had a quart of whiskey which he, Pitts and Bob drank before going into the bank. Cole and I never touched liquor in our life, and were shocked to hear that Bob had indulged. Had we known about the whiskey, the whole ghastly affair never would have occurred.

Cole asked what had gone wrong inside the bank that caused the two shots to be fired. At that time we did not know that anyone had been fatally shot.

Frank said, 'There was a lot of shooting and yelling going on outside and I thought I better do as the boys said and get out of there. When I started toward the door the man on the floor stood up; he was pointing a small revolver at me. I still had my gun in my hand so I aimed for his shoulder and fired. His gun went off as he dropped to the floor. His bullet was high, I guess; it didn't come anywhere near me. I don't know how badly he was wounded or if at all. This man did not do what I told him. He was the one who said there was a time lock on the vault, and he was lying. I then ran across the floor as Pitts yelled for us to run for it.'

No one spoke after Frank finished talking. We mounted and rode on. Later in the day we stopped again to rest. A cold steady rain had set in and it was miserable.

The robbers had to keep going. Posses from Northfield and elsewhere were in pursuit, and the officials at the state capital were also asked to assist. Governor John S. Pillsbury offered a $1,000 reward for the surviving bandits. He later raised this offer to $1,000 each, dead or alive. The bank and various corporations also offered cash rewards.

Back in Northfield, grief over Heywood's untimely death was widespread. He had been greatly liked and respected, and was a member of the Board of Carleton College. President James W. Strong of Carleton placed Heywood's body in a carriage and drove it to his residence. Mrs. Heywood showed herself worthy of the occasion. When she learned of how her husband had been killed, she said, "I would not have had him do otherwise."

On Sunday, September 10, two funeral services were held in honor of the murdered bank employee. During the morning the large auditorium of the high school was filled despite the prevailing rain and mud. The funeral eulogy, given by the Reverend D.L. Leonard, pastor of the Congregational Church, was so magnificent that people talked about it for months.

Later, the funeral service at Mr. Heywood's home, conducted by President Strong, paid equal testimony to the character of the deceased. Heywood was then buried in the Northfield Cemetery at the southern end of the city. His grave was marked with an appropriate headstone.

Coroner Waugh of Faribault held an inquest on the bodies of the two outlaws. He said, "The two unknown men came to their deaths by the discharge of firearms in the hands of our citizens in self-defense and in protecting the property of the First National Bank of Northfield."

The bodies of the dead outlaws were carried to the open square, which was soon overcrowded with the curious morbid. Bill Chadwell was described as five feet nine inches tall, with auburn hair, slim and muscular. People tried to cut off pieces of his clothing or locks of his hair. What happened to the compass and gold watch that were in his pockets at the time of his death is anyone's guess. Clell Miller was taller, about six feet three inches tall, with auburn hair and fair skin.

That night, in an obscure corner of the cemetery, two boxes were buried. No one troubled to determine whether the boxes were full or not, but we know that Clell Miller's body found its way back to Missouri, where it was claimed by his father. It was later buried in the Muddy Fork Cemetery, north of the James farm.

It was customary in those days to donate the bodies of dead criminals to medical colleges to further the study of anatomical science. Young medical student Henry W. Wheeler, who had shot and killed Bill Chadwell, thought this was a good idea. When Bill's body was taken off the street at Northfield, Wheeler asked for it. His request was granted, and he took the corpse to the University of Michigan at Ann Arbor. It was missing an ear, which someone must have whacked off. Today this same ear is on display under a glass case in the museum at Northfield.

After his graduation, Dr. Wheeler took the skeleton of Chadwell with him to Grand Forks, North Dakota, where it hung from a hook in his office, in line with the custom of that day. When a young reporter

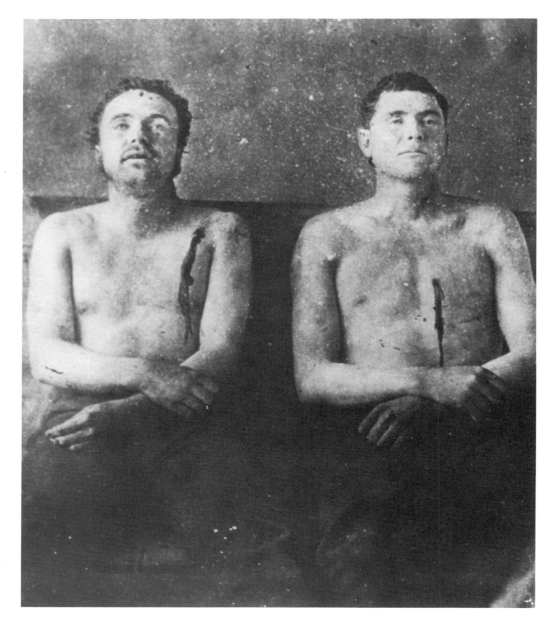

Dead at Northfield: McClellan (Clell) Miller (left) and Bill Chadwell (alias William Stiles).

learned of this he wrote a good newspaper story about it. One day an elderly gentleman came to Dr. Wheeler's office and asked to see the skeleton. After some questions it was determined that this man was the father of Bill Chadwell, alias Bill Stiles. The old man was visibly shaken when he learned the truth of the matter. The skeleton remained in Dr. Wheeler's office until it was destroyed in a fire.

Lost in an area unknown to them, the Youngers and the Jameses floundered from pillar to post, going in circles most of the time. The loss of their guide Chadwell devastated them. On Friday, near Waterville, they exchanged shots with a posse near the swollen Cannon River. The following Monday found them resting in a deserted farmhouse a few miles from Mankato. They had traveled fewer than fifty miles in five days.

Early Thursday morning, Jesse James, in a

high state of agitation announced he wanted to leave Bob and Jim Younger because they were too badly wounded to handle, and were leaving a trail of blood for the posse to follow.

"Either leave your [Cole's] brothers or kill them, for they are making a trail of blood and slowing down our flight."

This so enraged Cole that there would have been a shoot-out on the spot, had Bob not called out to prevent it. Frank, stepping close to Jesse, slapped him across the face, saying, "Don't you ever make a remark like that again unless you want me to forget that I am your brother."

At that point it was agreed that the Youngers and Pitts should proceed in one direction, and Frank and Jesse in another. Frank and Cole remained firm friends for the rest of their lives.

The news of the outlaws' whereabouts was brought to Sheriff James Glispin of Watonwan County, and Colonel Thomas L. Vought at Madelia by a young man named Asle Oscar Sorbel. He had seen the four fugitives at the Blue Earth River near Madelia.

Here is Jim Younger's verbatim statement regarding the brief fight that ended the career of the Youngers:

> Our horses were spent and made little progress due to the mud and rain. We must have bypassed Faribault on some farm-to-market road. Later I learned we were between Mankato and Madelia and off the main road when the posse caught up with us about daylight. We made our last stand against a large posse headed by Sheriff James Glispin along the Watonwan River. He later became a dear friend of ours.
>
> The posse surrounded us as we lay in some thick brush, a short distance from our horses, cutting off our escape. We were under heavy fire; our ammunition was almost gone. Bob shouted to me, 'This is senseless, we cannot hold out any longer.' I could not speak. Cole was unconscious and as I learned later, Pitts was dead. By an odd fate he, like Frank and Jesse James from Northfield uninjured. How many times he was shot by the posse I do not know.

Cole was hit numerous times. The first was in Northfield when he ran to the bank door to urge the boys to come out. The bullet lodged in his hip. Some of the bullets fired at him by the posse he has never had removed. Bob was wounded twice and I was shot in the mouth; I was shot four times.

The wounded outlaws were taken to Madelia in a wagon. There, they were treated and placed under guard. On order from the surgeon general, Dr. Frank W. Murphy, Charlie Pitts' body was shipped to the Rush Medical School in Chicago. Dr. Henry Hoyt, of St. Paul, took the body. He wanted a skeleton to hang in his office and the school had refused to accept it, owing to its damaged condition.

In order to whiten the bones to the desired color, Dr. Hoyt put the body in a box and submerged it in Lake Como. He also put some heavy stones in with the body and carefully marked the spot where he let it down.

In March of 1877, Dr. Hoyt accepted a position in Las Vegas, New Mexico (where he once sold a horse to Billy the Kid). He forgot all about Pitts' bones whitening at the bottom of Lake Como.

One day a friend handed him a newspaper clipping reporting the discovery of the remains of a murdered man found in Lake Como. The news article stated that a young muskrat trapper named August Robertson had found the box in the lake. Robertson reported it to the St. Paul Police who labeled it a foul murder. It was almost a year before Dr. Hoyt returned to St. Paul, where he informed the Chief of Police of what had happened. The story was verified and the puzzle solved.

When Dr. Hoyt moved to Chicago from New Mexico he took along the skeleton of Charlie Pitts. One day it disappeared, never to be seen again, although there is now a skeleton in a museum in Savage, Minnesota that some folks claim is Pitts.

When they had recovered enough to be moved, the Youngers were taken to the jail at Faribault, Minnesota, to await trial. Their attorney strongly urged them to plead guilty, and thus escape capital punishment. When the three brothers appeared before Judge Lord on four indictments brought against them, they pleaded guilty and were sentenced to life imprisonment at the state prison at Stillwater.

On Monday evening, September 16, 1889, Bob Younger died of consumption. He had spent thirteen long, dark and dreary years inside prison walls—all that time a model prisoner, faithful and docile. Funeral services were held in the prison chapel. Bob's loyal sister, Henrietta Younger Rawlins, took his remains to Lee's Summit, Missouri, and buried them in the Younger cemetery lot.

Many prominent men and women tried to have Jim and Cole released or pardoned. Among them was Cora Lee McNeill Deming, Jim's old sweetheart and now a

Bob Younger after his capture in 1876

Cole and Jim Younger were photographed at Faribault, Minnesota jail after their capture for the Northfield bank robbery. Jim first said his name was Carter to throw off his identity but the ruse failed. Some writers have erroneously stated, therefore, that one of the robbers was named Carter.

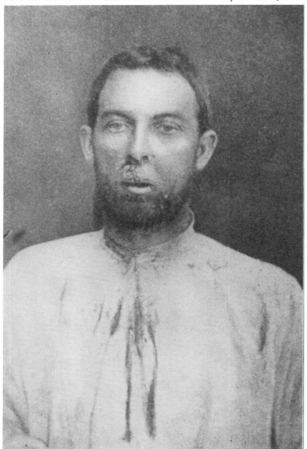

Left to right: Bob Younger, sister Henrietta, Jim, and Cole Younger at Stillwater, Minnesota prison, 1889.

widow, although she chose to remain in the background. Another driving force in the cause was George M. Bennett, then attorney for James J. Hill and the Great Northern Railroad.

In 1901, the Minnesota State Legislature passed a bill providing parole for any life convict who had been confined for twenty years. The bill enabled Jim and Cole to appear outside the prison walls on July 14, 1901, but it was of little use to Jim in his wish to marry Cora Lee. The pardon was conditional and did not permit Jim or Cole to leave the state of Minnesota.

Jim's and Cora Lee's meeting must have been terribly painful. Then, on Friday, October 18, 1901, Cora Lee married Mr. Bennett and moved to South Dakota. It was a shame she could not have seen into the future, for within two years Governor Van Sant issued Cole a full pardon with the stipulation that he could never exhibit himself for monetary gain or return to Minnesota.

When Jim requested a full pardon on October 13, 1902, he was refused. On Sunday afternoon, October 19, 1902, Jim's dead body was found in his room at the

Reardon Hotel in St. Paul. He had fired a bullet into his brain. Mr. and Mrs. C.H. Hall and Henrietta Younger Rawlins took his body to Lee's Summit, Missouri, and buried him in the Younger cemetery plot. Funeral services for Jim were held in the same church that held them for his brother Bob in 1889. Pallbearers were C.W. Wiggington, O.H. Lewis, H.H. McDowell, Sam Whitsett, William Gregg, and William Lewis—all old neighbors of Jim's and comrades in arms during the Civil War.

Cole returned to Missouri for the first time since 1876 on Sunday, February 14, 1903. His first social call was to the home of Mr. and Mrs. Thomas Monroe. Lizzie Daniels had married Monroe, a prominent businessman, and had raised a fine family during Cole's incarceration.[1] It must have been a sad occasion.

---

[1]This information is appearing here for the first time anywhere.

Captain W.C. Bronaugh fought to free the Younger brothers from prison.

Newspapers covered the suicide of Jim Younger.

DAILY REVIEW, MONMOUTH, ILL

MONDAY, OCTOBER 20, 1902

KILLS HIMSELF.

James Younger, One of the Famous Younger Brothers Commits Suicide.

St. Paul, Minn., Oct. 20.—James Younger, one of the famous Younger brothers, compatriots of Jesse James, committed suicide Sunday by shooting. Younger was recently paroled from the Stillwater penitentiary, where he and his brother, Coleman, were serving life sentences for participation in the Northfield bank raid in 1876. Under the terms of the parole the brothers were not to leave the state, and since their release they have been engaged in business of various sorts. James Younger has suffered much from old wounds, and several months ago an operation was performed for the removal of a rifle ball from his neck.

He left a letter to the press in which he gives as a reason for his act despondency over continued ill health and separation from his friends.

Cole tried his hand at everything from running a Wild West show to selling coal stoves and gravestones. He also spent time traveling the midwest and giving talks on "How Crime Does Not Pay." Cole finally bought a home for Harry Younger Hall and Nora on Market Street in Lee's Summit. It has since been razed to make room for a bank parking lot.

A year after the death of Frank James, Cole Younger died at Lee's Summit in the house he'd bought for Harry and Nora. He was survived by three sisters: Mrs. Helen Kelley of Amoret, Missouri, age 84; Mrs. Martha Ann Jones, Dennison, Texas, age 81; and Mrs. Sallie Duncan, Kansas City, Kansas, age 71.

Chapter Thirteen

Escape from Northfield

Jesse and Frank were in alien territory with one horse between them. On Thursday night, September 14, 1876, they rode close to Lake Crystal where, during a driving rain, they were fired upon by a young man named Richard Roberts. The horse bolted, throwing both riders to the ground, but it was dark and they managed to escape into the muddy field.

Then, on September 25, Dr. Sidney Mosher, whose office was at 407 Jackson Street, near the high school, in Sioux City, received a call.[1] He was asked to attend Mrs. Robert Mann, who was seriously ill and in need of a goiter operation. She lived about twenty miles northeast of Sioux City. Dr. Mosher went to the Broadbent livery stable at noon to secure a horse for his journey. At the stables, a group of men were discussing recent events, especially the raid on the Northfield bank and the pursuit of the outlaws. Dr. Mosher listened for a while, then mounted his bay mare and set out for the Mann home.

Dr. Mosher rode all day and about four o'clock he was in the vicinity of Kingsley. The doctor did not know the exact location of the Mann home. Seeing two men on a nearby ridge, he called to them as he approached. When he was within a few yards of the two men he found himself looking into the barrels of their weapons.

"Hands up!" they commanded.

Dr. Mosher was puzzled by this behavior. The face of the shorter man quivered and the doctor thought these men must have been looking for the outlaws and mistaken him for one of them.

"What do you want with me? I'm Dr. Mosher on a sick call to the Mann home."

"We know who you are. You are a detective from St. Paul. I think I will have to shoot you. I am Jesse James," said the smaller man. "I think you have a posse out there in the woods ready to pounce on us."

Dr. Mosher, sitting on his horse with his hands above his head, had to do some fast thinking.

"Why don't you search me to see if I am armed?" he suggested.

He was ordered off his horse and searched. Dr. Mosher was wearing a new suit and had neglected to transfer some of his more personal things from his old suit to the new one. All he carried was a small box containing a scalpel.

"I still think I will shoot you. There is nothing here to prove you are who you claim to be."

"Ride back to the next farmhouse and ask them to describe Dr. Mosher of Sioux City. Ask them if there is not a Mrs. Robert Mann who is very ill and if Dr. Mosher is not on his way to treat her."

[1]It was the author's good fortune to know Dr. Sidney P. Mosher, of Sioux City, who was the son of the doctor kidnapped by the Jameses after the Northfield raid. This younger Dr. Mosher related the circumstances leading up to the confrontation between the Jameses and his father, Dr. Mosher.

The plan seemed to find favor with Jesse. Mounting Dr. Mosher's horse, Jesse rode away. In a short while he returned, grinning. The doctor said it was the first and only time he ever saw Jesse grin; all the while he was sullen and morose.

"All right, Doc. I guess you are who you say you are. We will have to keep you for a while. We don't want to shoot you, but we will kill you quick if you try to give us the slip or if you don't obey orders. You will ride between us and you are not to speak (except) when you are spoken to."

At suppertime, around six o'clock, they stopped at a farmhouse and Jesse told farmer Wright that Dr. Mosher of Sioux City had a breakdown and wanted to borrow a saddle. The farmer knew about Mrs. Mann. He brought out his best saddle. Dr. Mosher had to take it, well knowing that Wright would never see it again.

Later that evening the three men noticed a light some distance away. Apparently it was not the Mann house. Jesse told Mosher that was where he was supposed to go, and he was to remain there all night.

As they stood there, Jesse ordered the doctor to strip. Frank James also began to remove his clothes. Dr. Mosher was given Frank's clothing and told to put it on. Frank was taller than Dr. Mosher and the trouser legs had to be turned up. Also, Frank's coat was a fine one, but the tail had been peppered by buckshot. When they had effected the change of clothing, Jesse told the doctor to head for the light and not to look back. The doctor raced off, running as best he could. Frank's shoes were too large, and with his trousers too long, his coat flapping in the wind, poor Dr. Mosher must have made a spectacle.

The next morning Dr. Mosher was taken to Sioux City in a wagon. Later that day he visited the Mann home and performed a successful goiter operation on Mrs. Mann.

Dr. Mosher was interviewed shortly afterward by the editor of the *Sioux City Democrat,* G.W. Hunt, who had great admiration for the James boys. The editor figured out the probable trail of the outlaws by taking advantage of his friendship with Deputy Sheriff Dan McDonald, who let him see dispatches concerning the freshness of the fugitives' trail. Hunt hoped very much to interview the bandits before Sheriff John McDonald caught up to them.

Dr. Mosher had described the two men to Hunt—a further help. Dr. Mosher gave the following descriptions:

> The smaller man, Jesse James, was about thirty, I should say, with full-face whiskers of a dark brown color, worn short at that time. He had snappy blue eyes. His face was roundish, with a stubby nose. He was not a large man—medium height and weight. Appeared to be nice-looking and evidently hot-tempered.
>
> The second man was tall, apparently a few years older than the other, his brother. Had blue eyes also, face was angular, and he was rather thin. He wore a beard with sideburn cut, smooth chin, needing a shave at that time. Sandy color hair and moustache. No resemblance between the two.

Hunt feared the overzealous officers might get to Jesse and Frank first. He successfully discouraged James Wall's scheme to capture the outlaws. Wall planned to patrol the Missouri River with four skiffs, held close enough to discover any other skiff that might attempt to glide through by night. The editor feared Wall's plan might work, for he knew that Frank James was wounded, and that the outlaws might steal a skiff to float down the river to Missouri. That's exactly what they did do, a little later, and a little farther south down the Missouri, but in a skiff the editor himself helped steal.

Next day he took care of Sheriff John McDonald's posse. He described his adventures for his astounded readers by using the nonspecific "we" when referring to himself—with no byline, of course. This is what Editor Hunt reported.

> . . . We discovered that, Sheriff McDonald and a well-armed party were on the fresh

and well-defined scent of the Jameses and must capture them if not thwarted. Hitching up our team, we started out after the sheriff's party, soon overtaking them, and a little strategy succeeded in turning them off in another direction.

Within one hour from that time, and within four miles of the village of Woodbury, on the Sioux City and Pacific Railroad, we espied two men leisurely riding toward us. When we were within a couple of hundred yards of the advancing horsemen, we stopped our team in the road and awaited their coming.

They first saluted us and then eyed us keenly, intently by apparently casually examining us and our outfit. This being done, we said, 'Gentlemen, we know who you are; have been looking for you, but don't seek your capture.'

We then briefly stated to them our business as a newspaper man, satisfied them we were unarmed, and that under certain circumstances we could be trusted. We told them we wanted an account of the plan by which they undertook to rob the Northfield bank, their adventures since, the biographies of all their associates who had participated in the Northfield raid, and other such items as would be interesting to the readers of the newspaper which were at the time representative, and in return that we would facilitate their escape from the country.

The proposition at that moment seemed so novel, and at the same time so ludicrous to them, that both brothers indulged in a hearty laugh. By mutual or tacit acquiescence we seemed to understand each other.

Fearing that we might happen to meet some of the numerous parties scouring the country for our then companions, at our request one of them tied his horse behind our wagon and took a seat beside us, while the other rode alongside.

Driving to a small body of timber a short distance below the village of Woodbury, and adjacent to the Missouri River, their horses were turned loose with some other stock found grazing there, the saddles, bridles and blankets placed in a hiding place, the two men took their seats beside us and we drove for a few minutes in the direction of Sioux City, when suddenly the elder of the James, espying some men on horseback in the distance requested us to turn our ponies in a southern direction; he gave us a reason that the farther we went north the more of the country was woke up against them, and that they desired to get out of that section of the country by the shortest and quickest possible way.

That night we camped at a point adjacent to the Missouri River, nearly opposite the village of Sloan, not desiring to risk the chances of stopping at a house. During the night they proposed and we acceded to an oath of pledge that we would not under any circumstances reveal what facts they gave us until their safe arrival among friends, of which fact they could acquaint us either by telegraph or letter, and in addition, under certain other circumstances pending the arrest and trial of the Younger brothers, we would not disclose certain other information given us.

That night we all slept together in a bed made of prairie grass, we being favored with the honored position in the middle of our two celebrated guests. After a sound night's sleep, at daybreak, we hitched up our team and kept on down the Missouri Valley in the direction of Council Bluffs, Iowa.

Having resided on the upper Missouri for nearly twenty years, the greater part of which have been engaged in public life, we were known personally to nearly every resident in the section of country in which we were driving with our two companions, and of course the fact of their riding with us disarmed all suspicion as to who they were.

Reaching the Little Sioux River, we drove along its banks to about where it empties into the Missouri River. That evening it was decided by the James brothers to secure a skiff, which, fortunately for them, happened to be moored at a stake by a small cabin.

We were appointed a committee of one to visit a neighboring house to purchase several dozens of eggs, some pounds of butter, and such bread, potatoes, etc., as we could obtain. Having the previous evening purchased some tea, coffee, sugar, crackers, etc., in the store of Ed Haakinson at Sloan, the boys well prepared for the journey.

The arrangements for traveling were, that they should float along at night, and during the day pull their skiff into some timbered or unfrequented nook in the river; that after reaching Nebraska City they would float down the river in the daytime, as the interest in their capture was not awakened so far south.

Having fulfilled our part of the contract, we were pleased to say that the James brothers did theirs by imparting to us facts, which events since transpired has rendered it impossible at the present to give to the public without violating our pledge.

The James boys made a safe retreat down the Missouri and reached St. Joseph, Missouri, in just eight days from the time we parted with them. At the latter place they were cared for by friends.

There is one ennobling feature about the once powerful but now dismembered banditti, that for years they have been the terror of railroad, express, and bank corporations. They never take, only in self-defense, a human life. They have never appropriated a dollar from other corporations who could afford it. They have, within the past two years, distributed and spent among friends, many of them poor, upwards to a quarter of a million dollars, and not one of them has ever been known to contract an obligation of whatever character that has not been complied with.

The *Sioux City Democrat's* editor, carried away by his admiration for the James brothers, failed to justify his regard for them in the Northfield bank raid during which several persons were killed. Whether or not this editor saw fit to divulge the secrets given to him by Jesse and Frank James, and the reaction of Sheriff McDonald when he learned he'd been tricked, are facts lost to history. We know that this account, incredible as it might seem, is a true eyewitness account of the James brothers' escape after Northfield.

Chapter Fourteen

Singing Rails Again

After the Northfield fiasco, Jesse and Frank gave Missouri a wide berth for a time. They hid at the Sayers' home in Kentucky, or at their uncle George Hite's. These were still too close to their stamping grounds, though, so they made for Texas, where they had a refuge called the Rest Ranch. It was in the Pecos River country—a rugged and isolated land, with the Staked Plains and salt plains to the northeast, mountains to the west, and a frontier outpost, Fort Lancaster, far to the south.

It was a safe spot, but it was also very solitary, except perhaps for a raiding party of Comanches or a gang of Mexican border bandits. Frank and Jesse got restless, so they headed toward the Rio Grande and Mexico, passing over mountains and across deserts to the Mexican state of Chihuahua. They camped near a small town called Carmen, a favorite stopping place for miners and traders whose mule trains were loaded with treasure from the nearby mines in the Sierra Madre, which surrounded the town on three sides.

At Carmen, Jesse and Frank were joined by three more men. All five behaved well and tried to make a favorable impression on the local residents. They kept up their pistol practice, often by shooting a pig or a chicken strolling at some distance. Before the farmer knew about his loss, he was always paid generously in cash.

The sojourn at Carmen was not without

When James Butler Hickok was a peace officer in Abilene, he made a pact with Jesse and Frank James not to bother them when they came to town, so long as they robbed nothing in Abilene. This pact was respected by both parties and the boys rubbed elbows with Hickok at various times in the local saloons.

purpose. A train of pack mules carrying silver came into town, accompanied by twelve men acting as guards, along with the mule drivers. The five outlaws spooked the mule train guards with harrowing tales of Indians and highwaymen lurking along the road between Carmen and the U.S. border, toward which the pack train was headed.

The owners of the train and treasure were at first suspicious, but they were reassured by the favorable opinion the villagers had formed of the five campers. They took Jesse and Frank and their three companions on as guards and struck out north.

Several evenings later, when the train had stopped for the night and the honest, if somewhat simple, guards had stacked their rifles at one end of the camp, Jesse gave the signal to attack. The two guards posted at the stack of rifles were killed, and the outlaws commandeered all the weapons. The owners of the train, the mule tenders, and the legitimate guards had to surrender. Jesse's men departed with the silver, leaving the pack train stranded at a place since called *La Temido,* the place of fear. Off went the outlaws southwest to their more happily named headquarters—Rest Ranch, leaving the bewildered Mexicans cursing a blue streak at the *gringo diablos.*

On another tour of northern Mexico, in the spring of 1877, Jesse and Frank visited Piedras Negras, just across the river from Eagle Pass, Texas, and a favorite rendezvous for rogues of all descriptions. Passing through the town, they were attacked by a mob seeking to avenge the death of Estevan Sandoval, a man killed by Jesse and Frank on a previous trip. The mob fled after Jesse and Frank, who launched a violent two-man counterattack and shot four of the mounted men in the mob from their saddles.

The Jameses rode on toward the Rio Grande to the north, but were waylaid that same evening by determined remnants of the Mexican attackers. Jesse received a slight bullet wound, his first since his Civil War days.

At Monclova, a large town in Coahuila, they called on an old Confederate guerrilla friend who had exiled himself and married a Mexican girl. The newlyweds gave a dance in honor of their visitors. Among the dancers were two men who recognized the honored guests as Frank and Jesse James. One of the men who recognized them was an American resident of Matehuala; the other was an officer in the Army of Mexico. Jesse took note of their scrutiny and their early departure from the dance.

The Mexican lieutenant and the American went to the encampment of a Mexican brigade near the town. They enlisted the assistance of the commanding officer in an attempt to capture the notorious Jesse and Frank James. They said that United States authorities were offering enormous rewards for their capture. About eight troops were dispatched to surround the house where the ball was in progress. Then, several army officers entered and demanded that the James boys surrender.

It was an inept maneuver. Outclassed in the use of pistols, the officers and their enlisted guard were shot at. The ball was in an uproar, and in the confusion, Jesse and Frank escaped and headed for Rest Ranch.

The ranch was well-stocked with cattle, and defending the herd against thieves sometimes led to gunplay. A locally noted bandit in Nueva Leon, Juan Fernando Palaciois, decided to raid the Jameses' herd, as well as the herds of several of their neighbors. He corralled a sizeable number of cows and, with his thirty confederates, took them across the Rio Grande into Mexico. Jesse and Frank went after the rustlers, found them, and recovered the cattle. The free-shooting brothers shot ten of the Palaciois band in the process.

Palaciois could not stomach losing ten of his men at the hands of only two ranchers. He decided to follow them into Texas. Palaciois was close of their heels when a troop of horsemen loomed up ahead of him, and ahead of Frank and Jesse. The

Jameses might have been trapped, but the troop of southbound horsemen was not a detachment of Mexican brigands, but a company of Union cavalrymen on patrol. The soldiers were under the command of Colonel Ranald Mackenzie, Civil War hero and Indian fighter. They joined forces with Jesse and Frank and routed the rustlers. It was a strange twist for the two Union-hating James boys to pose as law-abiding Texas ranchers, and not only be rescued by Union troops, but also praised as community heroes.

Many sources say that the James brothers' trips into Mexico and their owning a cattle ranch near the Mexican border are pure fiction. However, Jesse's letters and a description of the ranch by a visitor promoted by General Jo Shelby, show these claims to be accurate. Jesse sent the following letter to Jack (Jackson) Bishop in Texas, an ex-Quantrillian and a good friend of the Jameses.

> Rest Ranch, Texas
> January 23, 1877
> Dear Jack,
>   We had a little fun on the other side of the line lately. A lot of Greasers came over and broke up several ranches. Some of us were down that way, and "the cowboys" wanted us to help them and we done it. Some of our cattle had been taken, and I don't owe the yellow dogs anything good anyhow. Well, we left some half dozen or more for carrion-bird meat. We brought the cattle back. I was confounded glad when we met some cavalry out after raiders. There was a big lot of them motley scamps, and we would have had a pretty rough time, I expect. But the sneaks got back as fast as they could. You would have enjoyed the racket.
> As ever yours,
> J.W.J.

General Shelby's friend, who was permitted to see the ranch after being blindfolded during the long ride there, described it this way:

> Before me lay a broad, green valley, bounded by a line of high hills toward the northeast,

and widening toward the southwest. A beautiful grove of timber skirted the nearby stream which meandered through the valley. Situated beyond the stream and trees on a gentle slope rested one of the most beautiful homes I had ever seen. The house was two stories in elevation, surrounded by young fruit trees and cultivated fields. A short distance hence stood the barns and other outbuildings, all in tip-top shape. In the mansion I met Mrs. Frank James, a charming and hospitable woman, eager to please. I asked no questions as to Jesse's wife, but I could tell this apparently was the home of Frank James, Jesse merely a visitor when the situation demanded it. Later, in my own mind, I felt that Rest Ranch was located in the Pecos River Country, with the Staked Plains and salt plains to the northeast, mountains to the west, and a frontier outpost, Fort Lancaster, far to the south. I would have given a year of my life to have been able to pinpoint the location of the ranch, as well as being able to live there for a few months.

GLENDALE, MISSOURI

One of the most celebrated train robberies attributed to the James boys happened at the Glendale, Missouri, station, in the central part of Jackson County on the Chicago and Alton Railroad. On October 8, 1879, newspaper headlines blared reports of another train robbery committed by the James bunch. One even mentioned the Youngers as the originators of the attack. This shows how firmly the public was convinced that the Jameses and Youngers had a hand in every robbery characterized by boldness and ruthlessness. The Youngers were all locked up in Stillwater Penitentiary, where they had been for nearly three years.

Glendale was a lonely wayside station in the western part of Missouri, some twenty miles from Kansas City, and on the Kansas branch of the Chicago and Alton Railroad. It was wedged in between rugged and beautiful hills, in a region soaked with bloody deeds committed by both Confederate and Union guerrilla forces during the Civil War. The outlaws had picked the best station on the line between Kansas City and Chicago for their robbery. The tiny hamlet consisted of the station house and a general store operated by M. Anderson—who also served as the postmaster—and a blacksmith shop.

The bandits had no trouble corralling the entire population of the little place before setting the stop signal on the tracks alongside the depot. To make sure the engineer would stop the train, the desperadoes also piled timbers and debris on the track.

It was a little after 7 o'clock. The robbers had now been in Glendale an hour, anxiously awaiting the train's arrival. The prisoners in the station house wondered what would happen next, especially to them. They did not appreciate the fact that they were about to witness an epic event.

At 7:45 p.m., the rumbling steam giant rolled into the station and stopped. The engine was at the water tank. Two of the masked men rushed to the cab and demanded the coal hammer. At this point, John Greenman, the conductor, came to the platform expecting to hear new orders, on account of the lowered green signal. One of the robbers rushed at him with a cocked pistol and was soon joined by another. Both were masked.

The whole gang, headed by the long-bearded man, gathered at the door of the express car. One had a sledge hammer and started to break down the door that William Grimes had locked from the inside when he first suspected trouble. Grimes had also taken the money from the safe and put it in his satchel. He had swung the safe door shut and was making for another door when he was struck down with a revolver butt. In a moment the faithful Grimes lay senseless on the floor.

The outlaws grabbed Grimes' satchel, and ransacked the safe. In a moment the great train robbery at Glendale was over. The robbers netted between $35,000 and $40,000 in less than ten minutes. The train was ordered to proceed after the prisoners had been released.

Many sources stated Frank and Jesse James engineered the entire Glendale affair, but in a confession given by Tucker Bassham that appeared in the *Kansas City Journal*, November 7, 1880, only Jesse and Ed Miller are mentioned. Most people, some in the know, said the following men participated in the robbery: Jesse James, Edward Miller, Robert Woodson Hite, William Ryan, James Andrew Liddil, and Daniel Tucker Bassham. There is ample evidence from various sources to show that Frank tried hard to persuade Jesse not to return to Missouri or to engage in outlawry after three years of comparative peace. Therefore, the reports that Frank James was in Tennessee at the time of the Glendale robbery could well be true.

One of the law officers most determined to capture the gang who robbed the Glendale train was Major James Liggett, at that time marshal of Kansas City. He engaged the services of George W. Shepherd, a former Confederate guerrilla, who had been on bad terms with Jesse James for years. Shepherd had fought bravely at the Battle of Wilson's Creek and Pea Ridge during the Civil War. Marshal Liggett circulated the news that Shepherd was one of the men wanted in connection with the Glendale robbery. The deception was effective enough to permit Jesse to take Shepherd into his band, though he did have misgivings. Had Jesse known of Shepherd's hatred for him, he would never have accepted him.

Shepherd's desire to kill or capture Jesse began soon after the Civil War when Ike Flannery, Shepherd's nephew, came into an inheritance of several thousand dollars. He never got a chance to spend it, however, for he was killed and robbed near Glasgow, Missouri. Several housewives in the vicinity said that shortly before Flannery's body was found, they saw him riding in the company of Jesse James and Jim Anderson. Jesse readily admitted he had been with Ike, but claimed they were attacked by Federal militiamen who had killed the boy. Jesse made the story stick with the law officers, but Shepherd was not convinced. He trailed Jim Anderson, who, he was certain, was a partner in the murder, and found him in Austin, Texas. Anderson, unsuspecting, joined Shepherd in several drinks on the lawn of the Texas state capital. Here Shepherd cut Anderson's throat. Before his life bled away, Anderson said Jesse had helped commit the murder.

Shepherd escaped punishment for slaying Anderson, because many people in that vicinity hated Anderson, and it was difficult to concentrate the blame in any one quarter. Shepherd returned to Missouri but his chance to fully avenge the death of his nephew by wiping out Jesse James did not come for a number of years. The Glendale trail robbery and Marshal Liggett's plan gave him that chance—or so he said at the time.

At Benjamin Marr's home, some twenty miles from Kansas City, plans were made to rob the bank at Empire City, but they were never carried out because someone apparently learned of the plan. Checking the area, Jesse found armed guards all over the place. Soon after, about thirteen miles south of Galena, near Short Creek, Shepherd stated he fired a shot and killed Jesse James. In turn, Jim Cummins had fired and wounded Shepherd in the left leg below the knee. It was further reported that Cummins had been wounded in the right side. The surgeon who furnished these facts stated he had performed the operation on Cummins.

Jim Cummins later said that Shepherd never fired a shot at Short Creek—especially at Jesse James. According to Cummins, when Shepherd returned from Empire City, he was slightly drunk, and

since Cummins had already ascertained that the bank was guarded, he and Miller distrusted Shepherd and planned to kill him. They fired at him as he rode into camp, but he escaped.

Jesse's mother said she believed him dead, or pretended to believe so, to put people off the track. In later years she said the wound had been an ugly one and that her son had been disabled for a long time because of it. As it happens, Jesse was not heard from for almost a year; subsequent facts clearly disproved Shepherd's claim that he killed the outlaw.

Yet another story appeared in connection with the Shepherd affair. On March 6, 1882, the following item appeared in a Kansas City newspaper:

A sensation was created here among the police and county officials by the fact that George Shepherd, the ex-guerrilla and bank robber, who claimed to have shot Jesse James, the notorious outlaw, at Joplin, just after the Glendale train robbery of 1879, had proved a traitor for that trouble. He now admits that his wound in the leg and the account of the killing was all a put-up job with the James brothers, for the purpose of procuring the large rewards offered. The plan to get the reward money having failed after long perseverance and much swearing, he now says he would no more shoot Jesse James than he would his own brother.

This is just another of the puzzles that probably never will be solved. Naturally, Jesse's friends were compelled to admit he'd been shot to keep Shepherd in good graces with the authorities. With Jesse's nature being what it was, it's doubtful that Shepherd would have lived very long after the affair, if the story had been true.

In any event, the robberies that occurred over the next few months were strong evidence that the James boys were still on the prowl.

Chapter Fifteen

Final Years of Outlawry

THE GLASGOW STAGE–EDMONSON COUNTY, KENTUCKY

The Glasgow Stagecoach holdup occurred on September 3, 1880, as Sam McCoy was driving it from Mammoth Cave to Cave City, Kentucky. As the stage passed through a desolate stretch along the way, two mounted men emerged from cover, and with leveled guns ordered McCoy to pull his teams to a halt. Passengers were: Judge R.H. Rountree and his daughter, Elizabeth, of Lebanon, Kentucky; P.S. Rountree, his nephew from Fairmount, Minnesota; J.E. Craig from Lawrenceville, Georgia; S.M. Shelton from Chattanooga, Tennessee; and several others.

After the bandits had relieved the passengers of their valuables, one of them passed a bottle of whiskey around and insisted on each victim taking a drink. This was typical of Bill Ryan, a member of the James gang and known as "whiskey-head." The other robber, with his pleasant, flattering speech to the ladies as they reboarded the coach, sounded like Jesse James.

The two outlaws then galloped off in the direction of Cave City and robbed another coach that had just left for Mammoth Cave. The only occupants of this stagecoach were a black preacher and the driver. When the first stage reached Cave City, a posse was formed at once. It diligently searched the territory with the usual results—nothing.

Guerrilla Tom Hunt was accused of being involved in the Glasgow Stage robbery and was identified as Jesse James. He was later released from prison when the truth became known that he had not been with Jesse at the time and certainly was not the outlaw.

Courtesy of Charles Rosamond Collection

Lieutenant-Governor James E. Cantrill issued a proclamation offering $500 for the arrest of the two robbers. Of course the

Jim Cummins
Courtesy of Charles Rosamond Collection

Dick Liddil (real name James Andrew Liddil) surrendered to Sheriff Timberlake in January, 1882, and turned state's evidence against the James brothers.

reward money was an incentive for all the amateur sleuths in the area. G.W. Bunger, a deputy sheriff of Ohio County, appeared in Cave City with a suspect, T.J. Hunt, who was an ex-guerrilla known as "Guerrilla Tom." His trial was held on November 20, 1880, and he was bound over for the Barren County Grand Jury, which indicted him in April, 1881. The case did not come up for trial until March 31, 1882, when the jury declared a verdict of guilty. Hunt was sentenced to three years in the penitentiary at Frankfort, Kentucky.

Oddly enough, at the very time of Hunt's trial, Jesse James was shot and killed by Bob Ford. Jesse's picture was carried in all the papers throughout the country, and Judge Rountree instantly saw he'd made a mistake in identifying Hunt as Jesse James. Thereafter, the judge tried to correct his mistake by working for Hunt's release.

When Jesse was killed, he was wearing Judge Rountree's watch and Mrs. James was wearing Miss Rountree's diamond ring. This also puts to rest stories that Frank James and Jim Cummins were the two bold outlaws who robbed the Mammoth Cave Stage.

Judge Rountree's efforts in behalf of Hunt were successful and he was granted a new trial. Charles and Bob Ford signed affidavits saying Jesse James and Bill Ryan were the two men who had robbed the stage. Dick Liddil also signed an affidavit to the same effect; another was obtained from Bill Ryan himself, who was serving a term in the Missouri State Prison for his implication in the Glendale train robbery.

On May 1, 1882, Governor Blackburn of

Kentucky granted Hunt a full pardon. The state legislature passed a bill awarding Hunt $1500 for the time he spent in prison. Hunt eventually returned to his home town in Pike County, Illinois.

Some historians maintain Ryan was an asset to the James gang, but a study of his life, his foolish surrender, and the cause of his death, leads one to believe that he was a liability, as Frank had always claimed. Of course, liquor and jobs don't mix—the Northfield raid had adequately demonstrated that. Just so, it was Ryan's fondness for liquor that got him arrested and ultimately confined in the Missouri State Penitentiary. Perhaps Jesse's high regard for Ryan resulted from Ryan feeding his vanity.

Frank, on the other hand, always predicted that such a drinking man would cause trouble for the gang and it would be best to let him go. It was near White's Creek, not far from Nashville, that Jesse and Frank discussed Ryan. Frank was living at the Felix Smith place, on Hyde's Ferry Pike, under the name of Frank Woodson (the name Woodson was taken from his kinsman, one-time governor of Missouri, Silas Woodson). It was in this locality, too, that Frank spent three weeks in 1879, seriously ill and under Dr. Bank's care. Frank looked like an honest farmer hauling lumber for the Indiana Lumber Company. Jesse lived some distance away, using the name Howard (the name Howard was taken from that of Dr. John Black Howard, Kentuckian and close friend of the James family). He and Ryan visited Frank frequently.

MUSCLE SHOALS, ALABAMA

In March of 1881, the Jameses were in Selma, Alabama, living incognito at the St. James Hotel on Water Street. They registered as the Williams brothers and took separate rooms as a precaution. They had come to visit a friend of the family, John Norris, and Jesse also wished to consult a specialist there on the trouble he was having from his lung wounds. The manager of the hotel, James Dedham, later said that both Frank and Jesse were polished gentlemen and he never once had reason to doubt they were what they said they were.

On Friday, March 11, 1881, United States Army Paymaster Alexander G. Smith walked out of the Campbell and Coat Banking Company, Florence, Alabama, swung a heavy saddlebag over the back of his horse, mounted, and rode down the muddy street toward the engineers' camp at Bluewater. The camp was situated on the Tennessee River several miles downstream, toward Tuscumbia.

As Smith rode leisurely along the towpath that paralleled Muscle Shoals Canal, several miles from Florence, three masked horsemen with pistols drawn sprang out of the brush, disarmed him, grabbed the saddlebag, and tied his hands behind his back. They took his watch and $221 from his pocket. Then, strangely enough, they returned the watch and $21 to the victim. They extracted $5000 from the saddlebag, making the total haul $5200.

Thus the Missouri outlaws had successfully accomplished their only robbery in the deep South. Their partner in crime at Muscle Shoals was Bill Ryan, a fearless braggart whose liking for whiskey sometimes made him a dubious ally.

About twenty miles from the scene of the holdup, the men stopped in a dense, deeply secluded spot. The bandits dismounted, squatted on the ground, and carefully divided the $5200 equally among them. Smith later stated that near Bull's Mill the loud-mouthed bandit wanted to shoot him, but the younger man would not hear of it. After dividing the money, the bandits untied Smith's arms and remounted their horses. As they sped away in the darkness, one threw Smith his overcoat shouting, "Pass the night comfortably, Mr. Smith."

The bewildered paymaster wandered all through the thick, black, unfamiliar forest.

Toward dawn a terrible thunderstorm struck the area, causing the lost man more discomfort. Finally, on Saturday, Smith stumbled into Bluewater Camp, weary and ill. He was informed that several parties had gone in search of him, but with the coming of the storm, had given up, believing him dead.

Throughout the night the bandits stretched their tired horses across Alabama into South Tennessee. There, in the Nashville–Waverly area, where they had been living under the names of B.J. Woodson and J.D. Howard, they felt themselves comparatively safe.

On March 16, 1881, Ryan rode pell-mell into White's Creek and stopped in front of the general store operated by J. Maddox. Loudly he stomped into the saloon section of the store and demanded the best liquor in the house, declaring he could and would pay for what he drank. Naturally a bottle of "the best" was placed before Ryan, as he scattered several gold coins on the bar. In several hours he was very much intoxicated. He began to boast of his identity and created a general disturbance. The efforts of Maddox to quiet him were unsuccessful; the owner, W.L. Earthman, was also unable to cope with him. Ryan shouted, "Don't you know who I am? I am an outlaw, rip-snortin' Tom Hill, that's me." Surprisingly, though, he had sense enough to give a fictitious name.

Ryan started to jerk out his guns, but Mr. Earthman jumped behind him; held his arms to his side and tried to talk some sense into him. At this point someone

The James brothers visited the home of John Green Norris, 622 Alabama Avenue, Selma, Alabama, while Jesse was being treated for a case of granulated eyelids. Jesse and Frank had been friends with them when the Norris family lived in Missouri.

Courtesy of R. Rosenberg

called the blacksmith, whose shop was next door. He was a burly and powerful black man and he quickly disarmed Ryan and searched him. They found over $1200 in gold on him. This find, in connection with Ryan's boast of being an outlaw, led them to believe he was telling the truth. There was no identification on his person, however, so he was turned over to the Nashville police. It was not long before photographs of the talkative Ryan were being sent all over the country. The Kansas City police were quick to see that "Tom Hill" was Bill Ryan. They reported to William H. Wallace, Prosecuting Attorney of Jackson County, Missouri.

Ryan was returned to Missouri and convicted on the testimony of Tucker Bassham.

Officials of the Ryan Trial
Courtesy of T.T. Crittenden

Captain M.M. Langhorne, Deputy Marshal, guarded the prisoner, Bill Ryan, during the trial.

Amazon Hays, Deputy Marshal, guarded the witness, Tucker Bassham, during the trial.

Colonel John N. Southern, Lawyer, ex-Confederate, assisted the State.

Cornelius Murphy, Marshal of Jackson County, Missouri, superintended the selection of the jury.

W.G. Keshlaer, brought Bill Ryan from Tennessee.

There were threats against the life of Wallace during the trial, but he could not be intimidated; he was the first to succeed in trying a member of the James gang and getting a conviction. Both Frank and Jesse took no chances. Even if Ryan did not divulge their presence in Tennessee, the detectives might guess the truth. The morning after Ryan's arrest, Jesse and Frank met near Nashville. Their families went into seclusion somewhere in Missouri. Frank and Jesse shook hands and then the two rode off in opposite directions.

Some historians have declared that Bill Ryan was a member of the James band who robbed the train at Blue Cut in September of 1881, not far from Glendale, Missouri. It would have been impossible for Ryan to be there, for he was at that time in jail awaiting trial for the Glendale robbery of 1879. The official records show that he was convicted of robbery in the first degree in Independence, Missouri, Jackson County, on October 15, 1881, after having been arrested early in 1881. He was sentenced to twenty-five years during the August term of Court that year, under Cause No. 1954. He was received at the Jefferson City Prison on October 16, 1881, as prisoner No. 2677. Governor Morehouse commuted his sentence to ten years with benefit of the 3/4 law[1] on January 4, 1889. Ryan was released from prison on April 15, 1889.

Ryan returned to the Independence area and stayed with an uncle, John McCloskey. One day he went into town and began drinking heavily at the Mahan and McCarthy Saloon on Main Street. His whiskey-clouded mind brought back memories of his old war comrades, and he wanted to go to Blue Springs, where a number of them could always be found. He borrowed a fast mare from Tommy Mahan and was soon on his way. Riding like the Headless Horseman of Washington Irving fame, he galloped along the road to Blue Springs. A section of the road ran through some heavy timber. The next morning the horse trotted home alone. When friends went to investigate, they found Ryan dead, his head smashed. He had either been thrown from the dashing horse or he had struck his head on a low-hanging tree limb.

WINSTON, MISSOURI

On Friday evening, July 15, 1881, the Chicago, Rock Island, and Pacific train left Kansas City, with its usual complement of passengers but with a lighter treasure than usual, both in freight and bullion. In fact, there was not more than $2000 in currency and a few bars of silver, which were too heavy for anyone to carry off in a hurry. The express agent was Charles H. Murray; the conductor was William H. Westfall;

WM. H. WESTFALL.

William H. Westfall was killed at Winston.

---

[1]Prisoner is eligible for parole after serving 3/4 of his sentence.

Wolcott was the engineer; Frank Stamper was the baggageman.

It was said that the chief motive for robbing this train was vengeance on Westfall. It was reported that he had, on several occasions, acted as a guide for the Pinkertons in their attempts to arrest the Jameses, one time being the raid on the James-Samuel home at Kearney.

At Cameron four passengers boarded the cars, and at 9:30 p.m. the train reached Winston, where more passengers boarded, along with several railroad employees. One of them was Frank McMillen, a stonemason of Wilton Junction, Iowa. It was dark now, and the train had not gone far out of Winston when the murderous work began. The seven men who had boarded the train at the previous two stops were well-stationed. Three of them rode in the smoking car, and two were on the rear platform of the baggage car. Two more were on the front platform of the baggage car, where they could keep an eye on the fireman and the engineer. The bell connected to the engine was pulled, presumably by a frightened passenger. The fireman, guessing the trouble, said to the engineer, "Give her hell." The engineer suddenly turned around and became aware of two masked men with drawn revolvers, seemingly rising from the pile of coal in the tender. Suddenly the fireman and the engineer leaped from the train onto the cowcatcher, where they hung on for dear life as the bandits fired at them. Finally they escaped into a nearby woods.

William Westfall was collecting tickets when a masked man, believed to have been Frank James, dressed in a linen duster and wearing a straw hat, followed by two others, came into the car, yelling, "You are

Winston Depot

my prisoner! You are the man I want!'' Westfall was shot in the shoulder, and when he turned, the man fired again but missed. Another robber fired the shot that killed Westfall as he staggered out on the platform and rolled to the ground.

Harry Thomas, an eye-witness and brakeman on the train, said he boarded the train at Cameron on his way home to Trenton, and that the robbery had occurred between Cameron and Winston. He had this to say:

> All of the shooting occurred in the smoking car. I sat in the rear of that car and could see all that went on. Westfall was sticking a check-stub into a passenger's hatband, leaning over. Before he could straighten up, the revolver went off, and I saw him stagger past me out to the platform, and that was the last I saw of him until I found his dead body by the side of the track.
>
> I don't think the man shot Westfall intentionally. He was shooting recklessly around the car and stood facing the south side so that he could command both sides of the car. He shot principally into the roof. When Westfall was shot the robber swung his pistol around over his head and fired as he brought it down, so I think it was accidental. The bullet went in at Bill's right shoulder and came out on the left side of the chest, having passed directly through the heart.

Samuel Gibbons stated that McMillen and his partner were sitting on the platform when a shot broke through the window. When McMillen lifted his head to look through the window another bullet struck him in the forehead, killing him instantly.

In the express car Charles Murray was forced to surrender the key to the safe while the outlaws held him and Stamper under their guns. They stuffed the money into an old grain sack but grumbled in disappointment at finding only a small sum.

"Is this all you got?" demanded the apparent leader.

"You've got it all except the silver bricks," replied Murray.

"Damn you and your silver bricks," retorted the bandit, striking Murray a blow with his pistol. Even so, Murray must have felt elated, since he knew the robbers could not carry off the heavy silver bricks.

The bandits had not intended to rob the passengers, so the night's work netted them very little. About a mile from Winston the robbers stepped off the train and disappeared into the woods.

In the underbrush near Sibley's Landing on Big Dog Creek, a short distance from the scene, a crumpled piece of paper was found. This proved to have been dropped by one of the robbers. It read:

> Kansas City, July 12, 1881
> Charley: I got your letter today, and was glad to hear you had got everything ready for the 15th. We will be on hand at the time. Bill will be with me. We will be on the train. Don't fear. We will be in the smoker at Winston. Have the horses and boys in good fix for fast work. We will make this joust on the night of the 16th. All is right here. Frank will meet us at Cameron. Look sharp and be well fixed. Have the horses well gaunted. We may have some running to do. Don't get excited, but keep cool till the right time. Wilcox or Wilcott will be on the train. I think it best to send this to Kidder. Yours till and through death.
> Slick

William Pinkerton, when asked at his Chicago office what he thought of the Winston robbery, said, "The work undoubtedly was done by Jesse and Frank James, who are the only survivors of the James and Younger gangs, the remainder being dead or in the penitentiary. Jesse James lives in Clay County, Missouri, and he can gather a party to rob a train in Clay County in about two days. He has a thorough knowledge of the country, and if need be he will be secreted by the citizens for months so as to avoid arrest.''

Marcus M. Lowe, an attorney for the railroad, said he felt certain that the outlaws had been Jesse and Frank James, Jim Cummins, Dick Liddil, Wood Hite, Clarence Hite, and probably Robert and Charley Ford. A. Kimball, general superintendent of the Rock Island Road, issued the following statement:

The Chicago, Rock Island and Pacific Railroad Co. will pay a reward of $5,000 for the arrest and conviction of the parties who stopped one of its passenger trains near Winston, Daviess County, Mo., on the night of July 15th; killed the conductor and another employee and robbed the express; or a proportionate amount for the arrest and conviction of any one of them.

Strangely enough, at the time of the Winston robbery, there was not one dollar outstanding in reward money for the James boys or members of their band. During Governor Hardin's administration nearly all the rewards offered by the state were withdrawn. Then the private corporations withdrew their incentives, after which Governor Phelps wiped out the few offers remaining.

On July 26, Governor Crittenden met with representatives of the leading railroads at the Southern Hotel in St. Louis. Realizing he was unable to offer a reward large enough to entice men to capture Jesse James, Crittenden asked the railroad officials to provide the needed assistance. After a four-hour session, it was agreed that the railroads would furnish $55,000 reward for the capture of the seven train robbers, or $5,000 reward for the arrest and conviction of each member of the gang. The proclamation further stated an additional reward of $5,000 would be paid for each of the James boys, and a further reward of $5,000 each for their conviction.

A diligent search was made of the entire county by Sheriff Brown Crosby of Daviess County and his men; it was to no avail. Not

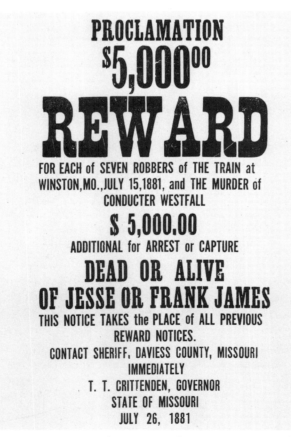

Missouri "reward poster" for Jesse or Frank James

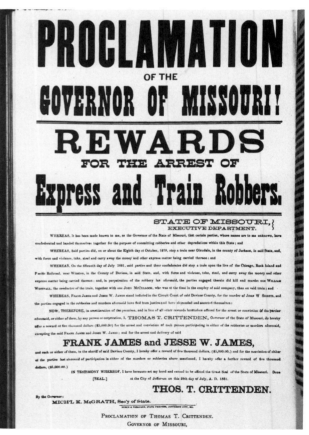

Missouri warrant for Jesse or Frank James

a dollar of the stolen money was recovered, nor any of the robbers caught.

Many people shook their heads in disgust and amazement, muttering that the bandits were still on the loose.

BLUE CUT

On September 7, 1881, the Chicago and Alton train, en route from Chicago to Kansas City, was robbed by twelve bandits near Glendale, Missouri, The train was brought to a halt in a deep ravine called Blue Cut, a spot where the Missouri-Pacific line crossed the track of the Chicago and Alton line.

The robbers accosted Engineer L. Foote and Fireman John Steading. The express messenger, a young man named Henry Fox, sensing a robbery, leaped from the express car and hid in the high weeds. All the bandits were masked. The leader wore a white sack with eye-slits over his head. He called to Fox that he would kill Foote and Steading if he did not appear with the key to the safe. Fearing that the robbers would carry out their threat, Fox came back and was knocked unconscious. The leader seemed particularly annoyed when he found only about $2,500 in the safe.

During the looting of the express car, Conductor Joel M. Hazelbaker had warned the passengers that the bandits probably would go through the cars and take their valuables. This way some of the passengers were able to hide their money and jewelry before the outlaws entered the cars. Hazelbaker's own statement might be of some interest: "When I reached the sleeper I told Burton, my brakeman, to flag down the train following. I knew there was a freight train after me, and it would wreck my train, and I knew that train must be stopped. Burton said he did not like to go but the brave fellow went just the same. We dropped off together, and they began to fire at us. Shots whistled all around us. I think there were probably twenty shots fired at us

altogether. We finally succeeded in flagging down the freight train just in time, and I went back and, climbing aboard the sleeper, took a back seat and waited to be robbed."

Hazelbaker further stated that the gang swore a great deal and seemed to center their rage on him. The leader, who said he was Jesse James, put a pistol under the nose of the conductor and said, "Damn you, smell of that! That's the pistol I shot Westfall with at Winston! Now, listen, all you dogs, the next reward that is offered we'll burn your damn train, and don't forget it. We'll cut the Pullman loose and save it because Pullman is white, and never offered a reward like you damned railroads and no-good governor of Missouri, but we'll make a bonfire of your train as sure as you live." The conductor also stated that six bandits were in the sleeper and perhaps four or five more outside. He could not identify any of them for they all wore masks.

Engineer Foote gave some interesting testimony of the affair which should not be overlooked.

> Between three and four miles east of Independence is a deep cut, over which the Missouri-Pacific track crosses the Chicago and Alton, and it was just before entering the deepest part of this cut that I saw a pile of stones, probably five feet high, on the top of which was a stick, to which was attached a red flag, and behind the whole stood the leader of the robbers. Of course I stopped. I was then approached by four of the gang, besides the leader, who said, "Step down off that engine, and do as I tell you, or I will kill you." He then told me to get the coal pick, which I did, and after some parleying, but as a revolver was pointed at my head I could not refuse to obey.
>
> Then they marched myself and John Steading, the fireman, to the express car, and ordered me to break the door down, which I did. Messenger Fox had hidden in the weeds by the roadside, but they swore they would kill me if he didn't come out, and so I called for him and he entered the car with two of the robbers who forced him to open the safe and pour the contents into a sack.
>
> They seemed disappointed in not getting

more booty, and knocked Fox down twice with the butt of a Navy revolver, cutting his head in a fearful manner. They then marched us to the coaches where they kept us covered with revolvers while they robbed the passengers. After the last car was gone through they marched us back to the engine, when the leader said, "Now get back there; we will remove the stones. You have been a bully boy and here is a little present for you," and he handed me two silver dollars. I told them I would remove the obstructions, and the entire gang skipped over the embankment, and were out of sight in a twinkling.

In going through the passengers, each one was made to hold up his hands, and what was taken from them was put into a two-bushel sack, which was nearly full of watches, money, and other valuables. They didn't take anything from me.

The leader told me to take the $2 and drink to Jesse James or I would be killed. He also warned me to quit this road or I would be killed.

Descriptions of the bandits fit Jesse and Frank James. It is believed that this was the first robbery in which Frank participated since 1877. Matt Chapman, first to be arrested in connection with the Blue Cut robbery, stated that Jesse and Frank were there. Later, Dick Liddil, also in the gang, after surrendering with a promise of pardon, said both the James boys were there, along with Jim Cummins, Wood Hite, Clarence Hite, and Charley Ford. Others in the band were Andy Ryan, Ed Miller, and Matt Chapman.

On March 27, 1882, John Bugler, one of the Cracker Neck region citizens involved in the Blue Cut robbery, was arraigned at Independence, Missouri. Meanwhile, John Land, who also was under indictment in the same case, made a full confession, and implicated the James boys, Jim Cummins, Dick Liddil, and others.

John Land came to his just desserts by being shot and killed, not for his participation in the robbery. In 1909 a neighbor of John Land had been hunting near Land's property when one of his coon hounds became lost and strayed onto Land's property. When Land saw the dog he promptly took his shotgun and killed the animal.

In that area, on the Lexington Road (now Highway #24), where it crosses the Little Blue River, stood a small store and a sawmill. Everyone in the vicinity traded there. Several weeks after the dog-shooting incident, its owner was at the store. Even though he carried a shotgun no one questioned it since many men did carry guns of one type or another at the time.

As was his custom, John Land also appeared at the store, bought some groceries and headed for home in the Atherton–Sibley area. Land had just about reached the covered bridge over the Little Blue when the owner of the dead dog raised his shotgun and shot Land in the back.

Without saying a word to the folks at the store, the dog's owner walked home, past the Frank Baldus home, where he waved and spoke to the folks there. John Land's killer was arrested, tried, and sentenced to twenty years in the State Penitentiary at Jefferson City, Missouri.

The Blue Cut robbery was the last spectacular assignment the James brothers undertook, according to most authorities on their travels and practices. Time was running out for Jesse, and without Jesse's initiatives, Frank James would have dropped into less hazardous ways long ago.

According to the best available evidence, thieves seldom fell out with others in the James troupe. The division of the hauls, as far as is known, was made fairly and promptly, and complaints on that score were not heard from the ever-changing membership of the band. After the Blue Cut robbery, however, several partners exchanged harsh words. This led to the killing of Wood Hite, for he had complained about the division of the spoils. Another incident occurred on the Hite property between Dick Liddil and Wood causing further animosity in the group. Wood had accused Liddil of stealing from him and Jesse. Liddil denied the charge, so Hite suggested they shoot it out.

Strapping on their pistols, they walked

alone to the barn. Each man's stand was selected and no firing was to occur until each had reached his station. However, Liddil fired prematurely and missed. Hite immediately put a tree between himself and the would-be assassin. Liddil did the same thing, firing until his weapon was empty. When Liddil retreated toward the house, Wood began firing. Neither man was hit in the cowardly escapade, and the matter was smoothed over by family members.

Wood Hite was the son of Major George Hite, who had furnished Jesse and Frank sanctuary in his Logan County, Kentucky, home on many occasions. Wood was a favorite cousin of Jesse, and like Jesse and Frank he was quick to resort to a pistol when life got unmanageable. Wood Hite's mother had died and his father had married a widow named Peak, who was attractive and flirtatious. The marriage did not last long. The second Mrs. Hite left her husband in 1882. Among the men she started to romance after her marriage failed was Dick Liddil, although some sources reported she was in love with Jesse. No evidence exists to substantiate this rumor. Wood objected to the extra-marital romance and quarreled with Liddil. Only the interference of friends stopped another impromptu duel. Liddil hastened back to Missouri.

Another man became as enamored of Mrs. George Hite as Dick Liddil had been, and the stepmother reciprocated. A black servant named John Tabor frequently carried billet-doux from Mrs. Hite to her latest admirer. Wood Hite discovered the note-bearer on one of his errands and warned him against carrying any more notes for the fickle woman. Then Wood bitterly accused his stepmother of being unfaithful to his father. She denied this and threatened to retaliate for Wood's meddling by telling the sheriff of Wood's connection with the James boys. She never carried out her threat, as far as is known. Wood was not so conciliatory, however. He again caught John

Tabor acting as messenger for his stepmother and killed him as he had said he would. He hid the body in the bushes.

When the body was found, the stepmother swore out a warrant that she had seen Wood commit the murder. He was arrested and for some unknown reason he was confined by Marshal Jeter in an upper room of an Adairville hotel, instead of in the jail. It is said that Wood made his escape by means of a hundred-dollar bill.

Wood made his way to Missouri, where he stopped off at the home of Martha Bolton outside Richmond. Bob Ford and Dick Liddil had arrived sometime earlier in the evening of December 3, 1881, and were asleep in an upstairs bedroom when Wood Hite came to the Bolton place. Doubts exist as to what happened next. Dick Liddil's statements and confession and Martha Bolton's statements at the inquest over Hite's body on April 6, 1882 show definitely that the fight occurred in the dining room and not upstairs.

Part of Liddil's confession reads:

> I was staying at the Bolton home for several weeks and then Bob Ford and I crossed over to Jackson County at Missouri City. We went to McGraw's and stayed there about a week. He was out with the threshing machine when we got there, and I did not see him but once while there. We then went back to Mrs. Bolton's, crossing the Missouri River in a skiff. We arrived here Saturday night, December 3, 1881. Next morning I came down to breakfast, and Wood Hite, who had come from Kentucky, came down with Ford in a few minutes. When he came in he spoke to me and I told him not to speak to me, since he had accused me of stealing one hundred dollars in the division of the Blue Cut robbery money. I told him he said he could prove it, and I now wanted him to prove it. One thing led to another and then the firing commenced. He shot me through the right leg, and I fired five times at him, and snapped the barrel. I drew my other revolver when he commenced falling.

Martha Bolton stated:

> Bob Ford fired shots at Wood, but I didn't know this until afterwards when he exhibited

an empty chamber in his revolver. I recognize the body before me as that of a man who frequently (went) by the name of Robert Grimes, but his real name was Wood Hite. He was killed in the house in which I lived early in December, 1881; I do not know who killed him, though I was present when he was shot; it occurred between seven and eight o'clock in the morning. I had prepared breakfast and called the boys into the dining room; there were present Dick Liddil, Bob and Charley Ford, and Capline Ford, Wood Hite, and my little daughter. There had been some difficulty between Liddil and Hite a few months previously in Kentucky, but they appeared friendly while at my house until the shooting occurred. My back was toward the two men when they commenced shooting in the dining room, but I quickly turned and saw Liddil and Hite, the former standing near the kitchen door and the latter perhaps ten feet distant, on the east side of the room. Three or four shots were fired so quickly that the room was filled with smoke and I could not even see the men, but there were perhaps as many as ten shots fired in all. When the firing ceased I saw Wood Hite lying on the floor dead, and Liddil was holding his hand over a wound in his hip, from which the blood was flowing freely. Hite was shot in the head and must have died instantly. I do not know whether Robert Ford fired at Hite or not, but his pistol was in his hand and I suppose he shot at Hite one or more times. After the killing, my brothers carried the body upstairs and left it there until after dark, when Capline and Charles Ford wrapped the body in a blanket and carried it out of the house to the place where it was later found. Liddil was badly hurt and was assisted to a bed upstairs in the north room.

Dick Liddil's statement:

The shot that killed Wood Hite was through the head. It struck him almost two inches about the right eye and came out a little above the left ear. Bob claimed that his shot was the fatal one. Hite lived fifteen or twenty minutes, but did not speak. We carried him upstairs, and that night, December 4, Cap Ford and Bob Ford dug a shallow grave in the woods, about a mile from the house, and buried him. They did not use a coffin. My leg was too sore to allow me to help them. On the night of Thursday, December 29, Jesse and Charley Ford came down to Mrs. Bolton's, where I had been since I was wounded, and tried to get me to

go with them. I mistrusted that Jesse intended to kill me, and so left. Jesse and Charley left the next night for the old lady's (Mrs. Samuel), I was told. This was the last time I saw either of them. After the police raid on Mrs. Bolton's, early in January, 1882, I concluded to surrender. Negotiations to that effect were made, and on the night of January 21, 1882, by direction of Governor Thomas T. Crittenden, I surrendered to Sheriff James R. Timberlake, Clay County, Missouri.

The coroner's inquest of April 6, 1882, carried the following statement, as reported by Martha Bolton:

That Wood Hite came to his death by shots fired by parties unknown.

Both reports coincide very well, other than Dick Liddil failed to state that Charley Ford had been present at the shooting.

INCIDENT AT BARDSTOWN

It was summer, 1881, and hot as blazes in Bardstown, Kentucky, where, in a small room opposite the Ellis Hotel, two men waited patiently, but uncomfortably.

One of the men, a medium-sized fellow, was the famous Louisville, Kentucky, detective, Delos Thurman "Yankee" Bligh, high on the hate list of the Jameses. The other man was George Hunter, former city marshal of Bardstown, now a detective for the Louisville and Nashville Railroad. Of course, at that time, no railroad man wanted to pass an opportunity to capture Jesse and Frank James.

"Dammit, Bligh, it's hot as hell in here," complained Hunter. "How in the world do you know the Jameses are supposed to be in Bardstown at this time?"

"Because I happen to know that a code letter was sent to Sheriff Pence that they would be here around this time. Clarence Hite's in the pen for working with Jesse; told me how to decode such messages."

"How in hell would you recognize Jesse, anyhow?" came another irritated question.

Bligh laughed out loud. "Let me tell you

something, George. When a fellow makes a damned fool out of you, you never forget it. And I've still got the postcard to prove it." Blight went on to tell his companion about the time he had met Jesse at the railroad depot in Louisville; how Jesse had told him on the card who he was.

"Well, I'll be damned, what a lot of gall," grinned Hunter.

Nelson County was a safe place for the boys since their old Quantrillian buddy, A.D. (Donnie) Pence, was sheriff of that county and was friendly with his ex-buddies. Besides, Donnie Pence had married a Samuel girl, thus becoming related to Jesse and Frank through marriage. Also, Frank had saved Pence's life during a battle at Beulahville in Meade County during the Civil War. Pence became sheriff in 1871,

holding that position until his death in 1896. He operated a fifty-acre farm near Samuel's depot, where Frank and Jesse often visited, Frank also visiting the Sayers farm near Deatsville.

Detectives Bligh and Hunter were about to give up their vigil when suddenly Bligh looked alert. Pointing to two men walking toward the Ellis Hotel, he exclaimed, "There goes Jesse James now. The man with him is probably Frank!"

"Yes, and two men walking close behind. That's a lot to take on, Bligh," complained Hunter.

"We've got the element of surprise on our side; besides, be patient, we'll get some local men to assist us."

"Not if they know who you're dealing with, you won't."

"No need to tell them," assured Bligh.

Who the two men were with the Jameses never was really known. However, at Frank James' trial in 1883, turncoat Dick Liddil stated that he, Clarence Hite, and the James boys were in Nelson County about that time. Liddil also stated that in 1881 the James brothers, together with Bill Ryan and Jim Cummins, had visited the area of Bardstown.

Sheriff Donnie Pence

Sheriff Donnie Pence lived near Samuel's Depot, Kentucky.

At that particular point Donnie Pence and Ben Johnson (later a United States Congressman from 1907 to 1927) met near the hotel and engaged in conversation.

"Jesse and Frank are eating at the hotel," Pence told Ben. "Want to visit with them for a little chat?"

"By all means," replied Ben, now thoroughly fascinated by the stories which had been circulated about the famous outlaw brothers. He had also met Jesse while hunting quail with Pence, but Jesse was using the name of Howard then. "It will be a real pleasure talking to Jesse again."

About 500 feet from the hotel, Pence saw Bligh and Hunter, accompanied by two recruits, emerge from the house they were using as an observation post. Of course, Bligh was well-known to the sheriff.

"Ben, we're in trouble. Don't stop or look back, but that detective Bligh and a railroad man named Hunter, and two more men are near the hotel. They must have learned about Jesse and Frank coming here."

"Well, it seems to me that the only thing you can do is go into the hotel as though you never saw them, or go around the back and slip in," suggested Ben.

Taking the latter suggestion, Sheriff Pence walked to the rear of the hotel, quietly slipped in through the back door, and then warned the four outlaws in the dining room of the condition of affairs.

Ben Johnson strolled leisurely into the hotel lobby, completely ignoring the two detectives stationed on the sidewalk. As he moved slowly toward the dining room door, Pence came out and told him that the James boys would not slink out the back way like cowards, but would fight if they had to.

"Then there'll be hell to pay if this happens," said Pence. "Ben, this ain't your fight, are you armed?"

"Yes, I am, and if you side with the boys, then so will I."

As they were speaking, Bligh, Hunter and the two local men entered the hotel lobby.

Pence, from the corner of his eye, recognized the two Bardstown men; they were Bill McAtee and Tom Edson. Bligh and McAtee sauntered toward the north wall of the building; Hunter and Edson edged toward the south wall. Pence and Johnson walked to a corner near the dining room entrance.

While no weapons were displayed, some of the patrons felt an uneasiness in the air, fully expecting the whole area to erupt into a battle ground.

Several minutes elapsed. Suddenly the dining room door opened slowly. A sturdily built, blue-eyed man wearing a felt hat, his arms crossed over his chest, each hand hidden under his coat, walked into the lobby. It was Jesse James! The famous outlaw walked calmly toward the front door. Upon reaching it, he spun around on the ball of his foot, surveying the scene intently, facing the dining room door. Another man walked from the dining room. He was a taller man, lean and awkward, both hands also hidden under his frock coat: Frank James!

The detectives stood as though petrified, not making a move. They realized that to make the slightest suspicious move would bring a hail of lead down upon them.

Another outlaw then emerged from the dining room, walked to the front door, stepped out onto the sidewalk and disappeared. He had been instructed to get the horses from the livery stable. Then the last man came out into the lobby. Slowly the trio backed toward the door, no weapons visible. The detectives knew it was folly to try an attack now with Pence and Johnson at their rear. The horses were brought to the front of the hotel, where the outlaws leaped into the saddles, and with a loud rebel yell, darted off at a fast gallop. During the whole proceeding, not a word had been said by either side; not a shot had been fired by either side. What a thrilling experience for young Ben! It was Ben's last meeting with Jesse James.

There was little criticism on the actions of the lawmen. People were quick to realize what a dangerous position they had been in. Probably George Hunter put it best when he said this to Ben Johnson later on, "I'm a pretty good shot and so's Edson. But if Yankee Bligh had ever shot at anyone in his life, I do not know it. Against us were four outlaws and Donnie Pence, all crack shots, as well as yourself. We would have been caught in a crossfire if we had made a move, so you can see why we did not move a muscle."

At any rate, Bligh had the opportunity of seeing Jesse James a second time. (We wonder how he covered this chapter of his life, if he ever even wrote about it.)

Sheriff Pence died of typhoid pneumonia on February 25, 1896, and was buried at Stoner's Chapel burial grounds. Frank James was there, and the funeral was attended by one of the largest gatherings of bereaved friends to ever attend a funeral in Nelson County.

In 1969 the Ellis Hotel was torn down, and Donnie Pence's home was razed by its present owner, Charles S. Hayden, to make room for a larger and more modern home. The Pence home had once been the property of A.W. Sherman and when he sold it to Hayden, he insisted he be allowed to remove a window, sash and all, which bore the signature of Jesse James. On October 18, 1881, Jesse James had insisted on scratching his name and this date on the window pane since he had been accused of a train robbery in Texas, this same day he was in Nelson County, Kentucky.[2]

---

[2]Richard S. Brownlee, author of *Gray Ghosts of the Confederacy,* stated he could find a hundred window panes bearing the signature of Jesse James. Probably true, but the signatures would not be genuine, while that on the Bardstown pane of glass certainly is. The author has an original letter written by Jesse and mailed from Medora, Illinois, on April 18, 1880, to a friend in Laredo, Texas. This signature has been verified as being the same as that on the window pane. This was done by George G. Swett, noted examiner of rare and old documents. The handwriting is also the same as that appearing in the letter which Jesse wrote at St. Joe in 1882, under the signature of Thos. Howard.

Chapter Sixteen

Successful Plot

In June of 1881, Jesse James moved his family to Kansas City, where he rented a neat frame house on Woodland Avenue between 13th and 14th Streets. There he used the name of C. Harvard. So secret were his and his family's movement that no one except the Mims family knew they were living in Kansas City. John Mims was the father of Zee James, Jesse's wife.

The house on Woodland Avenue that the James family occupied for about three months was close to the scene of the dashing Kansas City Fair robbery of 1872. It was here also that the Winston robbery was planned. On September 13, Jesse used the name of T.J. Jackson and rented a house on East Ninth Street, in the first block east of Woodland Avenue. After living there a month, the family moved to 1017 Troost Avenue.

While Jesse was living in Kansas City, Mrs. Frank James and her son, along with one of Jesse's children, came to Kansas City and registered at the St. James Hotel. This was calculated to throw off suspicion. Frank went to 1017 Troost Avenue, where he stayed several days with his brother.

Jesse was less than sociable during his months in Kansas City. He was irritable and worried, for word had come to him that a one-time member of his gang was talking too much. Ed Miller was that garrulous alumnus until he was killed in Saline County, with Jesse personally acting as the executioner, according to rumor. Jim Cummins, though never proven to have been a member of the select company, knew a lot of details of its operations. When "Windy Jim" became too talkative, Jesse and Dick Liddil chased him into Arkansas, trying to shoot him.

Jim dodged, however, and backtracked into Missouri stopping at the home of Bill Ford for several days. Then one day he began to fear for some reason that Jesse was close by, so he saddled his horse and rode away. His hunch proved correct, for he had just ridden off when Jesse and Liddil rounded a bend leading to the Ford home. Bill Ford was not at home, but his wife and fourteen-year-old son, Albert, were there. They boy was Cummins' nephew, for Jim's sister, Artella, had married Bill Ford. Jesse inquired about Jim but was informed he had not been there for some time. Not at all satisfied that the woman and the boy were telling the truth, Jesse and Dick took young Albert Ford into the woods and tried to force the truth from him. However, they were unsuccessful and Jim Cummins escaped. Before Jesse could again catch up with him, that fatal day in St. Joe arrived. Cummins ended his days in 1929 at the Confederate Home at Higginsville, Missouri, since razed.

In the autumn of 1881, Jesse visited his home in Kearney. There he was accosted by Charley Ford, who was trying to escape

Charlie Ford

Courtesy of the N.H. Rose Collection

capture by the law, and Jesse agreed to shelter him.

Jesse then returned to Kansas City and made preparations for his family to move again. On November 5, 1881, the James' household effects were loaded in a wagon with his family and Charley Ford. Jesse started out for St. Joseph. En route, they again stopped at the home of his mother, where Robert Ford joined them, although he did not accompany them to St. Joseph, and probably did not know their destination at that time. They arrived on November 8, and rented a house at the corner of Lafayette and 21st Streets. The family used the name of Thomas Howard—it was the last of Jesse's many aliases.

On the day before Christmas they moved to a neat frame one-story cottage of seven rooms at 1318 Lafayette Street. The house was painted white, with green shutters, and romantically situated on the brow of a lofty hill east of the city. It commanded a fine view of the principal portions of the city, the river, and the railroads. It was adapted by nature for the perilous calling of Jesse James. The house was occupied formerly by City Councilman Aylesbury, and he rented

A picture of the James's home at the time of the slaying of Jesse James was taken from a cut in the *St. Joseph News-Press,* Sunday, November 19, 1919.

Courtesy of the
St. Joseph News-Press

it to the Jameses for fourteen dollars a month. Here Jesse played Santa Claus to his children that Christmas Day.

Jesse could not see into the mind of Sheriff J.R. Timberlake, head of law enforcement in Clay County, Missouri. Timberlake conceived the plan to enlist the aid of the Ford brothers in capturing or killing Jesse. The sheriff had learned that the outlaw was a frequent visitor at the Harbeson farm, the home of Martha Bolton who was the widowed sister of the Ford brothers.

The sheriff had good evidence that the Ford boys had participated in some of the train robberies guided by the masterful Jesse and Frank. Without confiding his plans to anyone, he dressed as a farm hand and rode into Ray County, Missouri, the location of the Bolton–Ford menage.

Robert Ford holds a Colt pistol. This gun was not the one used to kill Jesse James; the murder weapon was a Smith & Wesson.

During the day the sheriff hid out, but each night for about three weeks he crawled up to the side of the house and eavesdropped. Among the facts he learned during his nightly vigils was that Wood Hite, Jesse's favorite cousin, had been killed, though Jesse was as yet unaware of it and never did learn this fact. More significantly, the sheriff learned that Robert Ford, Charley Ford, and Dick Liddil were not truly friends of Jesse, but instead harbored grudges against him. He also learned that Robert Ford, even as a child, wanted to be the man to rid the world of the noted outlaw.

This knowledge guided Sheriff Timberlake in his next step. He went back to Kansas City and approached Mattie Collins, who claimed to be Dick Liddil's wife. Timberlake persuaded Mattie to get in touch with Martha Bolton, who in turn was to attempt to obtain the cooperation of Bob and Charley Ford and Dick Liddil in ending the career of Jesse James. The sheriff had a powerful persuader in the form of strong evidence linking the trio to several robberies. He sent the boys word that he knew who had killed Wood Hite. His trump card was his promise to the Fords that if they assisted in killing Jesse, the governor of the state could be influenced to give them immunity.

There is some evidence that the Ford boys did not wait for Sheriff Timberlake to build the trap for Jesse, but that Charley and Bob themselves approached authorities in Kansas City as early as the spring of 1881. They proposed a plan for netting the harried leader of the outlaw band. The scholars who purport to have evidence of the Ford boys' initiative also say that Charley and Bob argued that their killing of Wood Hite showed how they felt about Jesse himself. Others say that Charley Ford was unaware of the whole plot until it also happened.

The killing of Wood Hite, incidentally, was the cause of Jesse's last visit to Kentucky. He did not know his cousin was dead, but he was troubled by Wood's unexpected disappearance. He began to suspect various members of the old gang, but apparently it never occurred to him that the Ford boys and Dick Liddil could have any knowledge about Wood. In February of 1882, Jesse set out for Major Hite's home in Kentucky to start a search for his cousin. In sixteen days he rode his six-year-old chestnut gelding nearly 1100 miles. His arduous trip was fruitless.

He returned to St. Joseph and to his recent name, Thomas Howard. Besides Jesse's wife and children, Charley Ford was living in the house. He was known to the townspeople as Charles Johnson, a relative of Mr. Howard, although they were not really related. While Charley thus kept track of Jesse's whereabouts, Bob was spending much of his time in Kansas City with Police Commissioner Henry Craig, working out the details of the plot to murder Jesse.

Charley and Bob Ford were newcomers to the James brothers' orbit. Born in Fauquier County, Virginia, the Ford boys had come to Missouri in 1871 with their father, J.T. Ford, who settled first in Clay County and later in Ray County. These sons were often suspected of horse thievery and, as they grew older, it was whispered that they had also taken part in train robberies. In 1879, Charley and Bob Ford and Martha Bolton rented the Harbeson farm, near Richmond, Missouri. Here it was, in their first year of residence on the farm, that Jesse met the family. It cannot be said that Jesse and the Ford boys became fast friends on first sight, but it is apparent that a working arrangement of some kind did develop between them in the next two years.

On March 12, 1882, Jesse and Charley rode into northern Kansas and southern Nebraska. They had previously addressed a letter to J.D. Calhoun at Lincoln, Nebraska, in reply to the man's ad regarding the sale

Bob Ford

Courtesy of Pinkerton Files

Lincoln Journal gave a glowing account of the fine 160-acre farm he had for sale.

During their sojourn, Jesse noted that the bank at Forest City, Kansas, a small village, would be an ideal place to stage a robbery. However, Charley begged him to abandon the idea, claiming he was ill and would not be of much use in the venture.

Before returning to St. Joseph, Jesse and Charley made several visits to their old haunts in Clay and Ray Counties, Missouri. There Charley met his brother Bob, telling him they would do Jesse in at the first chance. Jesse was glad to have Bob as a member in a planned bank robbery at Platte City, Missouri.[1]

Jesse's mother, with intuitions even keener that those of Jesse, frequently

[1]Just three or four days before Jesse was killed, he and Bill Sallee, together with Charley Ford, stayed at the home of Scarlet W. Madding a farmer from Hardin County, Kentucky, whose place was just outside Platte City. Bill Stigers of St. Joseph, Missouri, told me that his Uncle Madding talked Jesse out of robbing the bank at Platte City while the Burgess murder trial was going on (scheduled for April 4, 1882). Scarlet Madding said he did not want such a thing happening so close to his home. This could be true, since the Madding family were close to all the ex-guerrillas; in fact, one of the Madding daughters married Joseph Todd, a grandson of Captain George Todd of Quantrill's guerrillas. Also, if true, it is doubtful that the Fords knew of it.

of a farm in that area. The letter was dated March 2, 1882, and signed "Thos. Howard, No. 1318 Lafayette St., St. Joseph, Mo." The ad that Mr. Calhoun had placed in the

FOR SALE—A very fine 160 acres. adjoining the town of Franklin, Franklin Co. Corners with depot grounds. Living springs; beautiful creek runs through it. 90 acres in body of finest bottom land: balance natural young timber. Mill within a mile. As good educational, religious. railroad and other facilities as any point in western Nebraska. $10 per acre. Address or call on J. D. Calhoun, Lincoln, Neb.   feb15d6&w1t

Jesse answered this newspaper ad.

warned him against trusting the Ford boys. She advised against his taking them into his group, and against his extending hospitality to them. Jesse had survived nearly fifteen years as an outlaw, partly by his ability to judge men. What did his mother, now grown gray and shrill, know about picking prospective partners in an outlaw troupe?

It is quite possible, as an analysis of the events in the last two months of Jesse's life shows, that Mrs. Samuel was warning Jesse against the Fords at about the same time Bob was in a new conference with officials in Kansas City, completing the plans against Jesse. Chief Thomas Speers, Kansas City Police Department, and Henry Craig felt they needed the backing of higher authority before they could promise immunity. They arranged for Governor T.T. Crittenden to meet with Bob Ford. This meeting between the governor and the volunteer assassin was held on February 22, 1882, at the St. James Hotel in Kansas City.

Bob and Charley made frequent trips to their home in Ray County while living with Jesse at St. Joseph. They had gone there the latter part of March to visit their relatives.

Late on the night of April 1, 1882, Jesse rode up to the home of Elias (Capline) Ford and called Bob outside. He told him he had work for him and the two rode away together. The next day Elias Ford notified Sheriff Timberlake that Bob had gone to St. Joseph, no doubt to make final preparations for the Platte City robbery. The sheriff notified his posse to be ready at a moment's notice and kept an engine steamed up so they could race to St. Joseph.

Sheriff Timberlake had warned Bob Ford to keep the papers from Jesse as much as possible, since some reporters were getting wind of Liddil's surrender, although news of it had not yet been published. When Jesse questioned Bob about Liddil's disappearance, Bob said he knew nothing about Liddil that Jesse didn't know. On the morning of April 3, Bob brought the papers in before breakfast. Jesse was seated in front

Chief Thomas Speers of the Kansas City Police Department pursued the James brothers.
Courtesy of the Kansas City Police Department

Captain Henry Craig, Police Commissioner of Kansas City, was very active in the downfall of the outlaw Jesse James.

of Bob, reading the *St. Louis Republican.* Bob finished scanning the *Kansas City Journal* and picked up the *Kansas City Times.* He almost dropped it as if it were a serpent, for the headlines, half a foot high, screamed out the news of Dick Liddil's surrender. Bob almost fainted at the suddenness of it. He made an effort to hide the paper under a shawl on the chair. Jesse walked over to the chair, removed the shawl, tucked the paper under his arm, and went into the kitchen for breakfast. Ford knew his game of deception was up. He moved around so that his revolver was close to his right hand.

Mrs. James poured the coffee and sat down at one end of the table. Charley Ford was at the other end, and the two children sat in front of him. Jesse spread the paper on the table, folding his arms and scanning the headlines.

"Hello, here! Surrender of Dick Liddil!" was all he said at first. Then he looked across the table at Bob, whose heart was in his throat and who thought he was about to die.

"Young man," Jesse went on, "I thought you told me you didn't know anything about Dick."

"I didn't!"

"Well," said Jesse, "it's very strange. He surrendered three weeks ago, and you were right here in the neighborhood. It looks fishy to me."

Jesse glared at Bob until the young man could stand it no longer. He got up and walked back into the front room. Jesse followed him. Bob later said that he thought the shooting would begin at once, but Jesse spoke placatingly. Many people wondered why Jesse did not kill Ford then and there.

"Well, it's all right anyway, Bob."

Instantly the real purpose of Jesse's new attitude flashed upon Bob Ford. The outlaw was not going to kill him in front of his wife and children but would dispose of him that night on the ride to Platte City. Mrs.

James was pregnant at the time, and Jesse did not want to upset her. (She later had a miscarriage owing to the stress of Jesse's murder.)

Jesse walked over to the bed and deliberately unbuckled his belt carrying his revolver, and threw it on the bed. It was the first time that Bob had seen Jesse not wearing his revolver. He had also removed a pocket pistol, which he threw alongside the belt on the bed. There was no doubt that Jesse wanted to impress upon Ford that he had forgotten the incident of the headlines, for he picked up a feather duster from the table and said, "Golly that picture is awful dusty."

Ford later stated that there wasn't a speck of dust on that picture that he could see. He also said Zee was such a good housekeeper that she would never have permitted it to begin with. Jesse then climbed upon a chair beneath the picture of a horse and began to dust the frame. Another mystery is why would Jesse have needed to stand on a chair when he could just as easily dusted the picture by simply reaching up from his position on the floor.[2]

Bob thought, "It is now or never. There he stands, unarmed. If I don't get him now, he'll get me tonight."

Bob pulled his Smith & Wesson .44 and leveled it. Jesse heard the hammer click as the gun was cocked and turned just as Bob pulled the trigger. The heavy bullet struck the outlaw immediately behind the right ear and tore through his brain. It shattered the skull in a shocking manner, and lodged just beneath the surface of the skin behind the left ear. In falling upon the floor a right angle wound was produced at the corner of

---

[2]The eternal mystery as to why Jesse would stand on a chair to "dust" a picture on the wall could be explained by the letter written by Margaret Shepherd. If Jesse was hanging a picture of the horse over the doorway, it is understandable that he would use a chair, since the nailing and positioning of the picture would require two hands at a height where it could not be done by a man standing on the floor.

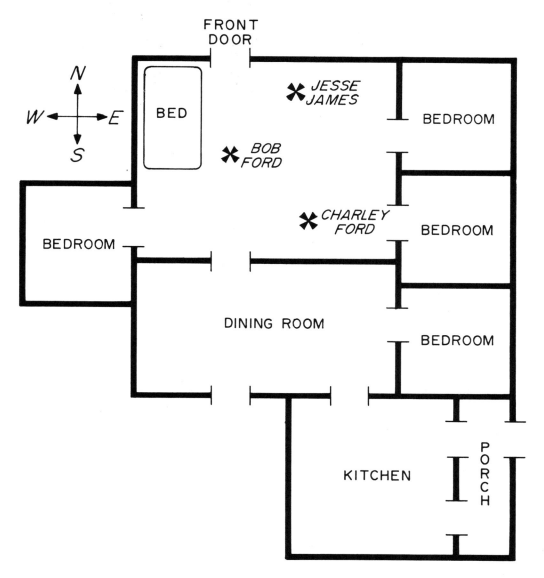

This diagram shows that Charley Ford was in the room when Bob shot Jesse. He was actually in the kitchen, but the story was amended to say he was in the room with Bob in order that Executive amnesty could also apply to him for the death of Jesse.

Courtesy of Jack DeMattos

Smith & Wesson .44 New Model No. 3 was used by Bob Ford to kill Jesse James. James had given the gun to Ford as a gift.

Courtesy of Grif Lingenfelder

the left eye, which for a time led many to believe that Jesse had been shot in the face.

Charley Ford ran into the room, and right behind him was Mrs. James, who began to mourn while she bitterly upbraided Bob.

"It was an accident!" cried Bob Ford.

"Yes, an accident on purpose. You traitor. Bob Ford, traitor! Traitor!" cried Mrs. James, and she tried in vain to wipe away the blood from the wound in Jesse's head.

Zee James was a neat and rather prepossessing person who had obviously been well reared among good and holy influences. She was slender, fair of face, with light hair, blue eyes, and a high forehead. She was wearing a neat-fitting calico. When she stood face to face with Ford's awful deed, she took the matter in a cool and philosophical manner. She may not have been entirely surprised; perhaps she had lived in expectation of this for a long time. The two children, Jesse Edwards and Mary, were brought into the room, and they grieved the loss of a father's love and protection as though they knew how it would affect their later years.

Ford ran from the house, leaped over the plank fence, and called to a passerby, asking him to notify the police that he had just killed Jesse James. He then hurried to the telegraph office and sent wires to Governor Crittenden, Sheriff Timberlake, Commissioner Craig, and several others, before Marshal Enos Craig of St. Joseph placed the Fords in the city jail.

Corydon F. Craig, the marshal's young son, took a fancy to the Fords, and he saw to it that they were furnished with cigarettes and various good things to eat during their brief stay in jail. After their release, Bob Ford presented young Craig with the gun he had used to kill Jesse James, as a token of his appreciation. Although all writers claim it was a Colt .45 caliber, improved pattern, it was not. It was a Smith & Wesson No. 3, New Model, nickel-plated, 6 1/2 barrel, .44 caliber, serial No.

Marshal Enos Craig of St. Joseph, Missouri was the officer who arrested Bob and Charley Ford after the killing of Jesse James.

Courtesy of St. Joseph Museum

3766, according to the testimony given by the Fords later on.

So much discussion has gone on as to the Dalton matter and the identification of the picture that Jesse was "dusting" that the following communication is an important addition to clear up this problem.

Poplar Bluff, Mo.
April 12, 1982
Dear Mr. Breihan

A short time ago you were on TV. On the same show there was a story about a man named Frank Dalton who claimed to be Jesse James. As you well know, the Shepherd family and James family were very close. My folks lived by Jesse when Bob Ford shot Jesse James in the back. My dad said he and his mom heard the shot and saw Bob Ford running from the house and heard Jesse's wife screaming. Dad and grandma ran over to James's house. Jesse lay on the floor dead. He had been standing up on a chair hanging a picture of a horse over a doorway. Dad was 22 years old at the time and he helped get Jesse ready for burial. I have seen my dad angry enough to fight over people claiming to be Jesse James. I do believe my dad. Therefore I will have to call anyone an imposter or a liar who would say he was not telling the truth. Dad said Jesse James helped my grandma through some really hard times. My grandpa was shot in the back by a Pinkerton agent who thought he was shooting Uncle Oliver. That was when my dad was eight. My grandpa lived six years with a hole in his chest. My grandma was lucky to have Jesse James for a friend and neighbor. Keep up the good work.

Sincerely

Margaret Shepherd

Chapter Seventeen

Following Jesse's Death

At ten o'clock on the morning of the murder, Assistant Coroner James W. Heddens was notified. He instructed Undertaker Sidenfaden to remove Jesse's remains to his establishment. As the body lay in a remote room of the building, reporters compared photographs of Jesse James with the dead man's features and searched for identifying scars.

They found two large bullet wound scars in the right side of the chest, within three inches of the nipple, a bullet wound in the leg, and the top of the left hand middle finger missing. Another identifying sign was a birthmark on the back of Jesse's right arm above the elbow, a dark brown spot in the shape of a potato. They also saw the results of Jesse's getting his left foot caught in the stirrup and dislocating an inside anklebone. It had never healed properly, but was pushed inward. This was probably the ankle injured at the Gallatin bank robbery.

Jesse was about five feet nine or ten inches tall, of a firm and compact build, but rather on the slender side, wearing a size thirty-two belt. His hair was dark, not overly long, his eyes blue, well-shaded with dark lashes. The entire lower portion of his face was covered by a full growth of dark or sunbrowned whiskers, which were carefully trimmed. His complexion was fair, and he was not sunburned at this time of the year in spite of his outdoor activities. He was clad in a business suit of brown cash-mere, which fit him neatly. He wore a shirt of spotless whiteness, with collar and cravat, and looked more like a substantial businessman than a noted outlaw.

Prior to the inquest an autopsy had been performed by Drs. George C. Catlett, Jacob Geiger, William Hoyt, and Assistant Coroner James Heddens. The cap of the skull was removed to permit a thorough exposure of the brain, which was found to be larger than average. Their report read:

> The bullet entered the occipital bone, immediately behind the right ear, and traversed the brain in a slightly upward direction, until it lodged in, but broke through the skull back of the left ear. It was found at the junction of the anture. The brain and skull were dreadfully shattered. Large pieces of bone were driven through the wound, which lacerated the entire cerebellum.

The bullet removed from Jesse's head remained in the Heddens family for many years. It was last displayed on the mantle at the home of Barrett Heddens. One day it just disappeared. It was also rumored that Dr. Heddens removed Jesse's brain, which he preserved and exhibited at the medical college. This is pure conjecture, however.

The inquest began at three o'clock that afternoon in the Circuit Court room of the courthouse. Mrs. James arrived in the custody of Marshal Craig. The two Fords had been kept in separate rooms until the jury summoned them for testimony. They then

Jesse James in death. Each group of three dots represents the locations of the two wounds received during the Civil War.

entered the court. Since their arrest was merely a formality, and they were afraid of attack by the public, they had asked permission to keep their guns even though they were in custody. Therefore, they were heavily armed when they appeared.

Six citizens of St. Joseph were impaneled for the inquest and heard testimony for two days. Mrs. Jesse James' principal contribution to the testimony was her admission that Thomas Howard, shot by Bob Ford, was indeed Jesse James. Her tears breaking forth repeatedly, she got it into the report that he had been an affectionate father and a thoughtful, loving husband.

Jesse's mother, Zerelda Samuel, arrived in St. Joseph early in the morning of the second day, and at the undertaker's request she identified the body as that of Jesse. Then she went on to the courthouse to testify. When she was asked if the body was positively that of her son, her answer in part was, "Would to God it was not!"

The air inside and outside the courthouse was tense. Rumors circulated that a force of armed outlaws was descending upon St. Joseph to avenge Jesse's death. The police guard over the Fords was reinforced.

Most of the witnesses at the inquest had little to contribute except to verify the identification of Jesse. Among those who appeared and said the subject of the inquiry was truly Jesse James were some of his fellow guerrillas of Civil War days; these included Captain Harrison Trow, Sam Whitsett, and Ben Morrow.

One of the identifying witnesses was Lamartine Hudspeth, a long-time friend of the outlaw. The Hudspeth home had been one of Jesse's favorite refuges when he was lying low. At the Hudspeth stable near the house, it was said, a fresh horse was always on hand for Jesse. On some mornings, when Hudspeth went out to the barn, the fresh horse was gone and standing in its place was a tired animal Jesse had left.

Bob Ford had much to say at the time of the inquest. He became so enamored of his descriptions of his semi-official law enforcement role that he continued his speeches for years. At the time of the inquest, however, he gave his basic story:

> So they say the dead man isn't Jesse James, do they? Then they are mistaken. I first met Jesse James three years ago, and I have made no mistake. He used to come over to the house when I was on my oldest brother's farm. Last November he moved here to St. Joe and went under the name of Thomas Howard. He rented a house on the hill, back of the World's Hotel, a quiet part of town and not thickly settled. My brother Charley and I had known nearly all the gang, but had never worked with them otherwise.
>
> I was in collusion with the detectives, and was one of the party that went into Kentucky and arrested Charles Hite last February. Hite got twenty-five years in the penitentiary. Jesse never suspected that we were false to him, and, as his gang was all broken up, he wanted new material and regarded us

favorably. Two weeks ago he came to Clay County to see his mother, Mrs. Samuel, who lives forty miles east of Kansas City. Charley and I told him then we wanted to join him and be outlaws, and he said all right. Charley came here with him a week ago Sunday, and I followed last Sunday night. We both stayed at his house, a one-story building with seven rooms.

> Governor Crittenden had offered a $10,000 reward for Jesse, dead or alive. We knew that the only way was to kill him. He was always cool and self-possessed, and always on the watch. During the day he would stay around the house, and in the evening he would go downtown to the news depot and get the papers. He said there were men here who ought to know him, but they never did. He took the *Chicago Tribune, Cincinnati Commercial,* and the *Kansas City Times* regularly, and always knew what was going on all over the world. About a week ago he read a piece in one of the papers that Jesse James' career was over, and Charley said he was awful mad about it. He said that he would show them, before long, that Jesse James was not done yet.
>
> He had not done any job since the Blue Cut train robbery, last September, and I don't believe he had over $700 or $800 in money. He was thinking of robbing some bank, nearby, and then running in under close cover. It was for this he wanted our help. We knew we had to kill him, but there was no chance to get the drop on him until this morning.
>
> His wife, and a boy of seven, and a girl of three, were in the kitchen. Jesse was in the front sitting room, where he slept. Never knew him to be so careless. He commenced brushing the dust off some picture frames, but stopped to take off his weapons, and laid them on the bed. There was a Colt's revolver and a Smith & Wesson, each .45 calibre. He also had in the room a Winchester repeating rifle, fourteen shots, and a breech-loading shotgun.
>
> As he turned away from the bed, we stepped between him and his weapons and pulled on him. I was about eight feet from him when he heard my pistol cock. He turned his head like lightning; I fired, the ball striking him in the head and lodging behind the left ear, as we later learned. Charley had his finger on the trigger, but saw that he was done for and did not shoot. Not one of us spoke a word. He fell dead at Charley's feet. We then got our hats, went to the telegraph office, and telegraphed what

we had done to Governor Crittenden, Captain Henry Craig, of Kansas City, and Sheriff Timberlake, of Clay County. The latter replied, 'I will come at once. Stay there until I come.'

Bob Ford's report differed somewhat from what he told reporters just after the shooting in that he said Charley was in the kitchen when he shot Jesse. It's possible that he revised his story at the governor's suggestion so that Charley could share in the reward and full amnesty.

At the inquest, Captain Craig substantiated his alliance with the Fords by saying, "The body corresponds with the description of Jesse James. I know the Fords. Bob Fork assisted Sheriff Timberlake and myself. He was not commissioned. Robert Ford acted through our instructions, and Charles was not acting under our instructions."

Sheriff Timberlake corroborated the identification of the outlaw, testifying, "We were personally acquainted. I saw him last in 1870. I knew his face. He had part of a finger off. I told Ford to get his brother to assist him."

Dick Liddil, one-time friend and later secret foe of Jesse, said after he was sworn, "I have seen the body and recognize it as the body of Jesse James. I have no doubt of it. His general appearance is that of Jesse James. His finger is off, as Jesse's was, and I recognize the scars in the side and thigh."

One important witness, never mentioned before, was Dr. George W. James, no relation to Jesse, but one of three doctor brothers who settled in Missouri. Dr. George James settled at Claysville, about six miles from the James farm. Dr. George James on occasion was called to attend the James family, once taking care of a finger that Jesse had accidentally shot the tip from. Governor Crittenden asked him to identify the remains. This is what he said, "Yes, it was Jesse, all right. The finger I tended was easy to identify."[1]

[1]The author thanks Jesse H. James, son of Dr. James H. James for this new and important information.

Most people had nothing but the utmost contempt for Bob Ford and for those who tried to foist him on the reading public as a hero and a law-abiding citizen. An analysis of the circumstances surrounding the killing and its causes shows that popular opinion reached the verdict that Robert Ford was the most contemptible coward ever to go unhanged.

After various witnesses gave their interviews the coroner's report read:

> State of Missouri
> County of Buchanan
> An inquisition taken at St. Joseph, in the County of Buchanan, on the third day of April, 1882, before me, James W. Heddens, M.D., coroner of the county aforesaid, upon their view of the body of Jesse W. James, then and there lying dead, S.H. Sommers, W.H. Chouning, J.W. Moore, Thomas Norris, William Turner, W.H. George, good and lawful householders in the Township of Washington, who, being duly sworn and charged diligently to enquire and true presentiment make, how and in what manner, and by whom the said Jesse W. James came to his death, upon their oaths do say:
> That the body of the deceased is that of Jesse W. James and that he came to his death by a wound in the head, caused by a pistol shot fired intentionally by the hand of Robert Ford, in witness whereof as well the jurors aforesaid, have to this inquisition put their names at the place and day aforesaid.
> James W. Heddens, Coroner
> S.H. Sommers, Foreman
> W.H. Chouning
> J.W. Morre Moore
> Thos. Norris
> Wm. Turner
> W.H. George

After two days of tension in St. Joseph, the crowds milling in and around the undertaker's to view Jesse's body began to thin out. The speculation as to whether Frank James would mysteriously appear and avenge his brother's assassination decreased as it became generally known that Frank was suffering from consumption and was supposed to be back east or in Texas.

The inquest over, the Ford brothers were confined to the St. Joseph jail, charged in a

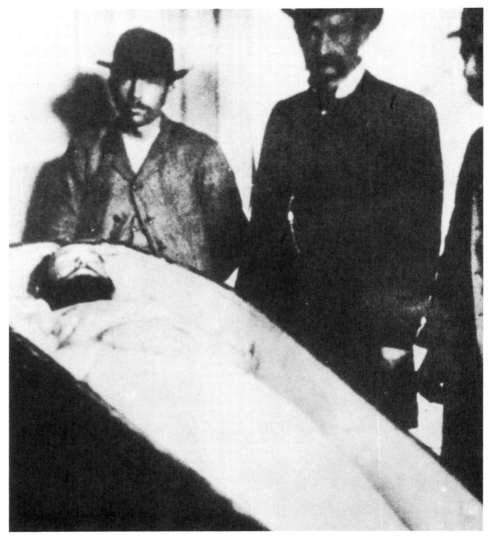

The body of Jesse James was viewed by hundreds of curious people.

Courtesy of R.F. James

warrant sworn out by Mrs. Jesse James for the murder of her husband, Jesse James.

On Wednesday, April 5, 1882, Jesse's body was released to his family, but only after Governor Crittenden had sent a message to O.M. Spencer, Prosecuting Attorney of Buchanan County, suggesting that he do so. There had been a dispute between the St. Joseph authorities and Sheriff Timberlake and Commissioner Craig regarding the disposition of the outlaw's remains.

At six o'clock a carriage drove up to the station. Mrs. Samuel stepped out and, leaning on the arm of an officer, walked to the train. She insisted on inspecting the baggage car to see for herself that Jesse's body had been placed on board. The funeral cortege was under the charge of Marshal Enos Craig. Members of the mourning party were: Mrs. Zerelda Samuel, Mrs. Zee James, the two James children, L.E. James (a cousin), and R.T. Mims, brother of Jesse's widow.

When the train reached Cameron, Missouri, at nine that evening, the special train that was to take the party to Kearney failed to arrive. Marshal Craig had the coffin removed into the caboose of a freight train.

The weary party arrived in Kearney just before daylight.

The body of Jesse James was taken to the Kearney Hotel and again exposed to view. Hundreds of persons had an opportunity to identify the bandit they had once known. It was the largest crowd Kearney had ever seen. On muddy roads men rode from afar on horseback and in wagons for the opportunity to view the mortal remains of the famous Jesse James. Trains stopped at the town so that passengers could disembark and view the outlaw, or walk for a few moments the streets that he had walked.

At 2:15 p.m. on April 6, the casket, a metallic imitation rosewood, with a plate on which was engraved the name *Jesse James,* was placed in an open spring wagon and driven toward Mt. Olivet Baptist Church, followed by a procession of twenty teams,

A page out of the ledger of the Sidenfaden Funeral Home of St. Joseph, Missouri shows payment of Jesse James's casket and shroud.
Courtesy of R.F. James

Reverend R.H. Jones of Lathrop, Missouri, read from the Scriptures of Job at the funeral of Jesse James.

Jesse Edwards James at the grave of his father when it was still in the yard of the homestead at Kearney, Missouri.

carrying members, relatives, and acquaintances of the James family. In the second wagon rode Mrs. James and her two children, Mr. Mims, and Mrs. Samuel; in the third wagon rode the pallbearers, Sheriff Timberlake, Deputy Sheriff Reed (long-time friend of Jesse), Charles Scott, J.B. Henderson, J.D. Ford (mayor of Liberty, Missouri, and no relation to the Ford brothers), Benjamin Flanders, and James Vaughn (an ex-Quantrillian, who later wrote a book claiming he was Frank James). Rumor had it that the fine casket was paid for in the amount of $250 by the "guilty consciences" of Sheriff Timberlake and Commissioner Craig. The ledger sheet of the Sidenfaden Funeral Home shows the entry of this $250 that paid for the casket of Jesse James.

The church was reached at three o'clock, where the body was received by the pastor, the Reverend J.M.P. Martin, of Kearney. He officiated at the services, assisted by the

Mrs. Jesse W. James stands at the coffee bean tree at the old homestead near Kearney, Missouri.
Courtesy of
W. Zink Collection

Center boulder is the grave of Jesse James. It has been replaced today by a ground level marker.

Reverend D.H. Jones of Lathrop, Missouri. After the services, which were concluded at 3:30 p.m., the procession started toward the early home of the outlaw, where the

The new headstone for Jesse's grave

remains were viewed by John Samuel, Jesse's half-brother, who lay wounded as a result of a recent saloon brawl, and Frank James.

At five o'clock the body was finally consigned to a very deep grave, dug opposite and near the kitchen, just inside the plank fence that separated the yard from the pasture and under a gigantic coffee-bean tree. The coffee-bean tree has since been destroyed by a bolt of lightning, and Jesse's remains were reburied in the Kearney Cemetery in 1902, at the request of his dying wife. It now rests between the graves of Dr. Samuel and Mrs. Zerelda Samuel. A beautiful and tall monument was erected at the site, but this has been replaced with a ground-level marker since souvenir hunters chipped away thousands of pieces from the stone marker over Jesse's grave, until it looked like an eroded little boulder tossed on the grass.

The James–Samuel home at Kearney still stands, unpretentious but comfortable, surrounded by the lush foliage typical of old-time Missouri farmsteads. In recent years the old cabin, built in 1822, completed in 1830, had fallen into bad disrepair. Efforts were made to seek contributions to restore the James home, to no avail. The old homestead was purchased from the last grandson of Mary James Barr by the Clay County Department of Parks and Recreation. They have renovated the old building and brought it back to its original state, minus a few logs that were totally destroyed. The Clay County Department also hopes to locate and replicate the sites of the old barn, ice house, and whatever other structures were originally on the site. They also sponsor a "Friends of the James Farm" club that one can join and assist in providing a "Jesse James Day" each year.

The seven-room house in St. Joseph was moved from its original location in the 1930s to the outskirts of the city, on the Outer Belt, alongside the Jesse James service station. Two of the original rooms have long since been removed. Today it stands at the rear of the Pattee House Museum in St. Joe. The old house also serves as a museum, with strongly commercial connotations. After Jesse's death, the owner of the house sold bloody splinters, from the boards on the floor where Jesse had fallen, for twenty five cents each. The supply of boards soon ran out and, to keep up the business, the owner replaced the boards with similar ones sprinkled with ox blood. One objectionable spiel that is given at the old home is to expound upon the bullet hole in the wall. The hole was "caused" by the one that killed Jesse James. The bullet that killed the bandit never left his head until the autopsy,

This is the last picture ever taken of Frank James. He is on his farm near Excelsior Springs, Missouri.

Courtesy of Robert James

hence no way could it have made a hole in the wall as claimed.

The fabulous Jesse James had been feared and hated as a robber and a killer, the latter stigma being rather far-fetched. Yet he came to be revered as an American Robin Hood. Perhaps this is partly owing to his devotion to his mother and to the persecution heaped upon his family and friends. At any rate, he has gone into folklore as a hero, and his memory is kept alive by the famed murals painted by Thomas Hart Benton in the state capitol at Jefferson City, Missouri. Even the popular folk song mentioned was written in his memory. The many pseudo Jesse Jameses have also contributed much to keeping the legend alive.

Chapter Eighteen

The Ford Brothers

On April 17, the Ford brothers were indicted for the murder of Jesse James. Robert was charged with murder in the first degree, and Charley with aiding and abetting his brother in the killing. Of course, it was all a formality. Even though they pleaded guilty and were sentenced to be hanged, they were given complete amnesty. As they were being released, Bob remarked, "Damn, it would have been a good joke on us if they really would have hanged us, wouldn't it?"

When Governor Crittenden pardoned the Ford boys for their crime, he committed a great political blunder. Apologists claim he knew nothing of it, but it was apparent that someone high in state political circles knew of the planned murder. Crittenden made himself the most likely suspect by stepping forth immediately in favor of the Fords.

Careful study of Bob Ford and his brother points to other motives for undertaking the assignment:

1. Bob's lifelong ambition to kill the noted outlaw.
2. Greed: the promise of the reward money.
3. Revenge on Jesse for the torture of Albert Ford.
4. Fear that Jesse would discover that Bob had killed his favorite cousin, Wood Hite.

The body snatchers who could not acquire Jesse's corpse for profitable display took the next best thing—Bob and Charley Ford.

At first, under the auspices of George H. Bunnell, and with a reluctant Charley, Bob toured the eastern cities. In September, 1882, they made their first public appearance, reenacting the murder of Jesse at 9th Street and Broadway in New York City. They then moved over to Bunnell's museum at Court and Remsen Streets in Brooklyn.

To easterners the act may have stood for the triumph of law and order in the Wild West. However, to Missourians and other Mid-Westerners from Ohio to the western border of New Mexico, the act appeared less noble. When Bob appeared in these areas he was sometimes booed, and sometimes threatened with lynching. Bunnell finally decided he had a poor investment. Bob then accepted an offer from P.T. Barnum to appear in his freak show. This did not last long.

Bob renewed his friendship with Dick Liddil. The two men went to Las Vegas, New Mexico, where they opened a saloon, thinking their notoriety would make them famous. The saloon, on Bridge Street in Old Town, was a miserable failure. Liddel then took employment with J.W. Lynch, famous horse-racing magnate, and toured the circuits with him, caring for his animals. Dick died a natural death in 1893, in Cincinnati, Ohio. His body was brought back to Missouri by his family, where it was buried at Independence, Missouri.

Charley did not endure self-exhibition very long. On May 6, 1884, Charley committed suicide at the home of his father, J.T. Ford, about a mile east of Richmond, Missouri. The wire Capline Ford sent to Bob was straightforward:

> Richmond, Mo., May 6
> Robert Ford,
> Charley shot and killed himself. Come home.

"Why do you think your brother killed himself?" was the question thrown at Bob Ford. Many wanted to know whether he feared Frank James would seek vengeance upon him for murdering Jesse James.

"The only thing I can think of is that he was depressed with his failing health. He was suffering from consumption, and frequently told me he never expected to get well. I know he came here last Thursday and wrote a letter to Captain Charles Ditsch in which he stated he was going to remain in Richmond until he got well. He also instructed the captain to forward all his mail to his parents' home. You know, the pain caused him to use a lot of morphine and I think this drug contributed to his death."

Bob Ford, however, tried to carry on what he called a good thing, by appearing in plays such as *How I Killed Jesse James.* He next went to Walsenburg, Colorado, where he opened a saloon. However, customers were few and he soon abandoned the venture. Eventually he arrived in Pueblo, Colorado, and opened a fancy honky-tonk in the section known as the Mesa. He was a good spender and had lots of barfly friends and a few respectable ones. Contrary to the old saying that only a coward will shoot a man in the back, he was not afraid, and he had the reputation of being the fastest on the draw of all the gang.

There was a clubhouse near the police station much frequented by city officials off duty. In those days Pueblo was a "wide open" town. Gambling was legal, and the faro dens were on the main street, Union Avenue, on ground floors adjoining bars. It was a tough town. There was some drinking and private gambling (poker, usually, at the clubhouse) and Ford was a frequent visitor.

Ford heard that Edward O'Kelley was talking about him, and he walked in a bar looking for trouble. This was in 1889, the year that O'Kelley was kicked off the Pueblo police force for drinking on duty and shooting an unarmed black man named Ed Riley. O'Kelley despised Ford for killing Jesse James, and he made no bones about this in conversation. This day Ford beat O'Kelley to the draw in an argument, but, instead of shooting him, Ford struck O'Kelley over the head with the barrel of his pistol and knocked him senseless.[1]

Ed's gun was on the floor and on his way out, Ford picked it up and took it with him, as if to add insult to injury. There were a number of O'Kelley's friends present, or else Ford might have killed Ed then and there.

This incident was a partial springboard for Ed later killing Ford. Some have claimed that Ford and O'Kelley shared a room and quarreled over a diamond ring that Bob accused Ed of stealing. Others took a more fatalistic stand, stating that Bob's death was the result of a Missouri vendetta. Romanticists claimed that O'Kelley killed Ford in a quarrel over a girl, but O'Kelley never cared for any woman in his entire life. This was confirmed by his own brother, Dr. Frank O'Kelley, a Missourian from Patton, who fought long for Ed's release from prison. (Dr. O'Kelley was a dear friend of the author.)

Dr. Frank visited his brother shortly after the fight in the saloon, but Ed said nothing to him about it. He heard it from Ben Crane. Frank O'Kelley replied, "Ed won't stand for that. He will kill Bob Ford for it."

---

[1]When men were "pistol whipped" in frontier days they were not whipped with the butt or grip smashing down on the skull, as movies pictured it, but were slugged with the barrel of the gun.

Stringtown, between Upper and Lower Creede, Colorado, 1893-94.

Courtesy of the Library of the Colorado State Historical Society

Dr. Howell DeWitt Newton, a travelling dentist, took this photo June 29, 1896 of Bob Ford's saloon in Creede, Colorado. Ford was killed here.

Courtesy of the Library of the Colorado State Historical Society

Ford soon left Pueblo and O'Kelley did not hear of him again until both appeared in the fabulous Creede (Colorado) gold and silver mining district. Here Ford again operated a saloon, while O'Kelley mooched what drinks he could and just loafed around the town. Creede at the time was just the name of the railroad depot; sections of the camp were known as Jimtown and Victor.

The arch-conspirator in the Ford–O'Kelley drama was Soapy Smith who owned the Orleans Club in Jimtown. He had taken over the town, appointing his brother-in-law, John Light, as marshal. Bob Ford owned the Omaha Club. The Gunnison Club was owned by Red McCune and his partner. Smith was angry with Ford and McCune because they would not "fix" their games in order to fleece the miners. He managed to have McCune killed one night, but was afraid to tackle Ford. Smith then approached O'Kelley, proposing that he kill Ford and became famous as "the man who killed the man who killed Jesse James." The idea appealed to O'Kelley; besides, he was still angry over the Pueblo incident.

The afternoon of June 8, 1892, was chilly and clear. Ford was alone at the bar so the Smith gang encouraged O'Kelley to saunter out into the street with a sawed-off shotgun hidden under his coat. Seeing Joe Duval, a local barfly, Ed called him over and asked him to have a drink with him. They walked together to Ford's bar, and O'Kelley shoved Duval through the tent opening ahead of him. When Bob turned his head to see who was coming, O'Kelley let him have it with both barrels, shooting him in the throat and almost taking his head off. Ford died in the arms of his Jimtown mistress, Ella Mae Watterson. It was 3:40 p.m.

The whole matter was prearranged and Marshal Light was right there, taking O'Kelley away at once, since some of the miners would have strung him up then and there. Soapy Smith managed to be in Denver on that fatal day, and, true to his promise, provided O'Kelley with legal counsel. It was to no avail, for Ed was sentenced to life imprisonment at the Canon City Penitentiary. However, by 1902, he was a free man again, largely because of the efforts of his younger

Ed O'Kelley, slayer of Bob Ford

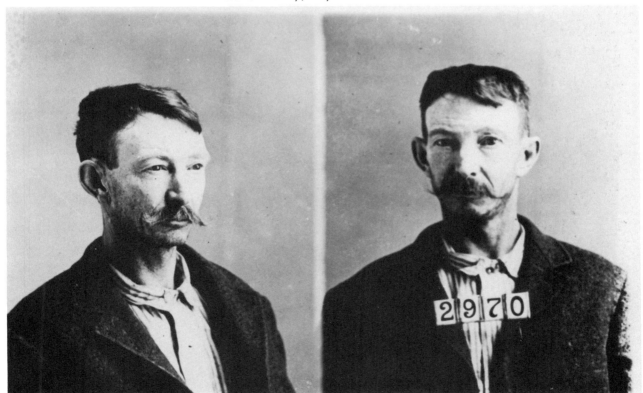

brother, Dr. Frank O'Kelley and the politi-cal clout of Soapy Smith.

Bob Ford was buried on the mesa south of the School Land.[2] In August, 1892, his body was exhumed and reburied at Rich-mond, Missouri, where his brother Charley also was buried. After seeing to Ford's proper burial, his widow, Dot Evans Ford returned to Creede the following month. There she became an entertainer at the Grand Theatre. She later married and moved to Durango, Colorado, with her husband, John Feeney. She committed sui-cide on June 15, 1902.

After getting out of prison, Ed drifted about the country. When in his cups, which was all too often, he bragged about how he

[2]School Land is a plat of land set aside for a future school.

had killed the man who bragged of killing Jesse James. He became *persona non grata* with his relatives, as well as his so-called friends. He stayed with Jesse James' son for a time in Kansas City—this young man tried to get Ed back on his feet.

On the night of January 13, 1904, Ed's destiny was played out in Oklahoma city. He got into a fight with a police officer named Joe Burnett. When he tried to pull a revolver on the officer, he was shot and killed in the scuffle. O'Kelley's body was taken to the morgue at Street & Harper's Furniture Store. There it was identified by those who had known O'Kelley, one being Otto Ewing of the Southern Club, who was at the scene when Ed killed Bob Ford. Later O'Kelley was buried in the Oklahoma City potter's field, unmourned and without rites.

Chapter Nineteen

Conclusion

In the history of internationally famous outlaws there is no parallel to the partnership of Jesse and Frank James.

Frank was a dangerous man in a tight situation. He killed the cashier at Northfield and many another man from Civil War guerrilla days onward, until "consumption" forced him to take up a quiet life on a Texas ranch shortly after Jesse was slain. His heart apparently had never been in bandit work. His happiest days were his two years near Nashville, midway in his bandit career. His next happiest days were after Jesse's death and the cessation of the several trials to which this older, Shakespeare-loving brother was subjected.

Outlaw Frank had been mechanical and listless, increasingly so after the Northfield raid, when his illness made steady inroads on his lungs. Bereft of Jesse, Frank surrendered to the law and stood trial on a number of occasions. In all his trials he was defended by excellent counsel. He displayed no outward fear and always went patiently through the court procedures.

Opinion was divided about Jesse. Many people thought he was a saint appointed for Missouri. Others thought he was the personification of the devil, but there is no division of thought about Frank James. As a gunman, he enjoyed a singular and unmitigated popularity, explained only by his quiet, mild personality, his slightly stooped posture, and the general belief that he had been commandeered by Jesse to commit lawless deeds. Frank's rides in a daycoach with a crew of deputy sheriffs and Major John Edwards, his friend, from one trial to another, were parades of triumph. Sick and wasted as he was, he did not care.

At Jefferson City, where he surrendered to Governor Crittenden, Frank was put on a train for Gallatin, Missouri. When night fell during the leisurely jaunt of the train he was taken to the old stone jail at Independence. The jailer, K. Holland, knowing Frank's penchant for the theatre, took him from his cell to a play at the Independence Opera House. The jailer was later discharged for this impropriety, but doubtless he felt repaid all his life for the companionship of an outlaw who had hung on the words of actors treading the boards in New York City, Philadelphia, and Baltimore.

Frank's most triumphant trial was at Gallatin, Missouri, where he was tried for alleged participation in the train robbery at Winston. He was held in the jail at Independence until this trial opened on August 21, 1883. The authorities thought the Winston affair was their strongest case against Frank James, since two men were murdered during that holdup.

Defending Frank James were some of the best legal talent in the country: Judge John F. Philips of Kansas City; James H. Slover; John M. Glover; Christopher T. Garner; Joshua W. Alexander; Charles P. Johnson;

William H. Rush. The prosecution was conducted by William H. Wallace, prosecuting attorney of Jackson County, Missouri, with the help of William D. Hamilton, John H. Shanklin, Marcus A. Low, Joshua F. Hicklin, and Henry Clay McDougal.

Days of examination and cross-examination followed, ending with a lengthy and eloquent speech by Mr. Wallace. The jury was given the case at 12:30 p.m. on September 6, and the court adjourned until 4 p.m. the same day.

Shortly after four o'clock the bailiffs in charge of the jury were notified that a verdict had been reached. Judge Goodman appeared surprised that a verdict had been reached so soon. The Gallatin Opera House which was used to hold the trial owing to the large crowd was almost empty when the jurors filed back into the room. No one had expected a verdict so soon. Judge Goodman called for the verdict, and William T. Richardson, the foreman, handed him the slip of paper. It read: "State of Missouri vs. Frank James—murder: we, the jury in the above entitled cause find the defendant not guilty as charged in the indictment."

Six hundred miles away, there was an old score to settle. Alabama had not forgotten the Muscle Shoals matter, and Federal Judge Krekel still held the Alabama requisition for Frank James. In February of 1884, the bandit was hustled aboard a train and under guard taken to Huntsville, Alabama. Bond had been refused by Judge Krekel.

Frank James languished in the Madison County jail until April 17 when some twenty government witnesses testified seeing three mysterious horsemen in the area in 1881. When Judge Bruce pointedly asked Paymaster Smith if he could identify Frank James as one of the men who had robbed him, he said, "I am not positive."

Defending Frank at Huntsville was General Leroy Pope Walker (esteemed Confederate hero and first Confederate Secretary of War), Richard Walker, R.B. Sloan, and James W. Newman. At three o'clock General Walker rose calmly and quietly to defend his client. He knew most of the jurors were ex-Confederate soldiers, so he expounded upon the heroic acts of Frank during the Civil War as a soldier and then guerrilla, the harsh treatment of his family by the Militia, and the ultimate crime of the Pinkerton attack upon the homestead.

At six o'clock on the evening of Friday, April 18, 1884, the jurors filed out of the room, slowly and solemnly. Almost immediately they returned with a "Not Guilty" decision.

By 1885 all official indictments against Frank James were dropped and the famous ex-robber became a full-fledged citizen and a free man. He became a race horse starter at county fairs in the midwest. At one time he was a slightly hammy actor in a Buffalo Bill type of traveling tent show which folded in a short time. When he was not earning an honest dollar as a showman, he was clerking in a store in Dallas or St. Louis. He spent his time quietly at the family homestead at Kearney, Missouri, or on a ranch at Fletcher, Oklahoma.

This ranch of Frank's, which he called a farm, was a favorite visiting place of his mother, Mrs. Zerelda Samuel. Whenever she boarded a train in Missouri she was given free passage, her only fare being a wave of the stump of her right arm. Once, after a visit, she boarded a train to return to her home at Kearney, but she was stricken with a collapsing heart en route. She died in Oklahoma City after being taken off the train, on February 10, 1911.

In 1915, thirty-three years after Jesse's death, Frank James died. After that his wife, Annie Ralston James, was never seen again in public. She died at a nursing home in Excelsior Springs, Missouri, on July 6, 1944, at the age of ninety-one. Her passing was noted on the news wires as a second item during a time when World War II raged.

Frank James proclaimed his innocence.

Courtesy of the Rosamond Collection

Although many a robber and robber band has passed over the land since the days of Jesse James, he is the outlaw whose feats seem destined to be remembered longest. The facts and fiction about Jesse and Frank James increase in volume every year, as research reveals hitherto buried or forgotten material. Lately the last of the old-timers who knew Jesse, Frank, and their mother, have been eager to contribute their recollections, lest it soon be too late for them to help complete the first-hand accounts of those stirring times in Missouri. Now all of these have gone across the Great Divide. Typical of these old-timers' remarks are the following from E.T. Estes, of Kansas City:

I well remember the tales about the James boys in my youth, and know some of them to be correct. Others are highly enlarged and made romantic. My mother was Katherine Williams, born January 29, 1825, the same date as the birthday of Mrs. Zerelda Samuel, the James boys' mother. My mother was baptized by the Reverend James, Jesse's father, in her later years. If Jesse had not been molested, he would have led a good Christian life.

Frank James owned this revolver.

Courtesy of the Bianchi Collection

Talking about the methods of Jesse and Frank in their outlaw work, Mr. Estes said, "David Duncan, who had a store at Cedarcreek, three miles from Jesse's and Frank's home, said he met them after the Liberty bank had been robbed, and first stated that Frank and Jesse were in the gang. Then he thought it best to say he did not know for sure, which was safer for him."

A myth that will probably live on long after the last contemporary of Jesse and Frank is dead is the perennial rumor that the boys left hidden treasure all over the Middle West, especially in the Ozark hills of southern Missouri and northern Arkansas. It apparently was never effectively communicated to people of the Missouri and Mississippi Valleys that, in total, the yield from the various robberies was far from an astronomical sum. Jesse lived modestly and died poor.

As late as 1948 there was a rebirth of the legend that loot hidden by the James boys was on the verge of being discovered. In

This house, near Garnett, Kansas, was supposed to be the retiring ranch for Jesse James and was to be called the "Jesse James Horse Ranch"—a name it bears to this day. This is the first prefab house in America. Jesse had it hauled piece by piece on a wagon (because he hated trains) from Kansas City. It has false doors, stairways, etc. and also a tunnel leading to an escape route.

Courtesy of Ed Fink

September of that year, a man cutting timber near Gads Hill, the scene of the train robbery three score years earlier, announced that he found a cave that had been Jesse's hiding place. Further, this wielder of the axe and saw said he found a fortune in gold coins in the cave. An investigation showed, however, that he had found only an old Civil War musket, a handful of two-cent pieces, and a crumbling book. As for the cave itself, the logger would not disclose its location. Under pressure he admitted to the Missouri State Highway Patrol officers that the entire tale was a fabrication. His confession included a disclosure that an "armored car," seen in his yard and described by him as a vehicle to carry away the gold in safety, was really nothing more than a newsreel camera truck whose operator had been lured to the house by the sensational yarn about the gold-filled cave.

There crops up, about as often as the gold discovery tales, a yarn that Jesse and his fellows sometimes led pursuers astray by having the getaway horses shod backwards, that the calks of the shoes of the horses were placed forward on the hooves. Some reputable historians of the period say the story is fantasy; others say it may well be true. That the James brothers were extraordinary characters and ingenious in their methods no one with the slightest knowledge of their feats will deny. It could be true that they devised a type of horseshoe that could be worn backward.

The getaway horses were usually tied up outside the town in which the robbery was scheduled, while conventionally-shod steeds were ridden into town. After the holdup, the outlaws would dismount from the horses they had used in the town and would ride away into the countryside on horses whose footgear made tracks in the opposite direction. As late as 1932, an aged blacksmith was still alive in Port Arthur, Canada, named George Kydd. He insisted not only that it was true, but that he himself had accepted commissions from the James boys to perform this variety of cobbling.

So the lore about this fabulous pair of robbers, Jesse and Frank, continues to live and to grow. To the accumulation of knowledge about the life and deeds of the brothers and their associates, historians add new facts from year to year, as well as new bits of unsubstantiated information that can be properly classified only as additional legend.

As a result of the viciousness of the enemies of the James family, Jesse Edward James, the outlaw's son, was blamed for the holdup of the Missouri-Pacific train at Belt Junction, near Leeds, Missouri, on September 23, 1898. However, T.T. Crittenden, the former Governor of Missouri who had so vigorously pursued the boy's father, staunchly testified to young Jesse's innocence. T.T. Crittenden, Jr., the son of the ex-governor and the man who gave young Jesse his first job, also worked diligently in the boy's behalf. Much evidence was produced pro and con, but finally Jesse's son was acquitted. After his release he opened a pawn shop which he was allowed to run to suit himself, and he got along very well. While operating the pawn shop Jesse's son attended night school, studying to become a lawyer. In June of 1905, he passed a successful examination before the State Board of Examiners. He was first in a class of thirty-seven. He then sold his pawn shop business and later moved to California, where he was a well-known and successful attorney.

For the record, more than forty Missourians of the Civil War era have been identified as one-time members of the celebrated robber group. Forty-five names have been verified: Jesse Woodson James, Alexander Franklin (Frank) James, Thomas

Coleman (Cole) Younger, James Henry Younger, Robert Ewing Younger, James Robert Cummins, Robert Woodson Hite, Clarence Bowler Hite, James Andrew Liddil, Daniel Tucker Bassham, William McDaniel, Thompson McDaniel, McClellan (Clell) Miller, Edward Miller, William Ryan, Jack Keene, William Miles, Samuel Wells, Samuel Pipes, Archibald Clements, Allen H. Parmer, James White, Joe White, George Shepherd, Oliver Shepherd, Hobbs Kerry, Isaac Flannery, James Anderson, William Hulse, John Jarrette, Bud Pence, Red Monkers, Bradley Collins, Jack Latche, William Chiles, J.F. Edmundson, Arthur McCoy, Andrew McGuire, Richard Burns, Payne Jones, William Keoughman, Charles Wilson Ford, John Hines, John Bishop, James Reed, and Robert Newton Ford.

There are many mysteries connected with Jesse's choice of associates. For instance, Bill Ryan, one of his favorites, was in personal habits everything Jesse feared and despised, yet Jesse loved him. Probably the key to Jesse's way of choosing can be found in the relationship between his mother and his stepfather, Dr. Reuben Samuel.

His mother was a woman of strong character, concealing several conflicts. Though born of a Protestant family, she was placed in a Catholic convent in Kentucky for some reason. Her Catholic upbringing during her formative years set a strong religious pattern in her life. It did not result, however, in a Roman creed that would oppose the Protestant atmosphere of the Missouri outlands where she went to live after her marriage. Nevertheless, her sense of religion was strong enough to make her a philosophic or religious threat to the beliefs of her first husband, Robert James. Of the Biblical injunctions, the Reverend James particularly favored to prefer meekness and abhor strife. His instinct of firmness in the Presbyterian-Methodist-Baptist creeds was reinforced by his wife's Catholic certainties.

It seems clear that from the beginning of the marriage, Zerelda "wore the pants." The

California Gold Rush of 1849 was a wonderful getaway excuse for a henpecked husband. Perhaps when Parson James set out for California to make his family rich the neighbors said, "There goes another henpecked husband toward the setting sun." Zerelda James took her husband's departure, as far as anyone knows, on faith.

Jesse probably inherited his tendency to dominate from his mother. To Zerelda he was not the favorite, for her first-born, "Mister Frank," held her best esteem. Modern psychologists would tell Zerelda that her openly-expressed preference was harmful to her children. Zerelda probably wouldn't have changed, anyway.

Frank always had a good visual memory, and words in print stirred his imagination. A line of poetry, with its rhythm and description of a scene in nature, would cause him to grow dreamy. He was likeable, even lovable, with the gentle, unemphatic air that lifelong tuberculosis gives. He was respectful and compassionate when listening to the mortal woes of his friends.

Jesse was too polite to jibe Frank over his dreaminess, but he resented his older brother's poetic instinct. Jesse's outlets were simpler—he found release in his adolescent years in shouting and hymn singing at brush-arbor revivals in the Missouri backwoods churches. Jesse was smooth. There was nothing hateful about him, except at times he would go into a fit of rage. Maybe his eyes were a bit too steely blue in anger for the easy-going Missouri mores. He tended to become tense—who wouldn't, with the law forever on the trail? The eyes of outlaw Jesse were never at rest, partially because of a granulated eyelid in his youth which never completely healed.

Jesse was the boss. Frank may have nominated members of the bunch, but it was Jesse who did the choosing.

The Last Jesse James . . .

One of the most publicized imposters of Jesse James was John James, who was not related to the family that fathered Jesse and Frank. John had affidavits to show that he was Jesse, like most seekers of this particular kind of fame. He had backers, too, who shared the proceeds of his appearances before sizeable audiences. His success went to his head, though, and he made one public appearance too many.

At a court hearing regarding his authenticity, members of the real James family suggested questions to test his knowledge of the family. Held in Excelsior Springs, Missouri, in the 1930s, the hearing attracted many old-timers who had known Jesse, and more particularly his brother Frank who lived until 1915. Even some members of the family were puzzled by John James's accuracy because in his answers he described incidents thought to be known only in the most intimate family circles.

He testified with such confidence that heads in the audience tilted in amazement. Was it possible that this aged man reappearing in Missouri was the noted outlaw whose career had presumably ended fifty years before?

Finally a question was put to the bold old fellow that unmasked his pretensions and revealed him for the hoax he was: "What was the name of Jesse James's half-brother who was killed in the family home at Kearney, Missouri, when Pinkerton detectives raided the Samuel place?"

John James was finally proved to be an escapee from a mental hospital in Illinois and died in Fort Smith, Arkansas in 1947. This man used the same papers when claiming to be Jesse James as did J. Frank Dalton in 1948.

Courtesy of the Rose Collection

John James did not know. He sat silent and the glory of his being acknowledged as the famous American highwayman faded. If he had answered, "His name was Archie Peyton Samuel," his pretense might have remained unshattered for a little while longer.

Out of the limelight and on to a drifter's life went John James after this climax to his short career as Jesse James. He was later identified as an escapee from an old soldier's home in Illinois. In 1947, a few months before the noisy introduction of J. Frank Dalton as the genuine Jesse, this John James died in Little Rock, Arkansas. His brief fame was not entirely fruitless, however, for the affidavits he used in his campaign soon found their way into the hands of J. Frank Dalton's promoters. They used them to contend, among other things, that Zerelda was not Jesse's real mother. In one instance Dalton's promoters even claimed that he was the same man as John James, despite the fact that John James was already dead.

Another of the many supposed Jesse Jameses is a man now buried in Brownwood, Texas, near the Mexican border which Jesse crossed during his travels. Many Brownwood citizens are firmly convinced that the local Colonel Henry Ford was the real Jesse James. At what date Ford arrived in the town not even his most ardent disciples know. There are even arguments over the date of his death: one defender claims that Jesse, alias Colonel Ford, died in 1914; another states that the Colonel died in 1898.

Examination of the Brownwood legend has not been so thorough as the J. Frank Dalton and John James myths. Perhaps detailed scrutinizing of the claim was not deemed necessary because of an abundance of particularly obvious contradictions. For example, proponents of Ford as Jesse said in later years he was visited in Brownwood by Cole Younger. The friendship between Cole and Jesse, what little there was to

begin with, had broken completely on the rocks of the Northfield, Minnesota, bank robbery fiasco.

Besides, the Brownwood legend proposed that Bob Ford didn't kill Jesse. On the contrary, Jesse killed Bob and then succeeded in convincing Missouri law officers in 1882 that Ford's body was his own. However, Bob Ford was thoroughly killed and thoroughly identified in 1892 in the Jimtown section of what is now Creede, Colorado, where he operated a barroom. The slayer was identified as Edward O'Kelley. O'Kelley's brother, who was still alive not too many years ago, vouched for this end to Ford's career, as many a newspaper file also attests.

Colonel Ford himself made no claims to being Jesse James. He was a man of some prominence in Brownwood: in 1891 he was president of the board of directors of the Brownwood Fair, and he was on the board of trustees of a local college. Jesse went up to the fifth grade only, so that should preclude his holding such positions to begin with. There appears to be ample proof that Frank James and Cole Younger were always good friends and visited Ford in Brownwood in their later years—but they visited Ford, not Jesse James.

Was Colonel Ford a short-term member of the Jesse and Frank James band of outlaws? Or was he a law-abiding citizen all his life who became acquainted with the James Boys as fellow guerrillas in the border warfare surrounding the Civil War? The latter seems more likely, since many ex-guerrillas did go to Texas after the war, including Jesse's own brother-in-law. At any rate, Ford's modest claim to being Colonel Henry Ford, civic-minded citizen of Brownwood, Texas, is in vivid contrast to the commercialized pretensions of the numerous, shabby and self-deluded frauds who wanted to be known as the famous Missouri outlaw.

On a hot evening in 1951 in the little town of Granbury, Texas, a very old man died. Just how old he really was no one knows, for he was an imposter and had faked his age as well as his identity. He claimed to be Jesse James, the most celebrated of American outlaws and the nearest thing America has to a Robin Hood.

A vast body of fact and folklore has grown up around the memory of Jesse James since he was shot to death in St. Joseph, Missouri, in 1882. Separating fact from fancy has been a self-appointed chore for historians of the life and times of Jesse James and his brother and partner in banditry, Frank James. These historians gave the old man who claimed to be Jesse a bad time of it for several years. By the time he died, he probably wasn't sure himself where and when he had been born.

After a couple of poor starts toward fame by trying to fool Texas that he was Jesse, the imposter tottered into full limelight in Lawton, Oklahoma, in 1948, when a newspaper there fell for his story. A sensational front page yarn was printed claiming that Jesse James, long thought dead, was indeed very much alive and living besides in the Oklahoma town. Press associations carried the news throughout the United States, and whenever there was a local historian who specialized in Jamesiana or nineteenth-century American outlawry, the telephone began to ring.[1]

The historians sighed at this appearance of still another pseudo Jesse James and patiently went to work on his pretensions. By the time he died in 1951, his carefully fabricated claims were sunk deep in a morass of confused and contradictory self-revelations. Tied like an anchor to the claims, and ready to bury them forever, were a number of historical documents that would never have been unearthed if this elderly imposter had not decided to have his fling at claiming to be Jesse.

Until he decided to be Jesse, the pretender's name was J. Frank Dalton. He continued to be stuck with this name, despite his attempt at a court hearing in Missouri in 1950 "to have his legal name, Jesse James, restored." Missouri Circuit Judge Ransom A. Breuer, presiding at the hearing in Union, Missouri, held that no ruling was in order, because if Dalton was really Jesse, he had never legally changed his name to Dalton anyway. The old man was taken back to the tourist-patronized caves whose owners exploited him, after Judge Breuer told Dalton to go home and pray for his sins if he were Jesse.

Research historians discovered that in 1939 Dalton had said he was born in Goliad, Texas, on March 9, 1848, while his father, a colonel in the United States Army, was en route to war with Mexico. The records of the United States Army do not show any Colonel Dalton in the Mexican

J. Frank Dalton's full name was probably Jeremiah Franklin Dalton, but he was referred to at carnivals as "Happy Jack Dalton."

[1] One scholar in St. Louis received nearly a hundred phone calls within a day or so after the story appeared in Missouri papers. I myself spent over three years in research of Dalton's claim.

Born at Louisville, Ky., April 17th., 1844.

JESSE W. JAMES AT 100

Jeremiah Franklin Dalton. The birthdate of 1844 shows this person was not the outlaw Jesse James (born in 1847). In reality, J. Frank Dalton was born near Lansing, Kansas in 1864.

War, or even any private by that name. Neither do any federal censuses or records of the state of Texas show Dalton born in Goliad.

Dalton was still claiming Goliad as his birthplace when he filed for a Soldier's Application for Confederate Pension with the state of Texas in 1947, and 1848 was still the year of his birth, according to his affidavit. When his application for a Confederate pension was turned down he became a live, if aged, exhibit for the promoters of tourist attractions outside of Texas. His birthplace and birth date were conveniently changed. He then claimed to have been born in Louisville, Kentucky, on April 17, 1844. Fortunately, the vital statistics of the Commonwealth of Kentucky are among the best in the United States, but the task of establishing this as a fact could not be done.[2]

Questioning the pretender continued from time to time. Finally he and his backers realized he ought to choose as his birthplace, the historically accepted place—Kearney, Missouri—and as his birthday, the historically accepted time—September 5, 1847. So, with a hand trembling with age and an attitude of befuddled exasperation, old man Dalton signed an affidavit saying he had really been born in Kearney on the day given as Jesse's birth in the James's family Bible.

How much was Dalton a faker? How much of his overly romantic oral autobiography did he himself believe? How much was his memory stimulated by his promoters? The answers may come years from now as historians who pursue the ramifications of the James story reveal new evidence. Or, the answers may never be known.

The whole story began in Austin, Texas, after several reporters investigated allegations of mistreatment of the elderly at a nursing home there. There Dalton was questioned by one eager young reporter who learned that Dalton had been an ex-Quantrillian and had known Jesse and Frank James and others of that raiding force. There are also letters from Dalton in the *Crittenden Memoirs* attesting to this, as well as his statements disclaiming those who came forth as the real Jesse James.

Regardless of the ultimate determination of the proportions of honest self-delusion and chicanery in the pretensions of Dalton (who was, incidentally, not one of the Oklahoma train-robbing Dalton Brothers), his saga contains much to make students of James history smile. For example, in one magazine Dalton wrote that he was tried

[2]I might mention that Charles Mason of St. Joseph, Missouri, told me in 1969 that J. Frank Dalton was his grandfather and that, in fact, he had been born in Jefferson County, Kentucky, never was an outlaw, and sometimes was called "The Kentucky Jesse James" since his real name was James.

and acquitted for implication in a train robbery at Muncie, Kansas. No one was ever arrested for that robbery, much less examined judicially.

He also claimed to be the author of numerous articles submitted to the University of Missouri. The Missouri Historical Society reports they have never found any such manuscripts.

He was proud of what was apparently an imaginary membership in the Knights of Pythias. In 1868, he often related, he was granted a life membership in this lodge at Chicago, Illinois. The Knights of Pythias records, however, show that in 1868 there was no such lodge in Chicago, or even in the state of Illinois. Lodge records of later years fail to disclose any member by the name of Dalton, or by the name of Carr, the name Dalton once said he used from time to time.

He was a Texas Ranger, he said, for a time after the Civil War. Here again the records fail to back him up. The Texas Rangers rosters list no officer by any of Dalton's several names. Indeed, he must have been a busy young fellow right after the Civil War, for he supposedly enlisted in the United States Army as a cavalryman in Kansas in 1866 and served for two years at Fort Harker, Kansas. Each of his claims received careful attention from historians. No Dalton or Carr appeared on the muster and enlistment rolls in the Adjutant General's office, nor in the militia at Fort Harker—between 1861 and 1868.

Pensions attracted him, and he was impartial to their source. He had been refused a Confederate pension, but on other occasions he said he was receiving a pension from the federal government. The historians checked that figment of the old gentleman's imagination with the United States Veterans Administration; no, he had never received a federal pension.

He was town marshal of Alpine, Texas, in 1868, he said. The Chief of Police at Alpine, when queried by the historians,

wrote, "The town of Alpine, Texas, was not in existence at the given time . . . Therefore, Dalton or Carr could not have been marshal then."

In his dreams, old man Dalton's fondness for the life of a law enforcement officer rivaled his career as Jesse James. He had been a deputy United States marshal, he said, serving at Fort Smith, Arkansas, under the West's famed "Hanging Judge" Parker from 1882 until 1889, rounding up desperadoes on the plains of the Indian territory. He had more historical facts to bolster that claim than others, for there really was a Frank Dalton who was a deputy marshal serving under the "Hanging Judge" in that period. Same name, but unfortunately for the pretender, a different man. The Deputy Marshal Frank Dalton at Fort Smith was a well-known character of Coffeyville, Kansas, where several of his brothers were killed in an attempt to rob two banks at the same time. The true Frank Dalton was killed at Fort Smith in 1887 while making an arrest. Historians have copies of a telegram dated November 30, 1887, containing news of the killing of this Dalton, and an acknowledgment of the news by the United States attorney general, who authorized offering a reward for the arrest of the slayer.

This Dalton who came into prominence as the alleged Jesse James in the 1940s was of course supposed to know something about the most notorious partners of the James Brothers—the Youngers of Missouri. The old man dutifully talked about the Youngers, presumably his fellow outlaws of nearly a century ago. Cole Younger, he said, in 1874 traveled to Osceola, Missouri, to visit Mrs. Henry Washington Younger, his mother. It was a tingling account of a desperado pursued by the law nevertheless risking all to see his mother. The story held up no better than the other Dalton yarns: Mrs. Henry Washington Younger, Cole's mother, died in 1870, four years before the brave and sentimental journey of her son.

Dalton, to be Jesse, had to know other

notorious characters of the past, such as Quantrill, the bloody guerrilla leader in the Missouri-Kansas border warfare. Dalton loved to upset history with his reminiscences, and he stoutly claimed that history was wrong in its account of Quantrill's fate. The guerrilla leader, Dalton said, was not killed in Kentucky, and not at the time generally believed.

However, the Army, which denied Dalton had enlisted and served in Kansas after the Civil War, likewise denied his statements about Quantrill's death. Quantrill, Army records show, was severely wounded on May 10, 1865. He died in a Catholic hospital in Louisville at 4:00 p.m., June 6, after being removed there from a military hospital in Louisville. Moreover, the records continue, he was buried in St. John's Catholic Cemetery (formerly called Portland Cemetery) in Louisville. Quantrill was never forgotten by the students of border warfare—they even kept track of his bones. In December, 1887, one W.W. Scott, a boyhood friend of Quantrill, removed them from Louisville, from where they traveled in many directions. The skull is still on display at the museum in Dover, Ohio. True, a lead box was buried in an unmarked grave in the Dover (then Canal Dover) Cemetery, but if it contained any (or just a few) of Quantrill's bones is a moot question.

During one of his pilgrimages to Missouri, Dalton carried an old photograph which purported to be a portrait of himself, his mother, and his brother Frank. This was a mistake, for authentic photographs of Zerelda James Samuel and Frank James were quite common. Furthermore, there were still a number of old residents of Kearney, Missouri, who knew what Zerelda looked like in the flesh before her death in 1911. Dalton's supposed photo of himself as Jesse with his mother and brother drew a barrage of cross-examination from local historians. Dalton retreated into a monumental yarn of explanation. There really had been, he said,

two sets of the James Boys. One set was blond with blue eyes; the other had dark complexions and brown eyes. Of course, the photo could have been of *his* mother and brother.

And while he was at it, the old codger tried to upset some other thoroughly established facts on the career of Jesse James. He stated that Jesse himself had never been in St. Joseph, Missouri, the town where Bob Ford shot him ("the dirty little coward, who shot Mr. Howard, and laid poor Jesse in his grave").

It would seem that such fantastic contributions to the history of American outlawry deserved little attention from serious students of the period. However, many people were gullible, and were willing to believe these pretentions. Thus each new wandering yarn of the old man was analyzed and disproved by the experts.

The city directory of St. Joseph in 1882 lists a Mr. and Mrs. Thomas Howard, living at 13th and Lafayette Streets. This bit of primary research was added to the volumes of contemporary news accounts, coroner's inquest hearings, legal identifications, mortuary photographs, and other material on the St. Joseph account of Jesse's life in the town as Mr. Howard.

The reader can see for himself the kind of investigation that disproves every claim of Frank Dalton, history's most recent pretender to the saddle-throne and mask-and-pistol scepter of Jesse James. Two exhibits appear in this book: a letter written on March 2, 1882, and signed by "Thomas Howard" in response to an advertisement in a Lincoln, Nebraska, newspaper offering a Nebraska farm for sale and a reproduction of the advertisement itself. Also, for the reader's comparison, a copy of a letter written by Jesse James to a friend in Texas is shown so that the handwriting can be determined to be that of "Mr. Howard."

This letter was made available by the James descendants some years ago. Dalton and his supporters, however, claimed the

AUTOGRAPH LETTER BY JESSE JAMES.

The only letter Jesse James ever wrote over the signature of Thomas Howard, was addressed to Mr. J. D. Calhoun, of the Lincoln, (Neb.) *Journal.* At great trouble and expense the original manuscript of this letter has been secured exclusively by the publishers of this authentic history; and the exact fac-simile of it here given is one of the most interesting relics of his extraordinary career ever given to the public.

(Copyrighted.)

Jesse James wrote to J.D. Calhoun in response to his ad about a farm.

Courtesy of Robert James

letter was a forgery, written to support the claim of Jesse's alleged residence in St. Joseph. That the letter is genuine is shown by the Lincoln newspaper files for the 1880s. The issue is available in which the advertisement appeared in enticing terms— "living springs; beautiful creek runs through it . . . finest bottom land . . . natural timber . . ." The description must have sounded good to Jesse. Perhaps he thought that after one more "examination" (bank holdup) he could retire to the farm for keeps. The letter from Jesse to Laredo should clinch this matter one and for all.

But that is getting into the story of the real Jesse James when there are still a few more lines to the story of Frank Dalton.

Jesse had been shot twice in the same lung during the Civil War. The wound would have left a permanent scar, so skeptics asked the pretender to let an X-ray be taken of his chest. He refused. Dalton's skin in the neighborhood of his chest bore no scars such as would have been caused by the shots that punctured one of Jesse's lungs. The lack of scars was easily explained by the masquerader; he said he had a skin graft performed on the scars in about 1890. Members of the medical profession report that skin grafting was not practiced that long ago.

When questioned about his supposed brother, Frank James, Dalton did not know his full name, which was Alexander Franklin James, sometimes called "Buck." In fact, he denied that Frank had much of a name at all until he was confronted with the census data from 1850 and 1860. Jesse also had a fingertip missing from his left middle finger; the most Dalton could display was a bent fingernail. (The real Jesse James had torn the end off his finger when he dropped a revolver as a boy. The Dr. James, no relation to Jesse, who had tended Jesse's finger attested to his handiwork at the inquest.)

Robert Franklin James, son of the outlaw Frank James, said of Dalton's claims, "Oh yes, this is not new to me. You see, I have had eleven Uncle Jesses since 1882. They bob up every once in a while. None of them has ever come to see me, though. They are too busy at fairs, rodeos, and making money out of it. At one time, two of them were operating this fraud at the same time. So far none has had the missing fingertip."

On the evening of August 16, 1951, the author, who had assisted in exposing the pretensions of this masquerader, was at the St. Louis County Courthouse when a man was brought in by a deputy sheriff to be booked for reckless driving. He was angry,

and said that if he had been driving at an excessive speed it was only because he was on his way to make funeral arrangements for his grandfather.

"Who is your grandfather?" he was asked. "J. Frank Dalton," he said, "and he died last evening in Granbury, Texas."

This was my first news of Dalton's death, and it was verified by the press. This wrote finis to the history of the last pretender. The final proof that Dalton was not the true Jesse Woodson James lies with the information provided by Lee Howk for the death certificate.

Jesse James wrote to Issac Hilton of Laredo, Texas.

Courtesy of Craig Fouts

A-1445 CERTIFIED COPY OF DEATH CERTIFICATE—CLASS 4 (Fits VS-112 Rev. 1-58)   25291 FOR SALE BY STAFFORD-LOWDON CO. FORT WORTH

TEXAS DEPARTMENT OF HEALTH
BUREAU OF VITAL STATISTICS
STATE OF TEXAS   CERTIFICATE OF DEATH   STATE FILE NO.

1. PLACE OF DEATH a. COUNTY	2. USUAL RESIDENCE (Where deceased lived, if institution: residence before admission) a. STATE	b. COUNTY
Hood	Texas	Unknown

b. CITY OR TOWN (if outside city limits, give precinct no.) | c. LENGTH OF STAY in 1 b. | c. CITY OR TOWN (if outside city limits, give precinct no.)
Granbury

d. NAME OF (if not in hospital, give street address) HOSPITAL OR INSTITUTION | d. STREET ADDRESS (if rural, give location)

e. IS PLACE OF DEATH INSIDE CITY LIMITS? YES ☐ NO ☐ | e. IS RESIDENCE INSIDE CITY LIMITS? YES ☐ NO ☐ | f. IS RESIDENCE ON A FARM? YES ☐ NO ☐

3. NAME OF DECEASED (Type or print)	(a) First	(b) Middle	(c) Last	4. DATE OF DEATH
	JESSE	WOODSON	JAMES	Aug. 15, 1951

5. SEX	6. COLOR OR RACE	7.	8. DATE OF BIRTH	9. AGE (in years last birthday)	IF UNDER 1 YEAR Months / Days	IF UNDER 24 HRS. Hours / Minutes
Male	White	Married ☐ Never Married ☐ Widowed ☐ Divorced ☐	4-17-1844	107	3 / 28	

10a. USUAL OCCUPATION (Give kind of work done during most of working life, even if retired) | 10b. KIND OF BUSINESS OR INDUSTRY | 11. BIRTHPLACE (State or foreign country) | 12. CITIZEN OF WHAT COUNTRY?
Louisville Kentucky

13. FATHER'S NAME	14. MOTHER'S MAIDEN NAME
Robert James Virginia	Zerilton Dalton Georgia

15. WAS DECEASED EVER IN U. S. ARMED FORCES? (Yes, no or unknown) | 16. SOCIAL SECURITY NO. (If yes, give war or dates of service) | 17. INFORMANT
James Lee Haulk

18. CAUSE OF DEATH [Enter only one cause per line for (a), (b), and (c).]
PART I. DEATH WAS CAUSED BY: Interval Between Onset and Death

IMMEDIATE CAUSE (a)   Hyperstatic   Pneumonia   3 Days

Conditions, if any, which gave rise to above cause (a), stating the underlying cause last.   DUE TO (b)   Old Age Nephritis   4 Days

DUE TO (c)

PART II. OTHER SIGNIFICANT CONDITIONS CONTRIBUITNG TO DEATH BUT NOT RELATED TO THE TERMINAL DISEASE CONDITION GIVEN IN PART I(a) | 19. WAS AUTOPSY PERFORMED? YES ☐ NO ☐

20a. ACCIDENT ☐ SUICIDE ☐ HOMICIDE ☐ | 20b. DESCRIBE HOW INJURY OCCURRED (Enter nature of injury in Part I or Part II of Item 18.)

20c. TIME OF INJURY | Hour Month Day Year a.m. p.m.

20d. INJURY OCCURRED While at Work ☐ Not While at Work ☐ | 20e. PLACE OF INJURY (e.g., in or about home, farm, factory, street, office building, etc.) | 20f. CITY, TOWN, OR LOCATION   COUNTY   STATE

21. I hereby certify that I attended the deceased from 8-10-51 19 to 8-15-51 19 and last saw the deceased alive on 8-12-51 19 Death occurred at   m. on the date stated above, and to the best of my knowledge, from the causes stated.

22. SIGNATURE	(Degree or Title)	22b. ADDRESS	22c. DATE SIGNED
Gus N. Lancaster	M.D.	Granbury	8-23-51

23a. BURIAL, CREMATION, REMOVAL (Specify)	23b. DATE	23c. NAME OF CEMETERY OR CREMATORY
Burial	8-19-51	Granbury

23d. LOCATION (City, town, or county) (State)	24. FUNERAL DIRECTOR'S SIGNATURE
Granbury Texas	Ben Estes

25a. REGISTRAR'S FILE NO.	25b. DATE REC'D BY LOCAL REGISTRAR	25c. REGISTRAR'S SIGNATURE
19	8-30-51	E.B. Price

IF DECEASED SERVED IN U. S. ARMED FORCES, FILL OUT THE FOLLOWING:
IS THE DECEASED REPORTED TO HAVE BEEN IN SUCH SERVICE?

NAME OF ORGANIZATION IN WHICH SERVICE WAS RENDERED?

SERIAL NUMBER OF DISCHARGE PAPERS OR ADJUSTED SERVICE CERTIFICATE?

NAME OF NEXT OF KIN OR OF NEXT FRIEND?

POST OFFICE ADDRESS?

IF DECEASED WAS MARRIED, FILL OUT THE FOLLOWING:
NAME OF HUSBAND OR WIFE | AGE IN YEARS

IF DECEASED IS AN UNIDENTIFIED PERSON, FILL OUT THE FOLLOWING:
COLOR OF HAIR? | COLOR OF EYES? | HEIGHT? In. | WEIGHT?

DEFORMITIES? | TATTOO MARKS?

OTHER MARKS OF IDENTIFICATION?

This is not the death certificate of Jesse James the outlaw. It is actually the certificate of death for J. Frank Dalton which was changed by an exploiter to suit his own purposes.

The certificate also backs up the statement made by Charles Mason when he said Dalton's real name was James. I, for one, cannot believe that the deceased's family would provide a false name. Apparently Dalton's name was Jesse W. James (I have checked four with that name during that period of time), but there the similarity to the Missouri outlaw ends. It states that Dalton's father was Robert James, born in Virginia; that his mother was Zerilton Dalton, born in Georgia; and that J. Frank had been born on April 17, 1844, in Louisville, Kentucky. It appears that if, in fact, Frank Dalton's name was Jesse James, then for reasons of his own he used his mother's maiden name.

A search of the Confederate records at the National Archives in Washington, D.C. reveals one Jesse W. James enlisting at Humboldt, Tennessee, on November 30, 1861, in the Tennessee 47th Infantry Volunteers, Company F. The muster rolls of Company F show that this James went AWOL a number of times, as he was listed on June 24, 1862, when his company was part of the 1st Brigade, 1st Division, 1st Corps, Army of the Mississippi. We next find this elusive Jesse being discharged on May 16, 1865, at Citronelle, Louisiana, and later residing at Russellville, Kentucky, for an unknown length of time.

On September 6, 1952, the following letter from Mrs. Stella James, widow of Jesse's son, Jesse Edwards James, was published in the *St. Louis Post-Dispatch:*

> I can remember eleven different men who claimed to be Jesse James since I have been in the family.
>
> Our family has never wanted publicity. We have no protection by law from these fakers, or as to the kind of books or motion pictures that are produced. We have wanted to live quiet and normal lives.
>
> I have four very fine daughters and four fine grandchildren. In all fairness to these young people, I hope you will give me a chance to disprove the story that Frank Dalton, who died last year in Texas, was really Jesse James.

(Confederate.)

47 | Tenn.

J. W. James

Pri___, Co. F., 47 Reg't Tennessee Inf.

Appears on

Company Muster Roll

of the organization named above,

for *May & June*, 186 2.

Enlisted:
When *Nov 30*, 186 .
Where *Humboldt*
By whom *Allison Esqr*
Period *12 Mo*

Last paid:
By whom *Capt Russell*
To what time *Feb 28*, 186 .

Present or absent *Absent*
Remarks: *In Gibson Co Tenn*

The 47th Regiment Tennessee Infantry was organized December 16, 1861, and re-organized May 8, 1862. It appears to have been temporarily consolidated with the 12th Regiment Tennessee Infantry (Consolidated) about October, 1862, but each company of the two organizations was mustered separately and under its original designation during the period covered by this consolidation.

About April 9, 1865, the 11th, 12th, 13th, 29th, 47th, 50th, 51st, 52d and 154th Regiments Tennessee Infantry were consolidated and formed the 2d Consolidated Regiment Tennessee Infantry, which was paroled at Greensboro, N. C., May 2, 1865.

Book mark: _____

(642)   G. E. Jones, Copyist.

Company Muster Roll of Tennessee 47th Infantry Volunteers shows one Jesse W. James AWOL. This was not the outlaw Jesse Woodson James.

When Orvus Lee Howk came out with the Dalton claim, he was using the same affidavits and story that were used by another man back in 1932.

I had read all of these affidavits and felt sure that Howk was using them as he had the same story about the man who was killed by Ford as being a Charlie Bigelow. I then called on Mr. Howk, incognito, of course, and asked Mr. Howk if this man was the same one who had made the claim in 1932. He said he was.

I then convinced him that this old man died in Little Rock, Arkansas. Later, Lee Howk sent a man who said he was Reverend Highley to see me, to say that if our family would claim this old man as Jesse James we would be paid $50,000.

Our answer to that was a letter to Mr. Howk by our attorney, stating he expected to bring a lawsuit to keep them from exploiting the old man in California. Mr. Howk then left Los Angeles; the old man, Dalton, was taken in charge by our police officers and placed in a rest home and later sent back to his home.

I want to assure you that if Jesse James had lived these many years he would have cared for his son and family and not have been exploited over the country for a few dollars that would be made from such an exploitation.

I can't help but feel that the reading public would like to hear the truth about this Lee Howk's story.

According to newspapers, the old-timer outlaw Al Jennings identified Dalton as the real Jesse James. His story was corroborated by John Trammell, at that time a one-hundred-year-old black man. The following statement is by Fred C. Pottorff, of Parsons, Kansas. Pottorff was related to Jennings by marriage.

June 16, 1955
I asked Al Jennings at his home in Tarzana if he thought J. Frank Dalton was Jesse James, and he answered, 'Hell, no!' I told him I believed I read somewhere that he had said this and he replied, 'Well, they paid me to say so, why not?'

When I contacted John Trammell in Choctaw, Oklahoma, he was living with the Rev. James Ellis. Since Trammell could not read or write, he dictated the letter to Reverend Ellis. Trammell had been a cook with the James band for many years and could verify without hesitation incidents as far back as 1879—incidents he could not have known if he hadn't been with Jesse and Frank.

July 25, 1955
Carl W. Breihan: My Friend
Now sir: J. Frank Dalton was not Jesse James. Jesse told me that he had some relatives by that name. Jesse went by some strange names when he did not want to be identified. He used the name of Reverend Jones in Mississippi and his brother Frank took the part of a doctor.
Yours truly
John Trammell

Over ten decades have gone by since Jesse was killed by a shot in the head as he dusted a picture on the wall of the little rented house in St. Joseph. He was nearly thirty-five years old when he died. The element of time precludes any new pretenders from coming forth. Before time ran out, playing the role of a resurrected Jesse James was a *flourishing* business.

Dalton was definitely the most noted of the eleven Jesse James imposters who surfaced after his death in 1882, but he was also the last.

Mrs. Ivy Long, court clerk deputy, issues a marriage license to John Tramell, 114-year-old Guthrian.

John Tramell (1951 photo) was actually the cook for the James gang, as verified by the author in his research in Wyoming. Near Cheyenne, there is a water ditch called "Negro John Ditch" due to the fact that Tramell watched it being built.

An all-time record for Logan county—and quite possible the nation—was established at the office of Mrs. Stella Hill, court clerk, this week when John Tramell, 114-year-old Guthrie Negro, applied for, and received, a marriage license.

Tramell, said he planned to marry a "child bride" of only 67 years, Mattie Moore, route 1, Meridian, Sunday afternoon.

Quite hale and hearty for his advanced years, Tramell, who lives at 510 S. Drexel, explained he was freed from slavery at Cat Springs, Tex., at the close of the war between the states. At that time he was 25 years old and had been working as a slave in Georgia, where he was born and reared.

Gradually, he worked his way north to Zanesville, Ohio, where he met and was employed as a cook for "Cap'n" Jesse James and his gang. This precarious occupation he followed for a number of years, later migrat-

ing to Oklahoma. He has been a Guthrie resident for the past 40 years.

Tramell says this is his fourth marriage—and, he hopes, his last. Questioned about his age at the time of his first venture into the sea of matrimony, the aged Negro said he had no idea; "In slave days, when a couple got married, all we did was step over a broom laid on the floor," he explained. "Sometimes the 'master' married us by reading out of a book—don't know what book it was, it could have been anything."

Although unable to read or write (Tramell signed his marriage license application with an "X"), he is accurate on dates and locations of events which took place in his life.

Although 114 years is a long long time to be alive, Tramell is as active and clear mentally as many men just half his age, and is living evidence of the belief that the "first hundreds years are the hardest."

Jamesiana

Mrs. Zee James stands with a collection of Jesse's boots and guns.

Courtesy of R.F. James

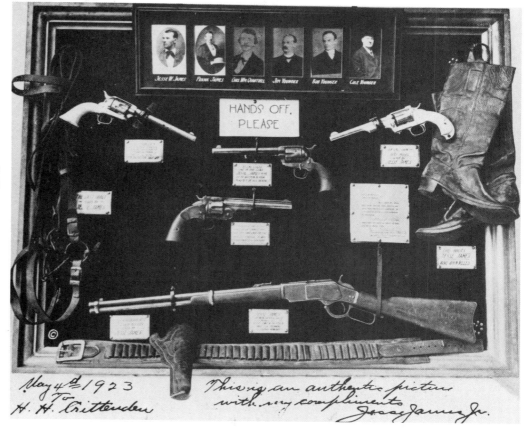

Display of outlaw guns belonging to Jesse and Frank.

Mementoes of Jesse's last days in St. Joseph are valuable. One bit of jewelry found by officials who searched the house after the slaying was a scarf pin on which were engraved the initials "J.W.J." It is now in possession of a St. Joseph friend of the family.

The most sought after souvenirs of Jesse's violent death were of course his guns. Guns allegedly owned at one time or another by him have shown up here and there, often disappearing again without a trace, and then reappearing. For many years the two guns which Jesse had laid on the bed in St. Joe remained in the possession of his wife, hidden in an old trunk. She had always told her two children not to dispose of them regardless of the price offered. Here is a history of two other guns Mrs. James had.

In Excelsior Springs, Missouri, some years after Jesse's death, there lived a phy-sician named Lowry who had been a friend of Jesse's mother, Mrs. Samuel. He was collector of Jamesiana and had filled a window in his office with photographs and relics of Jesse and Frank, partly as an advertisement for the James Farm at Kearney, for he was anxious to make the farm a tourist attraction for the sake of the family.

One Saturday night Jesse James' son, Jesse Edwards James, was en route to Excelsior Springs in an automobile when he met with an accident and was taken to this doctor's office for treatment. The wife of Jesse Edwards was away in Chicago, but she hurried home to be with her injured husband. In the meantime, the doctor had gone to the James homestead where the remaining guns of Jesse were kept, and he stated that Jesse's son had given him permission to use them but *only* as displays in his win-

This 1856 Colt Cap and Ball was the property of Jesse James.

dow, nothing more. Later he told Jesse's wife that the guns had been given him in payment for his medical services, although he was unable to produce a statement for services rendered. Before any action could be taken, the guns disappeared from the display window. Shortly afterward, the recuperating young Jesse and his wife left Missouri for a visit to California. They settled at Long Beach, later moving to Los Angeles.

The young Mrs. James returned to Excelsior Springs in 1932 to attend the hearing of John James, the imposter who wanted legal approval of his claim that he was the original Jesse James. She learned that the two revolvers she had seen in the doctor's window some years before were now hidden in his office safe. She filed suit to recover them, but when officers searched for the weapons they were gone. The physician was out of town, too . . . until Mrs. James departed for California.

Without ever having been seen by historians interested in the further travels of the two pistols, the St. Joseph revolvers have nevertheless been traced to United States Senator Harry B. Hawes, who obtained them from Dr. Lowry of Excelsior Springs. They were in turn passed on to Nick Longworth, the husband of Alice Roosevelt. I spoke with Alice Roosevelt about the guns years ago, but she had no knowledge of them.

Of course, probably the most important revolver was the one Jesse placed on the bed the day he was killed. This weapon was presented to the governor's son, T. T.

Crittenden, Jr. by Jesse's widow in appreciation for favors he had done for the family after Jesse's death. This is a Smith & Wesson, Schofield Model, .45 caliber, Serial #366, 1873. On the right side is scratched the name "Laura," said to be the name of an early sweetheart of Jesse James.

At Crittenden's death his widow disposed of all the souvenirs and reams of papers and notes dealing with the famous Missouri outlaw, remarking, "I'm sick and tired of hearing about Jesse James. I'm going to sell or destroy anything that reminds me of him."

She sold the Smith & Wesson to Miles Standish of Kansas City, a wealthy leather manufacturer and gun collector. His widow sold it to William O. Sweet of Attleboro, Massachusetts, along with Frank James' .44–.40 Remington Frontier Model pistol, which he had given to Governor Crittenden at his surrender.

Apparently men who own guns that are genuine Jesse James firearms are loath to publicize their prizes. The fake Jesse James guns are as numerous as the descendants of the Mayflower, or the beds in which George Washington slept.

Members of the James Family

	Born	Died
Robert Sallee James *Father of Jesse James*	July 7, 1818	August 19, 1850
Zerelda Cole James (Samuel) *Mother of Jesse James*	January 29, 1825	February 10, 1911
Alexander Franklin James *"Frank"—Brother of Jesse James*	January 10, 1845	February 18, 1915
Robert R. James *Brother of Jesse James*	July 19, 1845	July 24, 1845
Jesse Woodson James *"Jesse"*	September 5, 1847	April 3, 1882
Mary James *Sister of Jesse James*	October 3, 1848	August 17, 1866
Susan James (Parmer) *Sister of Jesse James*	November 25, 1849	March 3, 1889
Reuben Samuel *Stepfather of Jesse James*	January 12, 1828	March 1, 1908
Sarah Samuel (Nicholson) *Half-sister of Jesse James*	December 26, 1858	July 14, 1921
John T. Samuel *Half-brother of Jesse James*	December 25, 1861	March 15, 1934
Fannie Quantrill Samuel (Hall) *Half-sister of Jesse James*	October 18, 1863	May 3, 1922
Archie Peyton Samuel *Half-brother of Jesse James*	July 26, 1866	January 26, 1875
Zerelda Mims (James) *Wife of Jesse James*	July 21, 1845	November 30, 1900
Annie Ralston (James) *Wife of Frank James*	January 25, 1853	July 6, 1944
Jesse Edwards James *Son of Jesse James*	August 31, 1875	March 26, 1951
Mary James (Barr) *Daughter of Jesse James*	July 17, 1879	October 11, 1935
Robert Franklin James *Son of Frank James*	February 6, 1878	November 18, 1959
Mae A. James (nee Sandborn) *Second wife of Robert Franklin James*	February 6, 1902	April 19, 1974
Stella F. James *Wife of Jesse Edwards James*	February 27, 1882	April 1, 1971

Crime Chronology

February 13, 1866:   The Clay County Savings Association Bank of Liberty, Missouri, robbed of $58,000. A young boy killed.

October 30, 1866:   The Mitchell & Company banking firm of Lexington, Missouri, robbed of $2,011.

March 20, 1868:   The Southern Deposit Bank of Russellville, Kentucky, robbed of $14,000.

December 7, 1869:   The Daviess County Savings Bank in Gallatin, Missouri, robbed of $700. Cashier John W. Sheets killed.

June 3, 1871:   Corydon County, Iowa, invaded and county treasurer's office raided, no money obtained. Same day the Ocobock Brothers Bank in Corydon robbed of $6,000.

April 29, 1872:   Bank of Columbia, Kentucky, robbed of $4,000. Cashier R.A.C. Martin killed.

September 26, 1872:   Kansas City Fair cashier robbed at its gate of $8,000.

May 27, 1873:   Ste. Genevieve, Missouri, Savings Association, robbed of $4,000. Big money had been transferred to St. Louis the day before the robbery.

July 21, 1873:   The first train robbery west of the Mississippi and credited to the James gang. Train of the Chicago, Rock Island and Pacific robbed near Adair, Iowa. Engineer John Rafferty killed. Robbers obtained $26,000 from the express car and the passengers.

January 15, 1874:   Stagecoach robbery of passengers on the run between Malvern, Arkansas, and Hot Springs. Some $3,500 in cash and jewelry taken.

January 31, 1874:   Holdup of the St. Louis, Iron Mountain and Southern Railroad train at Gads Hill, Missouri. Loot taken from passengers and express car amounted to $10,000.

April 7, 1874:   The regular stage running between Austin and San Antonio, Texas, plundered and robbed.

September 6, 1875:   The bank at Huntington, West Virginia, robbed. Nearly $20,000 in valuables and currency taken.

July 7, 1876:   A Missouri-Pacific train held up and robbed at Rocky Cut, near Otterville, Missouri. $17,000 taken from two safes, plus an undetermined amount taken from the passengers.

September 7, 1876:   Northfield, Minnesota, Bank raided. Bookkeeper killed. Raid resulted in the capture of three Younger brothers and the killing of three other gang members.

October 8, 1879:   Robbery of the Chicago, Alton and St. Louis train at Glendale, Missouri, ending with arrest of Tucker Bassham. Between $35,000 and $40,000 taken.

September 3, 1880:   Glasgow stagecoach held up and robbed between Mammoth Cave and Cave City in Edmonson County, Kentucky.

March 11, 1881:   Government Paymaster Smith robbed of $5,200 near Bluewater, Alabama.

July 15, 1881:   Chicago, Rock Island and Pacific train robbed near Winston, Missouri, of a small sum. Conductor Westfall and an employee named Frank McMillen killed. About $2,000 taken.

September 7, 1881:   Train of the Chicago and Alton Railroad robbed near Glendale, Missouri, at Blue Cut. Amount taken from express car was $2,500 and from the passengers an estimated $3,000 to $4,000 in cash and jewelry.

Index

102.67
300.00
402.67
410.95
813.62